The
Garland Library
of
War and Peace

The
Garland Library
of
War and Peace

Under the General Editorship of
Blanche Wiesen Cook, *John Jay College, C.U.N.Y.*
Sandi E. Cooper, *Richmond College, C.U.N.Y.*
Charles Chatfield, *Wittenberg University*

Plans for World Peace through Six Centuries

by

Sylvester John Hemleben

with a new introduction
for the Garland Edition by
Walter F. Bense

Garland Publishing, Inc., New York & London
1972

Library of Congress Cataloging in Publication Data

Hemleben, Sylvester John, 1902–
    Plans for world peace through six centuries.

    (The Garland library of war and peace)
    Reprint of the 1943 ed.
    Bibliography: p.
    1. Peace. 2. International relations—History.
3. Security, International. I. Title. II. Series.
JX1938.H43 1972   327'.172   70-147411
ISBN 0-8240-0209-1

Printed in the United States of America

Introduction

To read Professor Hemleben's book today, less than thirty years after its first publication, is to be astounded by the gulf that separates the author's perspective from our own. A native-born American,[1] Hemleben had apparently no difficulty in equating the peace of Europe (which is what virtually all his Plans are about) with World Peace. And small wonder! He deliberately begins with "the first real peace plans of the early fourteenth century"; and he is writing in the midst of a war that was to end with the collapse of the most virulent expression of European nationalism and the beginning of the end of European world domination. His perspective is still the European perspective proper to these centuries. When a sometime American like William Penn is allowed to speak, he is represented by his Essay towards the Present and Future Peace of Europe — not his highly successful plan for keeping peace with the Indians — and even William Ladd's Essay on a Congress of Nations is addressed to "those Christian and civilized nations who should choose" to enter such a Congress; presumably the European states and such outposts of European civilization as might be found in the Americas. Of all the Plans discussed, apparently only Bentham's saw in colonies as such a

5

major obstacle to peace.

One of the fundamental differences between the world of Hemleben and our own is the virtual end of traditional colonialism. Most Africans and hundreds of millions of Asians have attained national independence in the three intervening decades. Europe is no longer the world. Nor is Europe even the preponderant world power. It is (somewhat unevenly) divided into two camps that depend more or less heavily on the two superpowers, the United States and the Soviet Union, both of which can be viewed as semi-European at best; perhaps they should be considered post-European. But crowding in behind the post-Europeans are Japan, China, India — potential superpowers that are distinctly non-European. And while the European-dominated League of Nations has passed into oblivion, its successor, the United Nations Organization, is dominated by a multitude of non-European states that could overwhelmingly outvote (in the General Assembly) all the actual and potential superpowers put together. The United Nations Organization has sanctioned some military operations, and may have helped prevent some others. But to regard it, in its present form, as an effective Plan for World Peace would stretch one's credulity.

Now the League of Nations and the United Nations Organization obviously constitute the model Hemleben had in mind for his Plans for World Peace. He knows that the only European peace to last for centuries was the Roman Peace, but that will not do as a model for modern times: "it was an enforced national peace, not a peace resulting from a league of independent nations." The Medieval Papacy and Empire likewise served the cause of peace; but they, too, will not do as Plans. A Plan for World Peace apparently must meet three criteria, according to Hemleben, in order to qualify. It must have been deliberately planned, it must be mainly political in nature, and it must recognize the principle of national or state sovereignty. Any one of these three conditions may well render a Plan for World Peace ineffectual today. To look to the more than six hundred years of European world hegemony for inspiration and guidance in building a peaceful world is surely more than a little sanguine. But Hemleben was not describing these Plans in order to show us how to build a world without war. As he indicates in his Preface, he is presenting these Plans in order to illuminate their failures, including that of the League of Nations. His work is essentially a competent and lucid summary of the chief Plans that meet his criteria. It provides an excellent introduction to them and valuable bibliographical aids for further study. But it leaves the reader to make his own analysis and does not really prepare him for the conclusion that "if peace is to be attained, men must turn to God for guidance and strength."[2]

Hemleben was criticized for this excursion into religion.[3] Hans Kohn regarded it as a "deviation from

7

the fundamental issue," which he saw in the establishment of effective international law and law enforcement machinery. Kohn thought that the "prevention of war on an international scale can be achieved in the same way as the prevention of private wars has been achieved in the national field." He thought the objective conditions for the prevention of war had come into existence, but not as yet the subjective conditions, "due to the confusion about the fundamental issues involved." Peace does not depend, according to Kohn, on social justice or economic equality or human perfection or faith in God. While it may not be possible to prevent all war — he cites the American Civil War as an example of war that broke out under conditions of relatively well-established law and law enforcement — most wars could now be avoided through the development of international law and law enforcement.

The relative merits of law and religion as means of pacification could be debated at some length. More useful, however, may be the realization of what both have in common. Both religion and law derive their effectiveness from one of two sources: from external force or from inward conviction. Beginning with Theodosius I, the Christianized Roman Empire imposed both its law and its faith on the "civilized world" by external force. A superpower, or a coalition of superpowers, may once again be able to do so. But it also may not; and whether or not such an imposition would really insure peace for any considerable length of time is certainly debatable. This leaves us with the second alternative: peace through religion or law based on inward conviction. When a person obeys the law not out of fear but out of a recognition that it is right that he should, and when he practices his religion not for the sake of tradition but for the sake of a love that is both human and divine, we say of him that he is a truly moral — and therefore a peaceful — person. And we might add, by way of explanation, that he is the recipient of divine grace, that he himself is "doing well," that he has good genes, that he comes from a good environment, or that his education has been a success. Now we have no control over God's sovereign gift of grace; our control of heredity and environment is severely limited; our part in determining whether others "do well" or not is also limited; but the possibilities afforded by education are very great indeed. John Dewey's insight that it is more important that children learn to "cope" with life and to "adjust" to others than that they acquire a vast store of objective knowledge has been of great value; perhaps we would be justified in regarding Progressive Education as a kind of Education for Peace on the personal level. It has not been an unqualified success; but it may well have pointed us in the right direction.

Can there be Education for Peace on the international level? If this involves teaching the nations or states themselves to "cope" with the world and to "adjust" to one another rather than to fight, such a *task is formidable indeed, yet not entirely impossible. In Europe, the task might have been easiest to accomplish when the various nations were emerging, under Papal and Imperial tutelage, in the earlier Middle Ages. In the later Middle Ages (ca. 1300-1517), Empire and Papacy were in eclipse, but an institutional framework for educating the emerging nation-states existed and almost flourished: the series of General Church Councils that mark this period as the Age of Conciliarism.*[4] *The Councils voted to meet at least once every ten years, they set up standing commissions on peace, they organized themselves by "nations," much as William Ladd was to propose some five hundred years later. One thinks of the young Nicholas of Cusa's* De Concordantia Catholica *as a Conciliarist Plan for World Peace that is not mentioned by Hemleben; when we add to it Cusa's* De Pace Fidei, *which urges recognition of all religions as expressions of the one true religion with but a variety of rites, something like a full-blown philosophy of peace emerges.*[5]

In the Age of Absolutism (ca. 1517-1776), the education of states should still have been relatively simple, for the state really was the monarch. Erasmus, Vives, and other humanists entertained high hopes of the young rulers that came to the leading European thrones in the early sixteenth century.[6] *While Hemleben devotes three pages to Erasmus, he fails to see that all of Erasmus's efforts to reform religion were at*

*the same time efforts to build a peaceful world; he
fails to mention the evangelical inspiration of
Erasmus and his emphasis on Education for Peace.
That absolute monarchy is the key to peace was the
conviction of both Thomas Hobbes and King James I
of England, who earned the title* rex pacificus *both
by his practice of peace and by his publication of a
Plan for both domestic and international peace.*[7] *The
most comprehensive Plan for World Peace through
education was developed in the seventeenth century
by Amos Comenius, bishop of the Moravian Brethren;
it remained in manuscript in Germany at the time
Hemleben wrote his book, but the Latin text*[8] *and a
Czech translation have since been published. Thomas
Campanella, an Italian whose Peace Plan centered on
the Spanish monarchy and was published in German
and Latin, has finally found a biographer who writes
in English; but the significance of his Peace Plan and
his conception of the Spanish monarchy's relationship to the Kingdom of the Messiah still invite further
study.*[9] *Hemleben barely mentions Francis de Vitoria
O. P. as possibly the true founder of modern
international law, but without identifying his distinc-
tive contribution, which was to redefine the "law of
nations" (which traditionally occupies the middle
position between natural law and positive or civil
law). The law of nations (*ius gentium*) had been
classically defined as prevailing among all men (*inter
omnes homines*), but Vitoria now defined it as
prevailing among all nations (inter omnes* gentes*).*

11

INTRODUCTION

Vitoria envisaged a kind of pluralistically structured universe, a community of communities, a world society made up of national societies, both being based on natural law.[10] *Grotius merely tried to spell out in some detail what the natural reason recognized by Vitoria required. But the results were disappointing: Grotius' natural law not only allows war but also nearly any means necessary to its success, though he sincerely tried to reduce both the frequency of wars and the barbarity with which they are fought (by his non-obligatory temperamenta).*[11]

But some of the early-modern advocates of natural law retained, or returned to, the classical Stoic conception of the law of nations as being based on the unity of mankind, rather than on the natural right of the state, which, in the Age of Absolutism, was of course easily transformed into the doctrine of the divine right of kings. Francis Suarez S.J., one of the Spanish successors of Vitoria, insisted on this "quasi-political and moral unity" of the human race as constituting the basis of the law of nations, and vigorously attacked the divine right of kings.[12] *In this respect he anticipated the Age of Revolution (since 1776), in which the state is identified with the people. This identification has rendered vastly more difficult the task of Education for Peace, at least from one point of view; for now it will be necessary to educate not just a few leading statesmen in a few leading countries, but all the people in every country.*

INTRODUCTION

But from another point of view, this very fact has also rendered Education for Peace more feasible; for while the people need *to be taught peace, they are now in a position to* demand *that they be so taught, and to* participate *themselves in the teaching. Basically, they will be guided by two insights: (1) Peace is not the natural state of the world — among nations no more than among individuals — but an ideal to be worked for; peace must be built. (2) War does not "break out," as we are accustomed to put it; it is made by man for reasons that can be investigated. Such investigation will almost necessarily begin with history. History used to be taught almost entirely in political terms, and here wars, and the various alliances and counter-alliances that precede and follow them, were generally the most exciting part. Today there is a growing interest in the history of peace — how wars end, why certain historical periods are more or less filled with the clamor of war than others, what means have been used or advocated to preserve the peace.[13] It would appear as though the more widespread experience of war — either first-hand, or second-hand, via realistic books, television, etc. — is contributing to the greater interest in peace and the tendency to look upon war itself as a crime. But merely historical peace research (such as the present volume) must be supplemented with other types of inquiry. Good work is being done in the sociology and psychology of war and peace, the influence of economics on religion is being rec-*

13

ognized, and philosophers and theologians are inquiring once again into the metaphysical foundations and the ethical implications of the phenomena of war and peace. Some educational institutions now sponsor such studies,[14] and undoubtedly others will follow their lead. The day may come when no student will want to graduate without at least one course in war/peace studies, to familiarize himself with the issues and alternatives, and to prepare himself to participate intelligently in the decisions that arise in this area, both on the personal level and on the level of public policy. Such courses need to go well beyond Hemleben's work. Yet his volume remains useful for at least two reasons. The Plans he describes stimulate us to formulate our own, and in a sense legitimate these by providing them with historical precedents. But more importantly, they encourage us to look for concrete structures and developments that might serve the cause of peace. We have suggested that in the later Middle Ages, the Conciliarist principle and in the Age of Absolutism the Legitimist principle constituted a force for peace, even though both might have been used more effectively. The same applies to the Federalist principle in the Modern period. In 1789, when the Age of Revolution began in Europe itself, the first great national product of that Age began to function on Federalist principles in America. Taken as a whole (despite the crisis of a great civil war), it has provided peace and prosperity along with popular rule and

respect for the rights of the individual. The question is, could the Federalist principle be extended beyond national frontiers, and if so, on what basis?[15]
Pope Paul VI, in his encyclical Populorum Progressio, *made the perceptive statement that today the name of Peace is Development. If we want to have peace, we must provide for development, and the Federalist principle affords perhaps the best basis for development. The essence of Federalism would seem to be the irrevocable delegation of certain powers to a central government, the elimination of certain barriers, particularly economic barriers, between the federal states, and the declaration of certain human rights that may not be violated by the union or the states. The United States of America and the Union of Soviet Socialist Republics are such federal unions that may not have reached their maximum development as yet. Economic interdependence will in the foreseeable future unite Canada to the United States, and the East Block countries (Poland, East Germany, Czechoslovakia, Hungary, Rumania, and Bulgaria) to the Soviet Union. Western Europe is likewise moving in the direction of regional federalism. Latin America would seem to constitute another area that must move, through revolution if necessary, towards federalism, and the countries of Africa and East Asia (i.e., east of India and China) are showing signs of regional consciousness that may eventually lead to federal unions. The region farthest from federal union is*

INTRODUCTION

South Asia, not least because of the efforts of Arabs, Israelis, and Pakistanis to build political structures not on geography but on racial and religious lines. One would hope that India and Turkey, states that seem to have learned the lesson of separation of church and state, would encourage the states lying between them to follow their example, for the sake of both church and state as well as in the interests of development and peace.

Peace depends on development, development depends on regional cooperation, and regional cooperation finds most effective expression and support in federal unions. Professor Hemleben thought that the Peace Plans he described pointed forward to the League of Nations and foreshadowed its failure. Perhaps the chief lesson we can learn from his book is that peace must be planned, and must overcome the extended egotism we know as nationalism. Christianity, royal conservatism, and national liberalism proved unable to unite Europe. What is uniting it today is the experience of a common economic development, beginning with the Marshall Plan and culminating in an expanding Common Market. Whether a United States of Europe will be formally proclaimed in the near future is of course uncertain. But two things are virtually certain. (1) Government will become increasingly concerned with economic planning, conservation of the environment, and protection of human dignity. Insofar as these concerns are being met on a regional basis, Federalism (formal

16

or informal) prevails. (2) The external security of a United Europe would seem to depend on its disarmament rather than on its armament. Japan has shown what economic progress a determined nation can make when it forswears the burden of large-scale military expenditure. Moreover, inasmuch as the Soviet Union has ever since World War II proclaimed the complete demilitarization of Germany as the price of its re-unification, it would be exceedingly risky for a United Europe in which West Germany would be the leading power, at least economically and population-wise, to embark on a heavy armament program that might be viewed by the Soviet Union as an intolerable threat to its own security. On the other hand, if a United Europe committed itself to complete disarmament, it is conceivable that not only East Germany but also the other East Block countries would be allowed to join if they so desired. The Soviet Union's self-interest – or more specifically, the security of its Western frontier – might be better served by a peaceful, truly United Europe with which it could enter into normal relations, than by a cordon sanitaire *of more or less captive nations that have to be invaded from time to time, or else permanently occupied, and whose cultural assimilation might prove very difficult.*

Walter F. Bense
Religion Department
University of Wisconsin – Oshkosh

17

INTRODUCTION

NOTES

[1] *Sylvester John Hemleben was born in La Crosse, Wisconsin, in 1902. He was educated at what is now the University of Wisconsin—La Crosse, at the University of Iowa (B.A. in History, 1927; M.A. in History of International Relations, 1928), and at Fordham University (Ph.D. in Political Science - International Relations, 1931). He pursued post-doctoral studies at Columbia, Harvard, Cambridge, and Munich. From 1931 to 1945 he served as head of the Department of Social Studies in the School of Education at Fordham, from 1945 to 1947 as editor of the Historical Branch of the Chemical Corps in the U.S. Department of War, and from 1947 to 1961 as Professor of History at the University of Southwestern Louisiana. In the 1960s he obtained two law degrees from the University of Mississippi (LL.B. with Distinction, 1963; J.D., 1968) and has been admitted to practice law in Mississippi (1963) and before the U.S. Supreme Court (1971). He taught at the University of Mississippi School of Law from 1963 to 1965, with specialization in International Law, Legal History, and Employees' Rights. He has authored and edited many books and articles. Since 1966 he has served as Professor of Political Science at the Brevard Community College at Cocoa, Florida, near Cape Kennedy.*

[2] *Most of these points were also made in Merle Curti's review of this book in* The Political Science Quarterly *58, 1943, pp. 317 f.*

[3] *Especially in Hans Kohn's review in* The Saturday Review of Literature *26, June 5, 1943, p. 37.*

[4] *Two early Peace Plans that point towards Conciliarism are those of Ramon Lull and Pierre Dubois; see Rafael Gibert, "Lulio y Vives, sobre la paz," La Paix II (Recueils de la Société Jean Bodin pour l'histoire comparative des institutions XV; Brussels, 1962), pp. 125-169 (French summary, pp. 167-169), and the bibliography cited there; and Pierre DuBois, The Recovery of the Holy Land, tr. by W.I. Brandt (New York, 1956). On Conciliarism, see Brian Tierney, Foundations of the Conciliar Theory (Cambridge, 1955), Hubert Jedin, A History of the Council of Trent, T. I.: The Struggle for the Council (St. Louis, Mo., 1957), esp. pp. 5-138, and Carl Andresen, "History of the Medieval Councils in the West," in The Councils of the Church: History and Analysis, ed. by H.J. Margull (Philadelphia, 1966), pp. 82-240, esp. pp. 172 ff.).*

NOTES

[5]*Cf. Maurice de Gandillac, "Der cusanische Friedensbegriff,"* Zeitschrift für philosophische Forschung *9, 1955, pp. 186-196; and, in English: J.P. Dolan, ed.,* Unity and Reform: Selected Writings of Nicholas of Cusa *(Notre Dame, Ind., 1962), Morimichi Watanabe,* The Political Ideas of Nicholas of Cusa *(Geneva, 1963), and P. Sigmund,* Nicholas of Cusa and Medieval Political Thought *(Cambridge, Mass., 1964), and the earlier works cited in these.*

[6]*Cf. Robert P. Adams,* The Better Part of Valor: More, Erasmus, Colet, and Vives on Humanism, War, and Peace, 1496-1535 *(Seattle, 1962).*

[7]*King James I of England,* The Peace-Maker: or, Great Britain's Blessing *(London, 1619). The Plan is related to King George Podiebrady's by J.V. Polišensky, "Bohemia, the Turk, and the Christian Commonwealth (1462-1620)," Byzantinoslavica XIV, (Prague) 1953, pp. 105 f.*

[8]*Jan Amos Comenius,* De rerum humanarum emendatione consultatio catholica ad genus humanum, ante alios ad eruditos, religiosos, potentes Europae *(Prague, 1966; 2 vols.); cf. Vaclav Vanecek, "Deux Projets Tchèques des XVe et XVIIe siècles relatifs à l'organisation universelle de la paix: Projet du Roi Georges de Podebrady et de J.A. Komensky,"* La Paix II, pp. 199-218, esp. pp. 212 ff.

[9]*Bernardino M. Bonansea,* Tommaso Campanella: Renaissance Pioneer of Modern Thought *(Washington, D.C., 1969). Cf. Luis G. Alonso Getino O.P., "La Sociedad de Naciones, segun Campanella,"* Anuario de la Asociacion Francisco de Vitoria *V, 1932/33, pp. 71-105.*

[10]*Cf. two articles in* La Paix II: *Willy Onclin, "L'idée de la société internationale en Europe occidentale avant Grotius," pp. 219-239; and Antonio Truyol y Serra, "La conception de la paix chez Vitoria et les classiques espagnols du droit des gens," pp. 241-273.*

[11]*Hugo Grotius,* De Jure Belli ac Pacis Libri Tres *(Paris, 1625), Book III.*

[12]*Cf. Bernice Hamilton,* Political Thought in Sixteenth Century Spain; A Study of the Political Ideas of Vitoria, De Soto, Suarez, and Molina *(Oxford, 1963). Suarez'* Defensio fidei catholicae et apostolicae adversus Anglicanae sectae errores *(Coimbra, 1613) was aimed directly at King James I.*

NOTES

[13] *The main institutional expression of this interest is the Conference on Peace Research in History, which was organized in 1963 and functions in conjunction with the American Historical Association. It is also an active member of the Consortium on Peace Research, Education, and Development. The Conference has published a* Bibliography on Peace Research in History *(1969) and plans soon to launch a quarterly review.*

[14] *See the* International Repertory of Institutions Specializing in Research on Peace and Disarmament *(Reports and Papers in the Social Sciences No. 23, published by UNESCO), and the supplementary list in the* International Peace Studies Newsletter *(published by the Center for Peace Studies at the University of Akron) vol. I, No. 1, Fall 1971, pp. 2-5.*

[15] *United World Federalists are the main group advocating the extension of the Federalist principle to world government. But the African states, for example, seem to correspond much more nearly to the states (or republics) that make up the United States of America (or the Union of Soviet Socialist Republics) than to these unions themselves. Some form of regional federalism would seem to be a necessary intermediate step between nationalism and world federalism.*

PLANS FOR WORLD PEACE
THROUGH SIX CENTURIES

THE UNIVERSITY OF CHICAGO PRESS
CHICAGO, ILLINOIS

*

THE CAMBRIDGE UNIVERSITY PRESS
LONDON

Plans for World Peace
through Six Centuries

By SYLVESTER JOHN HEMLEBEN

Head of the Department of History and Social Studies
School of Education, Fordham University

THE UNIVERSITY OF CHICAGO PRESS

CHICAGO · ILLINOIS

TO MY WIFE

PREFACE

W E ARE now witnessing one of the greatest wars in history. Freemen everywhere are resolved that this war shall not be fought in vain. Never again must a strong military power led by unscrupulous leaders be allowed to threaten the forces of liberty and endanger civilization itself. We must so organize the world that peace will be secure and free peoples will no longer need to live in fear of others. The hope of establishing a world order that will make war impossible is not new. There have been men of vision who have urged the necessity of a league to guarantee peace.

It is the purpose of this study to trace the historical background and development of the idea of an organization to secure permanent peace. It is obvious that it is impossible to consider here every plan that has ever been conceived. Only those were selected which the author thought to be of greatest importance or interest, although some of the minor plans are indicated from time to time. Doubtless, no two scholars will fully agree as to which plans should rightly be chosen. In the matter of selection there will always be room for difference and disagreement. The present endeavor has been guided by the thought that it is an attempt to give a portrayal of the peace plans of history in a work of sufficiently small compass to enable the reader to make a survey and a comparative study all within the covers of a single book.

The study begins with the first real plans of the early fourteenth century. It will be noted that the work is limited in scope to the plans previous to the formation of the present League of Nations. A consideration of peace projects since

World War I would necessitate a treatment in some detail of the immediate origins, the history, and the organization of the League and the Permanent Court of International Justice. Such treatment is patently impossible within the limits of space, and all that could be accomplished in a work of this size would be something akin to a textbook account, which is easily enough obtainable. The author trusts that at a later time he may be able to undertake a second volume dealing with the plans for world peace that were proposed after World War I. It is hoped that the present book may indicate why peace plans of the past have failed to be put into effect; and perhaps it will suggest why the greatest of all peace plans, the present League of Nations, has not achieved what was expected of it. If lessons can be derived from a historical study of the development of the concepts of international organization for peace, then this work may possibly make a contribution, no matter how small.

In the preparation of this volume I am indebted for suggestions and encouragement to Dean Francis M. Crowley and Professor Lawrence J. Mannion, of the School of Education, Fordham University; to Dr. Harold Larson, of the National Archives, Washington, D.C.; to Mr. V. J. Sacco, Federal Assistant District Attorney, Hartford, Connecticut; to Professors James Michael Eagan and Thomas F. McManus, of the College of New Rochelle; to Professor Albert Salisbury Abel, School of Law, University of West Virginia; and to the late Professor Parker T. Moon, of Columbia University. The greatest debt of all I owe to my wife.

SYLVESTER JOHN HEMLEBEN

NEW YORK CITY

CONTENTS

INTRODUCTION

THE conception of an international organization to preserve peace is not novel. Well-wishers of mankind have, from time to time, caught a vision of permanent peace and have offered their plans on how best to achieve it. The present work offers a study of some of the most important peace plans of history and attempts to trace through them the development of the idea of organizing world peace. Long before the appearance of definite written projects the foundations had been laid in the practices of federation and arbitration.

To the ancient Greeks we are indebted for the conception of federation for peace. Several federations, of which the Delphic Amphictyony is the most noted, furnished the nearest approach in ancient times to a working league of nations. Yet it would be somewhat hasty to entitle such federations as "leagues of nations" in the modern sense of the term, since membership was drawn wholly from Greece itself, and the interests of the members were not primarily political but religious. When it is realized, however, that the Greek political unit was the city-state, each independent of the other, federation among these independent city-states will appear as a true accomplishment in co-operation. In addition, we are indebted to the Greeks for frequent use of arbitration as a peaceful means of settling disputes and for the development of the general arbitration treaty. Although the Greeks had constant recourse to federation and arbitration, it is evident from a perusal of Greek history that peace was not the natural condition of society. The first approach to world peace was achieved under the Roman Empire; but the peace of the Caesars cannot be considered international, for Rome dominated the world and recognized no equals. The Pax Romana was an enforced national peace, not a peace resulting from a league of independent nations. In such a system there was no place for arbitration as developed by the Greek city-states.

With the crumbling of the Roman Empire and the coming of the barbarians, peace in the political realm was no longer possible. Christian Europe turned to the spiritual realm, and the church assumed leadership, effecting, in a very real way, a common unity of Christendom. Arbitration, dormant during the Roman period, was brought into use in the Middle Ages. The papacy provided Europe with a supreme and final arbiter. Parallel with this was the attempt to establish political unity under a universal empire. There appeared the Carolingian and the Holy Roman empires, each claiming to be the legal successor to the former Roman Empire. While world peace was never as completely secured either by the universal church or by the universal empire as that attained under the Roman Empire, the idea of the unity of civilization was a real force throughout the Middle Ages. The rise of the spirit of nationality and the birth of the modern national state system were potent factors in the breakdown of this conception. Rulers cast aside the political philosophy of the Middle Ages with its acknowledgment of the natural law and the compact and substituted, instead, a philosophy based on the Roman law. Their claims to absolutism were supported by a rising group of theorists who recognized no moral obligations and no limitations on the powers of the monarch. Reason gave way to sheer force, and the claims to absolute power made themselves felt in the international order as well as in the national. Any hopes that might have survived

5

for a world federation through religion were made impossible by the Protestant revolt, which produced rival and conflicting Christian groups. Europe lost a common international arbiter, and in its stead was raised the sovereign state, which alone was the judge of its own conduct and obligations.

HICAL NOTE

The reader who may be interested in making an introductory study of the peace idea in ancient times and a survey of the conception in the Middle Ages apart from written projects is referred to the following:

nsdon Grady, *Epigraphic Sources of the Delphic Amphictyony* (Walton, N.Y., 1931); Anton H. Raeder, *L'Arbitrage international chez les Hellènes* (New York, 1912); Charles Calvo, *Le Droit international théorique et pratique: précédé d'un exposé historique des progrès de la science du droit des gens* (Paris, 1880–81); Ferdinand Dreyfus, *L'Arbitrage international* (Paris, 1892); Coleman Phillipson, *The International Law and Custom of Ancient Greece and Rome* (London, 1911); W. L. Westermann, "Interstate Arbitration in Antiquity," *Classical Journal*, Vol. II (1907); Wallace E. Caldwell, *Hellenic Conceptions of Peace* (New York, 1919); Marie Mathieu, *L'Evolution de l'idée de la société des nations* (Nancy, 1923); Marcus N. Tod, *International Arbitration amongst the Greeks* (Oxford, 1913); Michael I. Rostovseff, "International Relations in the Ancient World," in Edmund A. Walsh (ed.), *The History and Nature of International Relations* (New York, 1922); Henry S. Fraser, "A Sketch of the History of International Arbitration," *Cornell Law Quarterly*, Vol. XI, No. 2 (1926); Elizabeth York, *Leagues of Nations: Ancient, Mediaeval, and Modern* (London, 1919); Edward Augustus Freeman, *History of Federal Government in Greece and Italy* (London, 1893); V. J. Lewis, "The Peloponnesian League," *New Commonwealth*, Vol. I, No. 6 (March, 1933); Jacques Hodé, *L'Idée de fédération internationale dans l'histoire: les précurseurs de la société des nations* (Paris, 1921); Jackson Harvey Ralston, *International Arbitration from Athens to Locarno* (Stanford, Calif., 1929); Victor Bérard, *De arbitrio inter liberas Graecorum civitates* (Paris, 1894); W. W. Tarn, "Alexander the Great and the Unity of Mankind," *Proceedings of the British Academy*, Vol. XIX (1933); Marie V. Williams, "Internationalism in Ancient Greece," *London*

Quarterly Review, Vol. CLVI (July, 1931); Louise E. Matthael, "The Place of Arbitration and Mediation in Ancient Systems of International Ethics," *Classical Quarterly*, Vol. II (October, 1908); George A. Finch, *The Sources of Modern International Law* (Washington, D.C., 1937); C. L. Lange, *Histoire de l'internationalisme* ("Publications de l'Institut Nobel norvégien," Tome IV [Kristiania and New York, 1919]); C. L. Lange, "Histoire de la doctrine pacifique et de son influence sur le développement du droit international," *Recueil des cours, 1926, III*, Tome XIII (1927); John Eppstein, *The Catholic Tradition of the Law of Nations* (Washington, D.C., 1935); C. van Vollenhoven, *The Law of Peace* (London, 1936); August C. Krey, "The International State of the Middle Ages: Some Reasons for Its Failure," *American Historical Review*, Vol. XXVIII, No. 1 (October, 1922); Loren C. MacKinney, "The People and Public Opinion in the Eleventh Century Peace Movement," *Speculum*, Vol. V (April, 1930); Paschal Robinson, "Peace Laws and Institutions of the Medieval Church," *Ecclesiastical Review*, Vol. LII (1915); R. F. Wright, *Medieval Internationalism, the Contribution of the Medieval Church to International Law and Peace* (London, 1930); William F. Roemer and John Tracy Ellis, *The Catholic Church and Peace Efforts*, study presented to the Catholic Association for International Peace by the History Committee (New York, 1934); John Eyre W. Wallis, *The Sword of Justice or the Christian Philosophy of War Completed in the Idea of a League of Nations* (Oxford, 1920); Frédéric Duval, *De la paix de Dieu à la paix de fer* (Paris, 1923); Maurice De Wulf, "The Society of Nations in the Thirteenth Century," *International Journal of Ethics* (Concord, N.H.), Vol. XXIX (January, 1919); Siegfried Frey, *Das öffentlich-rechtliche Schiedsgericht in Oberitalien im XII. und XIII. Jahrhundert* (Luzern, 1928); A. Mérignhac, *Traité théorique et pratique de l'arbitrage international* (Paris, 1895); Michel Revon, *L'Arbitrage international* (Paris, 1892); Comte L. Kamarowsky, *Le Tribunal international* (Paris, 1887); Mileta Novacovitch, *Les Compromis et les arbitrages internationaux du XIIᵉ au XVᵉ siècle* (Paris, 1905); John Gruber, "The Peace Negotiations of the Avignon Popes," *Catholic Historical Review*, Vol. XIX, No. 2 (July, 1933); John K. Cartwright, "Contributions of the Papacy to International Peace," *Catholic Historical Review*, Vol. VIII (April, 1928); Franziskus Stratmann, *The Church and War: A Catholic Study* (New York, 1929); Joseph Müller, "L'Œuvre de toutes les confessions Chrétiennes (Églises) pour la paix internationale," *Recueil des cours, 1930, I* (Paris), Tome XXXI (1931).

CHAPTER I

EARLY PEACE PLANS

PIERRE DUBOIS, lawyer and adviser to Philip le Bel, king of France, was the medieval herald of modern projects of world organization for peace.[1] Dubois was born in Normandy about 1255, attended the University of Paris, and became successful in the legal profession. His interest in writing, however, led him to give expression to his ideas concerning contemporary affairs in a succession of pamphlets between the years 1300 and 1314.[2] In his chief work, *De recuperatione Terre Sancte*,[3] written between 1305 and 1307,[4] Dubois advocated a federation of Christian sovereign states. A staunch supporter of his king in the latter's struggle with Pope Boniface VIII, it was only natural that Dubois's devotion to the crown led him to conceive an association of nations in which France would be the dominant member.[5] Whether this in Dubois's mind amounted to the establishment of a French overlordship is open to question. It would seem that, while he expected France to play the leading role in the federation, he was

[1] V. J. Lewis, "Pierre du Bois," *New Commonwealth*, I, No. 12 (September, 1933), 10.

[2] Charles C. Tansill, "Early Plans for World Peace," *Historical Outlook*, XX, No. 7 (November, 1929), 322.

[3] Pierre Dubois, *De recuperatione Terre Sancte: traité de politique générale, pub. d'après le manuscrit du Vatican par Charles V. Langlois* (Paris, 1891).

[4] Langlois, Introduction to *ibid.*, p. x. Dubois's work was first published in 1611. See Elizabeth V. Souleyman, *The Vision of World Peace in Seventeenth and Eighteenth-Century France* (New York, 1941), p. 3.

[5] Tansill, *op. cit.*, p. 322.

opposed to the creation of a world-state dominated by a single lord.[6] Although advanced by the greater part of his contemporaries,[7] he apparently saw that the hope of a revived Roman Empire was a dream that would but lead to disaster, and he therefore eliminated the conception of a universal monarchy as the solution.

The treatise, while purporting to deal with a plan for recovering the Holy Land, was more concerned with the general problem of European relationships. Peace among Christian rulers was considered a necessary prelude to the successful undertaking of a crusade. It is probable that Dubois used the subject of the Holy Land as a means of popularizing his work, but this does not necessarily imply that the subject of the crusade was a mere excuse for writing on other schemes in which he was more interested.[8] The idea of a crusade was being widely discussed at the time, and Dubois was only one of a number of writers in the first decade of the fourteenth century to reflect this interest. *De recuperatione* was divided into two parts. The first and longer part was dedicated to Edward I of England as one who was particularly interested in a new crusade.[9] This was probably meant as a circular to be sent by the French king to the European courts.[10] The second part was concerned with Philip's royal problems and was meant for him alone.

[6] Delisle Burns, "A Medieval Internationalist: Pierre Dubois," *Monist*, XXVII (1917), 108.

[7] C. L. Lange, *Histoire de l'internationalisme* ("Publications de l'Institut Nobel norvégien," Tome IV [Kristiania and New York, 1919]), p. 98.

[8] Eileen E. Power, "Pierre du Bois and the Domination of France" in F. J. C. Hearnshaw (ed.), *The Social and Political Ideas of Some Great Mediaeval Thinkers* (London, 1923), p. 147. Souleyman presents the controversy among scholars on this point (*op. cit.*, pp. 3–5).

[9] Burns, *op. cit.*, pp. 105–6. A survey of the plan is given on pp. 105–13.

[10] Frederick Maurice Powicke, "Pierre Dubois: A Medieval Radical," *Owens College Historical Essays* (London, 1902), pp. 175–76.

According to Dubois, war breeds war until war becomes a habit (par. 2). He considered war as the principal obstacle to progress and proposed the establishment of a council of nations to decide all quarrels by arbitration.[11] If the council disagreed (par. 3), nine judges were to be selected to settle the dispute. In order to prevent any direct influence by the disputants on the judges, three judges were to be selected by the council to represent each contestant and three from among the ecclesiastics.[12] Appeals could be carried to the pope.[13] Dubois was distinctly a pioneer, for he was the first to propose an international court of arbitration. He urged the kings and the general council to institute a boycott (par. 5) against a power making war, and he advocated concerted military action against the offending nation. In this recommendation Dubois preceded the sanctions of the Covenant of the League of Nations by over six centuries. After defeating the guilty people the European allies were to send them off to colonize the Holy Land! Because he advocated that the economic saving from the abolition of wars was to be expended for the establishment of international schools (par. 60), he may be considered one of the earliest proponents of international education.

[11] Stawell states that arbitration was more fully used in the time of Dubois than at any other period in medieval history and that Dubois was recommending a method which was tried and which he knew would continue to prove useful (F. Melian Stawell, *The Growth of International Thought* [London, 1929], p. 67).

[12] Dubois held, however, that a prerequisite to general peace was a reform of the church. He suggested as a first step that the pope deter the cardinals and bishops from going to war. Next he recommended the abolition of the temporal power of the popes, for then no one would need to go to war for the papacy, and thus a beginning would be made on the road to peace. Then he called for the confiscation of ecclesiastical property by the states, the wealth to be used for the common European civilization (Burns, *op. cit.*, pp. 110–11).

[13] Stawell (*op. cit.*, p. 65) points out that Dubois was writing when the "Babylonian captivity" at Avignon had already begun and that Dubois therefore expected the pope to be under the influence of the French king.

While in some respects Dubois was a pioneer, he was not
entirely original, as perhaps no one can be, for all are prod-
ucts of their age. The ideas which he advanced were current
in the Europe of his day. By some writers Dubois has been
bitterly assailed and by others just as stoutly defended.
Characterizations of his proposals, as one writer says,
"stretch the entire octave of praise and condemnation."[14]
One writer states: "When all is said and done there can be
few books more remarkable in their prevision of the future
than the *De Recuperatione*. . . . . Pierre Du Bois' book was a
prophecy rather than a programme."[15] Langlois speaks of
the Norman's conceptions as noble, elaborated dreams, be-
queathed with a very liberal intelligence, and animated with
a violent love for the good and the better.[16]

In contrast to Dubois, who proposed an assembly representative of the European powers, Dante, early in the fourteenth century,[17] in his *De monarchia*[18] called for the estab-

[14] Tansill, *op. cit.*, p. 322.

[15] Power, art. cit., in Hearnshaw, *op. cit.*, p. 163.

[16] Langlois, Introduction to Dubois, *op. cit.*, pp. xix, xx.

[17] *De monarchia* was not published until 1559 at Basel. Some scholars believe that the work was written prior to Dante's exile in 1302, probably in
Florence; some hold that it was produced between 1308 and 1314, heralding
the coming of Henry of Luxemburg to Italy; others maintain that it was one
of his last works and believe that it was composed between 1318 and 1321
(Aurelia Henry [ed.], Introduction to Dante Alighieri, *The "De monarchia" of
Dante Alighieri* [Boston, 1904], pp. xxxii–xlvi).

[18] Centuries before, Augustine had given to the world (A.D. 413–26) his
great work, *Civitas Dei*. While it has been called "one of the most difficult
books to read," nevertheless in design and execution "its grand idea is clear"
(A. J. Carlyle, "St. Augustine and the City of God," in Hearnshaw, *op. cit.*,
p. 40). This book became "the chief source" of disclosing the Christian attitude toward peace (Herbert F. Wright, "St. Augustine on International
Peace," *Catholic World*, CV [September, 1917], 745). St. Augustine had presented "for the first time in history" the plan of a great empire of peace binding the world and all nations together (M. Erzberger, *The League of Nations:*

lishment of a world-state under an all-powerful emperor. The Italy of Dante's day was distracted with quarrels and endless strife. Factions reigned within every city, and the turbulent country was divided and impotent. It was "in a strain of passionate patriotism that the 'De Monarchia' was written to show his [Dante's] countrymen the principles of government by which alone he believed safety could be found amid such dire peril."[19] The *De monarchia* was a political treatise "born of the special circumstances of his own time."[20] Dante raised "a passionate cry for some power to still the tempest"[21] that engulfed the civilization of his day, and he found the solution in a universal emperor. If, to Dante, the Middle Ages represented war and conflict, the empire meant peace.[22] In the realm of real politics he saw the

The Way to the World's Peace, trans. Bernard Miall [New York, 1919], p. 77; Louis Carle Bonnard, *Essai sur la conception d'une société des nations avant le XXe siècle* [Paris, 1921], p. 20). St. Augustine held the foundation of the City of God to be peace, and he presented the ideal of an earthly society which "should be an exact copy of the divine city where all is peace and unity" (Maurice De Wulf, "The Society of Nations in the Thirteenth Century," *International Journal of Ethics* [Concord, N.H.], XXIX [January, 1919], 219). On Augustine see further: James Brown Scott, *Law, the State, and the International Community* (New York, 1939), I, 184–95. In the thirteenth century St. Thomas Aquinas in his *Summa theologica*, dealing with the problem of peace and the problem of a just war and its characteristics, proposed to achieve the same end by exalting the papal theocracy. The writings of St. Thomas, along with Gratian, were the authoritative manuals in philosophy and theology and greatly influenced later writers (William F. Roemer, "The Scope of This Study Determined by a Christian Philosophy of Peace," in William F. Roemer and John Tracy Ellis, *The Catholic Church and Peace Efforts* [New York, 1934], p. 17). On St. Thomas see further: Scott, *op. cit.*, pp. 213–22.

[19] Charlton Wilkinson, "Dante's Vision of International Peace," *Nation and the Athenaeum*, XXX, No. 3 (October 15, 1921), 111.

[20] *Loc. cit.*

[21] Viscount James Bryce, *The Holy Roman Empire* (New York, 1904), p. 280.

[22] E. Sharwood Smith, "Dante and World-Empire," in Hearnshaw, *op. cit.*, p. 128.

embodiment of his hopes in Henry of Luxemburg,[23] who was crowned Emperor in 1308. In him Dante saw the ideal emperor who would rid the world of the evils from which it was suffering. The *De monarchia* was written in behalf of imperial power against the spiritual and has been termed by one author "a specimen of the writings which the conflict of Boniface VIII and Philip IV called forth."[24]

Dante explained his purpose in writing the treatise in the following words:

> But seeing that among other truths, ill-understood yet profitable, the knowledge touching temporal monarchy is at once most profitable and most obscure, and that because it has no immediate reference to worldly gain it is left unexplored by all, therefore it is my purpose to draw it forth from its hiding-places, as well that I may spend my toil for the benefit of the world, as that I may be the first to win the prize of so great an achievment to my own glory. The work indeed is difficult, and I am attempting what is beyond my strength; but I trust not in my own powers, but in the light of that Bountiful Giver, "Who giveth to all men liberally, and upbraideth not."[25]

Dante divided his work into three books. The first book dealt with the question whether a temporal monarchy is necessary for the well-being of the world; the second answered the question whether the Roman people assumed to itself by right the dignity of empire; while the third book undertook the problem of whether the authority of the monarch comes directly from God or from some vicar of God.

In the first book Dante maintained that the end of the

[23] V. J. Lewis, "Dante," *New Commonwealth*, II, No. 1 (October, 1933), 8.

[24] Mandell Creighton, *A History of the Papacy during the Period of the Reformation* (London, 1882), I, 30–31.

[25] Richard William Church, *Dante: An Essay to Which Is Added a Translation of "De monarchia" by F. J. Church* (London, 1879), p. 178. The following page references to the text of *De monarchia* are made to the Church edition.

civil order of mankind is "to set in action the whole capacity of that understanding which is capable of development,"[26] and that, in order to achieve this, mankind needs the calm and tranquillity of universal peace.[27] Where several means are ordained to attain an end, one of them should govern the others. There must be one to guide and govern, and therefore an emperor of a world-state is necessary.[28] "It is only under the rule of one Prince that the parts of humanity are well adapted to their whole" and adapted to the Prince of the Universe, who is one God.[29] Men are made in the likeness of God, and God is one. When the race is wholly united in one body, it is "most made like unto God."[30] Since the whole heaven is regulated with one motion and by one mover, God, the best state is one regulated by one law and a single prince.[31] There may be controversy between any two princes, and there should be a means of judgment; but one cannot be judged by the other if they are equal. Therefore, it is necessary for the world to have one monarch to whom all princes are subject, and thus controversies can be settled.[32] The universal monarch is most disposed to work for justice,[33] "for if he be really a Monarch he cannot have enemies."[34]

The human race is ordered best when it is most free.[35] "Men exist for themselves, and not at the pleasure of others, only if a Monarch rules; for then only are the perverted forms of government set right, while democracies, oligarchies, and tyrannies, drive mankind into slavery, as is obvious to anyone who goes about among them all. . . . ."[36]

[26] P. 184.

[27] Pp. 184–85.

[28] Pp. 185–88.

[29] P. 189.

[30] P. 190.

[31] P. 191.

[32] Pp. 191–92.

[33] Pp. 192–98.

[34] P. 198.

[35] Pp. 198–201.

[36] P. 200.

Mankind is best off under an emperor who is "the servant of all."[37] The monarch is the only one who can be fitted in the best possible way to govern, for he has nothing to tempt his appetite, as have other princes, and "in him there may be judgment and justice more strongly than in any other."[38] Dante indicated that, while there would be one supreme prince, this did not mean that the prince would direct every trifling matter in local government. Nations and states, Dante pointed out, have their peculiarities and therefore should be governed by different laws.[39] Only in matters common to all men would they be ruled by one monarch and governed by one law.[40] Dante thus allowed for local government. He held that "all concord depends on unity which is in wills."[41] There must be one will to regulate all the others. He concluded his first book by pointing out that Christ willed to be born when Augustus was monarch, "under whom a perfect Monarchy existed and the world was everywhere quiet."[42]

In the second book Dante claimed that it was the role of Italy to accomplish this political union. He first asked whether the Roman people assumed to itself by right the dignity of the empire. Answering in the affirmative, he stated that "what God wills to see in mankind is to be held as real and true Right."[43] Therefore, it was by right and not by usurpation that the Roman people assumed to itself the office of the empire over all mankind. It was fitting that the noblest people be preferred, and the Romans were the noblest.[44] Further, the Roman Empire was helped to its perfection by miracles, and therefore it was of the right. Whoever works for the good of the state, works with right as the

[37] P. 201.	[40] P. 205.	[43] P. 215.
[38] P. 203.	[41] P. 208.	[44] P. 216.
[39] Pp. 204–5.	[42] P. 209–10.	

end.[45] In bringing the whole world into subjection the Romans aimed at this good of the state, and thus they aimed at the end of right, the common good. Consequently it was by right that they assumed the dignity of the empire.[46] In addition, the Roman people were ordained for empire by Nature; if this were not so, Nature would have been untrue to herself, which is impossible.[47] The Roman people prevailed when all were striving for the empire of the world, which shows that the Romans conquered by the will of God.[48] Christ's birth in the Roman Empire proved that the authority of the empire was just. His death confirmed its jurisdiction over all mankind.[49]

In the third book Dante attacked the question of whether the authority of the monarch comes directly from God or from some vicar of God. Affirming his loyalty to the church, Dante wrote: ". . . . strong in the reverence which a dutiful son owes to his father, which a dutiful son owes to his mother, dutiful to Christ, dutiful to the Church, dutiful to the Chief Shepherd, dutiful to all who profess the religion of Christ—I begin in this book the contest for the maintenance of the truth."[50] He then refuted the contention that the authority of the empire depended upon the authority of the church, disposing of one argument after another.[51] Dante

[45] Pp. 220–23. [47] Pp. 233–34. [49] Pp. 251–55.

[46] Pp. 224–30. [48] P. 239. [50] P. 264.

[51] He refuted the argument drawn from the sun and the moon (pp. 264–70); the argument drawn from the precedence of Levi over Judah (pp. 270–71); the argument drawn from the crowning and disposition of Saul by Samuel (pp. 271–73); the argument drawn from the oblation of the Magi (pp. 273–75); the argument drawn from the power of the keys given to Peter (pp. 275–78); the argument drawn from the two swords (pp. 278–82); the donation of Constantine to Pope Sylvester (pp. 282–87); the summoning of Charles the Great by Pope Hadrian (pp. 287–88); the argument from reason (pp. 288–94).

declared that "man had need of two guides for his life, as he had a twofold end in life; whereof one is the Supreme Pontiff, to lead mankind to eternal life, according to the things revealed to us; and the other is the Emperor, to guide mankind to happiness in this world, in accordance with the teaching of philosophy."[52] It was Dante's contention that the authority of temporal monarchy comes down, with no intermediate will, from the fountain of universal authority and that this fountain flows from the abundance of the goodness of God.[53] In certain matters, however, Dante conceded that the prince was subject to the pope. "Let, therefore, Caesar be reverent to Peter, as the first-born son should be reverent to his father, that he may be illuminated with the light of his father's grace, and so may be stronger to lighten the world over which he has been placed by Him alone, who is the ruler of all things spiritual as well as temporal."[54]

Dante thus divided his work into three books: the first maintained that, just as there is one God over mankind, so there should be one supreme monarch to effect political union; the second asserted that it was the role of Italy to accomplish this political union; the third advised separation and independence of the state from the church, since the emperor derived his powers directly from God. It is to be observed that, while Dante proposed the union of mankind under the leadership of Italy, he was not suggesting autocratic rule or despotism, for he held that if the monarch exceeded his powers men would no longer need obey or respect him.[55] In this connection Miss York observes that Dante was influenced by St. Thomas Aquinas, who advocated self-government.[56] Stawell perceives elements in Dante's doc-

[52] P. 302.   [53] Pp. 303–4.   [54] P. 304.

[55] Robert Jones and S. S. Sherman, *The League of Nations from Idea to Reality* (London, 1927), p. 44.

[56] Elizabeth York, *Leagues of Nations: Ancient, Mediaeval, and Modern* (London, 1919), pp. 61–62.

trine which would lead to absolutism, as there was no provision for the election of the monarch and no opportunity
for the community to share in legislation on important
matters.[57]

Imbued, as he was, with medieval traditions, Dante envisioned a world-wide state with one ruler, unselfish as he
was all-powerful, who would suppress all tyrannies and
bring about universal peace. It was to the glory of the
former Roman Empire, with its Pax Romana, that Dante
turned for inspiration. "He imagined that the Roman
empire had been one great state; he persuaded himself
that Christendom might be such. He was wrong in both
instances; but in this case, as in so many others, he had already caught the spirit and ideas of a far-distant future."[58]
Dante has been called "the first great modern man";[59] and in
his conception of the organization of humanity in which the
different states would conserve their particularisms and their
autonomy, it has been claimed that he approached very
closely to contemporary thought.[60] However this may be,
his book has frequently been referred to, in the words of
Lord Bryce, as "an epitaph instead of a prophecy."[61] Dante's
philosophical treatise,[62] medieval in its conception and glori-
ous in its spirit, was impossible of fulfilment, for the subsequent appearance of the national states marked the passing
of cosmopolitanism.[63]

[57] Stawell, *op. cit.*, pp. 54–55.   [58] Church, *op. cit.*, p. 86.

[59] Edwin D. Mead, *Organize the World* (Boston, n.d.), p. 9.

[60] Lange, *op. cit.*, p. 74.   [61] Bryce, *op. cit.*, p. 280.

[62] The style of this Latin work appears to some as wearisomely disputative
(John Addington Symonds, *An Introduction to the Study of Dante* [Edinburgh,
1890], pp. 75–76).

[63] One writer declares that Dante's ideal "never has been, and is never
likely to be realised by a personal monarchy" (Lonsdale Ragg, "Dante and a
League of Nations," *Anglo-Italian Review*, II, No. 8 [December, 1918], 333).

Another outstanding political treatise of the fourteenth century[64] was the *Defensor pacis*. This famous anticlerical tract is generally attributed by scholars to a joint authorship, that of Marsiglio of Padua and his colleague, John of Jandun.[65] The work is more popularly known under the authorship of Marsiglio of Padua. The essay was divided into three "dictiones," that is, statements, which purported to show that peace was an indispensable benefit to human society. The first book devoted itself to a discussion of a working model of the "natural" state and the principal object of the state, which, the authors maintained, was the securing and furthering of peace. The second book examined the origin and development of the church, the supremacy of the Roman papal system, and its relation to the civil powers. Marsiglio and his collaborator attempted to establish the supremacy of the empire and its independence of the Holy See. They rejected any claim of papal supremacy over tem-

[64] Sullivan is of the opinion that the *Defensor pacis* was written in 1324. The plan is surveyed in James Sullivan, "The Manuscripts and Date of Marsiglio of Padua's *Defensor pacis*," *English Historical Review*, XX (1905), 293–307. Previté-Orton states that on June 24, 1324, the *Defensor pacis* was finished (C. W. Previté-Orton [ed.], Introduction to The *"Defensor pacis" of Marsilius of Padua* [Cambridge, England, 1928], p. xi). For a summary of the structure and contents of each dictio, *ibid.*, pp. xiii–xxvi; for the Latin text, *ibid.*, pp. 1–501; on the manuscripts, *ibid.*, pp. xxvi–xlii. The range of Marsiglio of Padua's reading is indicated from a study of the acknowledged quotations in C. W. Previté-Orton, "The Authors Cited in the *Defensor pacis*," in H. W. C. Davis (ed.), *Essays in History Presented to Reginald Lane Poole* (Oxford, 1927), pp. 405–20.

[65] A. C. F. Beales, *The History of Peace: A Short Account of the Organized Movements for International Peace* (New York, 1931), p. 23; Lange, *op. cit.*, p. 76; J. W. Allen, "Marsiglio of Padua and Medieval Secularism," in Hearnshaw, *op. cit.*, p. 170; Stawell, *op. cit.*, p. 58. Previté-Orton says that the share of John of Jandun "in the actual composition remains dubious; but he was at any rate considered equally responsible with Marsilius for the heretical opinions propounded in Dictio II" (Introduction to The *"Defensor pacis" of Marsilius of Padua*, p. ix). In Previté-Orton's opinion the main author is Marsiglio of Padua (*ibid.*, p. xxvi).

EARLY PEACE PLANS

poral affairs—over kings, lords, and princes. They vigorously attacked the papacy, which had gained its control, they charged, by a series of "usurpations." The work went so far as to encourage the seizure of church property by the secular power. It further stressed the supremacy of the civil power with regards to benefices, appointments, and other clerical matters. In the third book the authors summed up the results of the first and second. They believed that the supreme authority in the church should be a council appointed not by the pope but by the different Christian lands. The pope's pre-eminence was to be strictly honorary, and he was to be elected by the people or by their delegates, the princes. He was to have no power to define dogma or promulgate bulls.

The greatest contribution of the *Defensor pacis* perhaps may be said to be this discussion of the representative system. Marsiglio was primarily a political theorist employed in defending the rights of civil authority against what he represented as "encroachments" and "usurpations" of the Holy See.[66] The work was "a keen, bold and clear assertion of the rights of the State as against the Church";[67] but, as one writer has pointed out, it has little to do with the avoidance of war in spite of its pacific title, for "the peace with which the authors are concerned is rather the stability of the constitution."[68] Yet it has been called "one of the most remarkable treatises that remain to us from the Middle Ages."[69]

[66] Ephraim Emerton, *The "Defensor pacis" of Marsiglio of Padua: A Critical Study* (Cambridge, Mass., 1920), p. 16. It was the condition of northern Italy which Marsiglio of Padua believed was brought about by papal and ecclesiastical interference that chiefly prompted him to write the book (Previté-Orton, Introduction to *The "Defensor pacis" of Marsilius of Padua*, p. xiii).

[67] Creighton, *op. cit.*, p. 37.   [68] Stawell, *op. cit.*, p. 58.

[69] Bryce, *op. cit.*, p. 225. In relation to the "modern" ideas of government

In the second half of the fifteenth century George Poděbrad, king of Bohemia, proposed an international parliament.[70] He desired to bring about a general understanding to secure a lasting peace which would also limit the powers of the pope and the Emperor and protect Christianity against the Turks. The scheme, called after Poděbrad, was not so much the king's work as that of his chancellor and adviser, Antoine Marini, of Grenoble.[71] In 1461 Marini presented the plan to Rome. In this first project, it will be noted, there was no thought of eliminating the influence of the pope, although King George, who was a Hussite, expected that a conflict would ensue between himself and the papacy.[72] Rather, great weight was placed upon a crusade in which all Christian nations would participate and in which the papacy would assume a leading role. The prominence given to an expedition against the infidels is understandable, for it was but a few years since Constantinople had fallen (1453) into the hands of the Turks. While the alleged object was a crusade, it is possible that the Hussite king's primary purpose was to secure alliances for himself to

expressed in the *Defensor pacis*, it is to be noted that, although a "radical," he was not expressing new ideas and cannot be considered an innovator (Scott, *op. cit.*, p. 275).

[70] Ferdinand Veverka (letter), "United Europe Idea," *New York Times*, March 23, 1930, sec. 3, p. 5.

[71] John Kapras, *The Peace League of George Poděbrad, King of Bohemia* (Prague, 1919), II, Part V, 9; William Menzies Alexander, *League of Nations in History* (London, 1918), p. 2; Jones and Sherman, *op. cit.*, p. 44; W. Evans Darby, "Some European Leagues of Peace," in *Problems of the War* (Vol. IV [1919] of the *Transactions of the Grotius Society*), p. 172; Souleyman, *op. cit.*, p. 9. Souleyman concludes that the plan of Dubois might have been known to the king and Marini.

[72] Kapras, *op. cit.*, p. 7.

strengthen his position in a probable conflict with the papacy.[73]

The king of Poland approved the project in 1462, and a defensive alliance was made between Poland and Bohemia. The treaty provided that all disputes between the two powers should be settled by arbitration.[74] At this time the antipapal attitude was not as yet injected into the plan. In the same year, in negotiations at Venice, a similar league was proposed and favorably received by Bohemia, France, Poland, Hungary, Burgundy, and Bavaria. The Venetian representatives asserted that it was improper to exclude the pope from the league and from the expedition against the Turks.[75] In 1464 a great Czech embassy went to France,[76] and in the proposed federation no special place was assigned either to the pope or to the Emperor. The French king, Louis XI, was disposed to view the plan with high esteem, as he was not on friendly terms with the pope. The pope's party, however, was too powerful in France at this time to permit Louis to give his assent.[77]

The project called for a federation of Christian princes of France, Germany, Italy, and eventually of Spain to preserve peace among themselves and to protect Christianity against

[73] Percy Ellwood Corbett (trans.), Introduction to Desiderius Erasmus, *Institutio principis Christiani* ("Grotius Society Publications: Texts for Students of International Relations," No. 1 [London, 1921]), p. 11.

[74] Kapras, *op. cit.*, p. 10. [75] *Loc. cit.*

[76] The Latin text of the treaty of alliance and confederation (France, Bohemia, and Venice) to resist the Turks is given in Ernst Schwitsky, *Der europäische Fürstenbund Georgs von Poděbrad: Ein Beitrag zur Geschichte der Weltfriedensidee* (Borna und Leipzig, 1907), Anhang, pp. 49–60.

[77] V. J. Lewis, "The Bohemian Project of 1464," *New Commonwealth*, II, No. 3 (December, 1933), 10; Charles H. Levermore, "Synopsis of Plans for International Organization," *Advocate of Peace*, LXXXI, No. 8 (August, 1919), 266.

the Turks.[78] In the proposed federation the pope and the Emperor were not to be accorded their special position in the Christian world. The Emperor, if he took part in the league, was to be reduced to the same position as the other German princes, and given second place, as first was assigned to the French king. The pope was not even permitted to become a member of the federation, but he was expected to co-operate with the league in certain matters.[79] The project stipulated that the powers were to delegate to the federation their independent right of waging war, a provision which it is most unlikely our present-day sovereign states would adopt. The draft treaty presented to Louis XI provided that the member-states were to protect each other against attacks by nonmembers, and even without invitation were to use their influence to prevent war among nations not members of the league. If a nonmember refused to accept the decision of the confederation, the member-states were to wage war against it. The chief organ of the confederation was to be an assembly, which was to meet for the first time at Basel and later was to meet successively in all the countries of the league. The assembly was to be organized on a nationalistic basis. Each nationality was to be accorded one vote, and the various political divisions were not to be granted separate votes. Therefore, all princes of the same nationality would be obliged to come to an agreement before voting in the assembly.

King George's plan was one of the first to recognize the principle of nationality that was arising. The project was a definite breaking-away from the earlier idea of the world-state. The assembly admitted new members, passed rules and regulations concerning its own organization, decided questions of war and peace, provided for the army, directed

[78] Kapras, *op. cit.*, p. 13.　　　　[79] *Ibid.*

military action, and was even empowered to introduce military coins for the army. The assembly administered and disposed of conquered territories, raised funds, appointed the federal court, and possessed general legislative powers.[80] The other organ of the league was to be a tribunal or court of justice, which was to be by no means as important as the assembly. It was primarily a tribunal for the princes. The court was to co-operate with the assembly and to administer justice without undue formalities.[81] The confederation was to have its own badge, its own seal, as well as treasury and archives. The association was to be served by a number of officials, not to comprise a permanent staff, but selected from the country in which the confederation was meeting.[82] The plan of Poděbrad differed from previous plans in that it was actually proposed in treaty form to the governments of several countries. While it may be more complete and more exact than its predecessors, the project of Poděbrad, although sponsored by a king, remained, like the others, a mere proposal. Even a royal plan for a league of nations was without great influence on the politics and ideas of the day.

In 1513 a new peace plan, that of William of Ciervia and John Sylvagius, chancellor of Burgundy,[83] was prompted by the wars that were raging in Europe.[84] The project of Ciervia and Sylvagius called for a congress of kings at Cambray to consist of Emperor Maximilian, Francis I of France,

---

[80] *Ibid.*, pp. 14–15.

[81] *Ibid.*, pp. 15–16.   [82] *Ibid.*, p. 15.

[83] It seems that the first mention of this plan was in a passage in one of Erasmus' Latin letters. Editor's Preface to Erasmus, *The Complaint of Peace, to Which Is Added "Antipolemus"* or *"The Plea of Reason, Religion, and Humanity, against War"* (1st American ed.; Boston, 1813), pp. iii, iv.

[84] Frederick C. Hicks, "The Literature of Abortive Schemes of World Organization," *American Library Institute: Papers and Proceedings, 1919* (1920), p. 161.

Henry VIII of England, and Charles, the sovereign of the Low Countries. They were to promise to keep peace with each other, and in consequence peace would be kept throughout Europe. But, according to Erasmus, "certain persons" who profit by war made the realization of the plan impossible.[85]

This proved a great disappointment to Erasmus and occasioned his writing, upon the suggestion of John Sylvagius, the *Querela pacis*, or *The Complaint of Peace*.[86] The title in the original language is *Querela pacis, undique gentium ejectae profligataeque*, and we gather from internal evidence that the work was written about 1517.[87] Since Erasmus had little faith in treaties, he directed his plea to kings, whom he believed were the instigators of war.[88] As he reviewed the wars of the foregoing twelve years, he was led to assert that they were undertaken for the sake of kings to the detriment of the people, who often had little or no concern in their origin or prosecution.[89] The kings must have looked with disapproval upon this contention and were undoubtedly startled when Erasmus went on to say that wars should not be declared by the heads of governments "but by the full and unanimous consent of the whole people."[90] Erasmus was rather naïve in assuming that the "unanimous" consent of the "whole" people could be so easily obtained. He asked why kings did not reconcile their differences instead of resorting to arms,

[85] Editor's Preface to Erasmus, *The Complaint of Peace*, pp. iii, iv.

[86] *Ibid.*, p. iv.

[87] *Ibid.*, p. iii. The work was dedicated to Philip of Burgundy, the bishop of Utrecht, who acknowledged it under date of December 6, 1517 (Edwin D. Mead, "An Early Scheme To Organize the World," *Independent*, LXIII [August 29, 1907], 498).

[88] Erasmus, *The Complaint of Peace*, p. 16.

[89] *Ibid.*, p. 40.   [90] *Ibid.*, p. 55.

since there were laws by which disputes could be judged, since there were wise men, worthy prelates, and bishops whose advice could be sought and who could bring about a reconciliation.[91] Even if the arbiters were unjust, which was improbable, rival kings would suffer less injury than if they resorted to war, an irrational and doubtful means of obtaining a decision.[92] Erasmus thought that it was the special duty of the clergy to discountenance war. They should be engaged in the "humane work of preaching, recommending, and inculcating peace."[93] Erasmus would even have the clergy refuse burial in consecrated ground to all who died in battle. This, indeed, would have been drastic punishment for the people of his age.

The cosmopolitan sweep of Erasmus' vision, the dream of the unity of civilization so characteristic of the Middle Ages, is well expressed in the following:

Let the lovers of discord, and the promoters of bloodshed between nations, divided only by a name and a channel, rather reflect this world, the whole of the planet called earth, is the common country of all who live and breathe upon it, if the title of one's country is allowed to be a sufficient reason for unity among fellow-countrymen; and let them also remember, that all men, however distinguished by political or accidental causes, are sprung from the same parents, if consanguinity and affinity are allowed to be available to concord and peace. If the Church also is a subdivision of this one great universal family, a family of itself consisting of all who belong to that church, and if the being of the same family necessarily connects all the members in a common interest and a common regard for each other, then the opposers must be ingenious in their malice, if they can deny, that all who are of the same church, the grand Catholic Church of all Christendom, must also have a common interest, a common regard for each other, and, therefore, be united in love.[94]

[91] Erasmus, *Antipolemus*, p. 80; also letter of Erasmus to Anthony A. Bergis, abbot of St. Bertin, *The Complaint of Peace*, Appen., pp. 129–30.

[92] Erasmus, *The Complaint of Peace*, pp. 48–49.

[93] *Ibid.*, p. 57.   [94] *Ibid.*, pp. 63–64.

Erasmus was not "in the complete sense" a pacifist,[95] for he did not condemn all wars. He divided wars into two classes: the just and the unjust. He approved the just, or bona fide, wars, which he defined as purely defensive, such as those for repelling invasion and preserving public tranquillity.[96] However, the difficulty of determining whether a war is defensive or not is more perplexing a task than he realized. Erasmus was the greatest apostle of peace in his time; and, while his plea had no immediate effect in preventing war, it undoubtedly influenced his contemporaries. Erasmus failed to present a detailed plan for organizing peace, and he did not use the political machinery of his day to put some scheme for the preservation of peace into operation. His emphasis upon arbitration as a means of settling disputes was, perhaps, his greatest contribution in the interest of peace.[97] While his work failed to produce immediate results, it should be valued as undoubtedly attracting many to the cause of peace who would further the work and offer more detailed plans for accomplishing it. One writer has concluded that *Complaint of Peace* is "fresh and convincing material for the peace workers even of today."[98]

About the time of the publication of Erasmus' work an opportunity to secure enduring peace presented itself in the realm of actual politics. With the cessation of hostilities between England and France, Cardinal Wolsey, minister of Henry VIII, proposed a treaty to guarantee European peace

[95] J. A. K. Thomson, "Desiderius Erasmus," in F. J. C. Hearnshaw (ed.), *The Social and Political Ideas of Some Great Thinkers of the Renaissance and Reformation* (London, 1925), p. 162.

[96] Erasmus, *The Complaint of Peace*, p. 58.

[97] Corbett, Introduction to Erasmus, *Institutio principis Christiani*, p. 12.

[98] Arthur D. Call, "The Will To End War," *Advocate of Peace*, LXXXVI, No. 5 (May, 1924), 299.

↓ in order to combat the Turkish danger. The treaty[99] was ratified in St. Paul's Cathedral, London, October 2, 1518, by Henry VIII and the French plenipotentiaries. Later Spain and the papacy acceded to the agreement. Provision was made to allow all Christian princes to join the league. The contracting states agreed to take military measures against any power which threatened to invade or attack any member of the league, such action to be taken within two months. France, Spain, and England also were to employ their naval forces in subjugating the aggressor. Each league-state was to pay its own expenses and was to permit and assist the passage of an ally's troops through its territories. The treaty was not to be called into operation in case of civil wars.[100] But Wolsey's league, which lasted only one year, like Erasmus' *Complaint of Peace*, apparently had little actual influence in preventing war.

One of the most completely formulated peace plans of early modern times was the work of Emeric Crucé, *The New Cyneas or Discourse of the Occasions and Means To Establish a General Peace, and the Liberty of Commerce throughout the Whole World.* The original work is extremely rare; according to Crucé's modern editor, Mr. Thomas Willing Balch, there are only three known copies.[101] A copy of the first edition of 1623 and a copy of the second edition of 1624 are in the Bibliothèque nationale of Paris, and another copy is in the private collection of Charles Sumner in Harvard University.[102] We know little about the life of Emeric Crucé. He

[99] Text of treaty in R. C. McGrane, "A Sixteenth Century League of Nations," *Nation*, CVIII (March 8, 1919), 372.

[100] Lange, *op. cit.*, pp. 118–23.

[101] Thomas Willing Balch (ed. and trans.), Introduction to Emeric Crucé, *The New Cyneas* (Philadelphia, 1909), p. iii.

[102] The copy used by the present writer in this study is the 1623 edition in Harvard University Library: "*Le nouveau Cynée*" *ou discours d'estat représentant*

was born in Paris about 1590 and died in 1648. He was, according to some statements, a monk and widely read in the classics. In addition to *Le nouveau Cynée*, he published several works in Latin.[103] The name of the author for a long time was believed to be Emeric or Emery de La Croix.[104]

Cruce addressed his appeal to the monarchs of his day. Just as the old Cyneas of whom we learn in Plutarch's *Lives of Illustrious Men* was to show his monarch, Pyrrhus, the futility of war, so the new Cyneas was to lead the monarchs of his age along the paths of wisdom and peace. The new Cyneas, like the old, advised his royal master of the uselessness of war.

That if ambition induces him to waste his life, and that of his subjects, let him at least spare his honor, for which he worries so much, and look at the shame and the loss into which those who undertake war hurl themselves. They place themselves within an ace of their ruin. Only a little wind is necessary to push them into the abyss of misery: and when they are thinking they are in their celestial home at the height of their prosperity, a reverse of fortune will overthrow them suddenly, and from sovereigns will make them slaves. . . . . Histories testify, experience verifies that war rather hazards the reputation of a Prince than augments it.[105]

Cruce thought that the development of commerce between nations, necessarily making them more dependent

---

les occasions et moyens d'establir une paix générale et la liberté du commerce par tout le monde aux monarques et princes souverains de ce temps (Paris: Chez Jacques Villery, 1623; avec privilège du roy). The work was received by the Harvard Library, April 28, 1874.

[103] Balch, Introduction to Cruce, *op. cit.*, pp. vii–ix.

[104] In 1890 Mr. Justice Nys, the Belgian jurist, became aware of the existence of Cruce's book. It was he who restored to Cruce his true name (*ibid.*, pp. v–vii; Thomas Willing Balch, *Éméric Cruce* [Philadelphia, 1900], p. 25).

[105] Balch ed. of Cruce, *The New Cyneas*, pp. 28, 30. The following page references to the text of the plan are to the Balch edition.

upon one another, would make wars less frequent. He saw, too, that peace was necessary if commerce was to thrive. He interested himself, therefore, in the development of commerce and industry as essential in securing peace and advocated the construction of canals and the suppression of pirates.[106] In his conceptions of trade and commerce he was in some respects far ahead of his day. For the encouragement of commerce he advised great moderation in taxing import and export merchandise, especially commodities necessary to life, so that merchants might trade in them more freely and the people might have them at a lower price.[107] He believed that there was no occupation to compare in utility with that of the merchant, who increased his resources by great labor and often at the peril of his life, without injuring anyone, and who, therefore, was more worthy of praise than the soldier, who advanced himself through destruction and at the expense of others.[108] Side by side, in importance with commerce, he placed the industrial arts.[109]

Foreign wars are mainly undertaken, according to Crucé, for, first, honor;[110] second, profit;[111] third, reparation of some

[106] Pp. 62–76.

[107] P. 60.   [108] P. 58.

[109] In order to encourage artisans, Crucé recommended that an officer was to be established in all towns who would secure the names of those who excelled in some art in order that they might be appointed according to their capacity (p. 76).

[110] Crucé asked: "What reason is there to esteem so much a thing [honor], which only boasts of doing what the most imbecile animals can carry out? For to injure and kill is an easy thing" (p. 22).

[111] Where two soldiers are enriched, fifty will gain "only blows or incurable sicknesses." Princes only impoverish themselves by war (p. 32).

wrong;[112] fourth, "for exercise."[113] Crucé discerned another cause of conflict in exaggerated notions of nationality. He wrote with penetration:

> For how is it possible, some one will say, to bring in accord peoples who are so different in wishes and affections, as the Turk and the Persian, the Frenchman and the Spaniard, the Chinese and the Tatar, the Christian and the Jew or the Mohammetan? I say that such hostilities are only political, and cannot take away the connection that is and must be between men. The distance of places, the separation of domiciles does not lessen the relationship of blood. It cannot either take away the similarity of natures, true base of amity and human society. Why should I a Frenchman wish harm to an Englishman, a Spaniard, or a Hindoo? I cannot wish it when I consider that they are men like me, that I am subject like them to error and sin and that all nations are bound together by a natural and consequently indestructible tie, which ensures that a man cannot consider another a stranger, unless he follows the common and inveterate opinion that he has received from his predecessors.[114]

He did not consider religion one of the most weighty causes of war, as he believed that religion was generally used as a pretext.[115] Further, Crucé did not approve wars of religion. He said: "It does not belong to men to punish or correct the mistakes of faith. It belongs to Him who sees hearts and the most secret thoughts. The faults of the will are punishable by the civil law: those of knowledge, to wit, false doctrines

---

[112] Crucé held that "kingdoms have the same peculiarities as individuals, birth, growth, and decline." While kings should oppose valorously aggressors who attempt to deprive them of territory, they should resign themselves to the will of God if they are deprived of all their lands. "Let them therefore not complain of a misfortune common to all states." Even if they are in a position to take vengeance, they should resort to arbitration before taking up arms (pp. 38–42).

[113] The author thought that "men are naturally impatient of quiet, and especially men at arms." Those who go to war for the sport of it Crucé would send to the cannibals and savages (pp. 42, 44).

[114] Pp. 84, 86.   [115] Pp. 18, 20.

have only God for judge."[116] Crucé therefore believed that differences in religion should not make peace impossible, and he was ready to include in his confederation men of all religious beliefs—Christians, Mohammedans, Jews, and pagans.[117]

Crucé's plan[118] for securing peace called for an assembly to meet at some chosen city, where the ambassadors of the various sovereigns were to have their permanent residence. Differences arising between the nations were to be settled by the judgment of the whole assembly, after the ambassadors of the countries involved had pleaded their cases. It was expected that the other deputies would judge without prejudice.[119] In order to afford more authority to the decision, the advice of the great republics, like Venice and Switzerland, was to be sought. If any sovereign refused to abide by the decree of the assembly, he was to be brought to reason by all the other princes. Crucé suggested as a suitable location for the meetings of the assembly the city of Venice, because of its neutrality, its indifference to other princes, and its central location.[120] The question of the rank to be as-

[116] P. 98. Yet in another place Crucé said: "And of more recent memory, Luther and Calvin, what a mess have they not made with their tongues and writings, under pretense of reforming the abuses of Christianity? Such people must be anticipated, and forbidden to dogmatize either in public or in private, under penalty of rigorous punishment. For they attract the people which allows itself to be easily led off by the appearance of piety, as well as by the hope of liberty or a better condition" (p. 168).

[117] Pp. 34, 36.

[118] Louis-Lucas saw in Crucé's work three themes: first, the productive forces and liberty of commerce; second, general peace and international arbitration; third, monarchical liberalism and social organization (Pierre Louis-Lucas, *Un Plan de paix générale et de liberté du commerce au XVIIe siècle: "Le Nouveau Cynée" d'Eméric Crucé* [Paris, 1919], pp. 79–123).

[119] Balch ed. of Crucé, *The New Cyneas*, pp. 102, 104.

[120] P. 104.

signed to the ambassadors, who might be unwilling to yield to one another, was a question of much greater delicacy. Cruсé decided to give precedence to the pope, second place to the emperor of the Turks, third to the Holy Roman Emperor, fourth to the king of France, fifth to the king of Spain, and the sixth was to be contested between the kings of Persia, China, Prester John, the precop of Tatary, and the grand duke of Muscovy. The kings of Great Britain, Poland, Denmark, Sweden, Japan, Morocco, the Great Mogul, the monarchs from India and Africa, he stated, "must not be in the last ranks." Princes dissatisfied with this disposition had the right to apply to the assembly for correction. This appeal to the decision of the others would not diminish their sovereignty, but would add to the esteem in which they were held because they had voluntarily submitted themselves to the dictates of reason. In case the assembly were evenly divided and could not reach a decision, recourse was to be had to the deputies from the republics, who were to cast the deciding votes. Thus Cruсé disposed of the delicate question of the precedence of ambassadors.[121]

Cruсé's congress was the first to include both Christian and non-Christian princes, and well might he say in behalf of his scheme that

never was a council so august, nor assembly so honorable, as that of which we speak, which would be composed of ambassadors of all the monarchs and sovereign republics, who will be trustees and hostages of public peace. And the better to authorize it, all the said Princes will swear to hold as inviolable law what would be ordained by the majority of votes in the said assembly, and to pursue with arms those who would wish to oppose it. This company therefore would judge then the debates which would arise not only about precedence, but about other things, would maintain the ones and the others in good understanding; would meet discontents half way, and would appease them by gentle means, if it could be

[121] Pp. 104–18.

done, or in case of necessity, by force. By which means peace being generally established between Princes, there would remain nothing except to maintain it particularly in each monarchy: to which end all sovereigns would work for their part, and would not have much difficulty to make themselves obeyed by their people and hold them in check.[122]

Kings, he held, would no longer need to fear internal strife in their dominions, for they could call upon the other sovereigns for aid in suppressing rebellions and insurrections.[123] The principal means of obtaining general peace consisted in limiting the monarchies, "so that each Prince remains within the limits of the lands which he possesses at present, and that he does not pass beyond them for any pretences. And if he finds himself offended by such a regulation . . . . let him address himself to this great assembly, as to the most competent judge that can be imagined."[124]

Cructé, like Erasmus,[125] was a firm believer in the power of the monarch to abolish war.[126] If peace might only be published "by the orders of the king," the firebrands who wished to disturb peace would drop their arms at the bidding of the royal command. In an eloquent appeal to the monarchs he said:

One must abandon those barbarous customs, and show to the people the way of humanity and true honor, in order that they shall no longer live in a brutal way. It is necessary to make reason and justice reign, and not violence, which is only suited to the beasts. . . . . Let us replace the sword in the scabbard. It is not a question of maintaining everlasting

[122] Pp. 120, 122.

[123] P. 124. [124] P. 130.

[125] For comparisons with other plans, in particular Sully's and the Abbé de Saint Pierre's, see Hubert Pajot, *Un Rêveur de paix sous Louis XIII: Émeric Crucé, Parisien* (Paris, 1924).

[126] The pope should initiate the movement for peace. As to the Mohammedans, the king of France, on account of the reputation he has among them, "will more easily make them condescend to peace" (Balch ed. of Crucé, *The New Cyneas*, p. 342).

hostilities. . . . . That depends of your Majesties, Great Monarchs. You can appease all the troubles of the world, and place your peoples in obedience to the law of nature, and to your own. What do you ask in addition? Peace maintains you in grandeur, in respect, and in safety: on the contrary war diminishes all these things, and often takes them away, together with honor and life.[127]

And like the old Cyneas, the new Cyneas advised his royal master: "If you had subjugated the whole world, a thing which has never happened to any one, and will never happen, finally you will be forced to repose yourselves, since war is waged to obtain peace."[128]

Crucé was a follower of the divine-right-of-kings theory.[129] He believed that sovereigns must not be controlled in their actions and that, if they did evil, it was for God to punish them, not for the people, who owe unquestioned obedience.[130] He considered kings the lieutenants of God, amenable only to God. To Crucé it was a sacrilege for subjects to murmur against kings, to attack them or their jurisdiction. Kings were to be revered and obeyed without any distinction as to their virtue or wickedness. Crucé had little respect for democracies, in which he thought the evils of monarchy were to be found more excessive. Cabals, corruptions, and crimes were common occurrences in democracies, "where the best orators do what they choose, the virtuous are suspect, the magistrates are ill respected, the factions are advanced, justice is sold to the highest bidder, and negligently administered." All this Crucé beheld in the object lessons of Athens and Rome.[131]

[127] Pp. 134, 136.   [128] P. 136.   [129] Pp. 168, 170.

[130] It was better to have "a catarrhal head" for a prince than not to have any at all. If necessary, the people could make humble remonstrances to the ruler (pp. 176, 178).

[131] Pp. 172, 174.

Unlike most authors of peace plans, Crucé gave attention
to insuring internal peace as a necessary condition to international concord. He was vitally interested in a well-
ordered government. To achieve domestic tranquillity
Crucé suggested certain requisites, namely: a moderate
government; punishment of the wicked; reward of merit;
nourishment of the poor; regulation of trials; public, but not
gratuitous, provision of grain; lawful recreation; the cen-
sure.[132] Crucé's perspicacity is reflected in the breadth of his
recommendations. He opposed dueling, "a beastly custom."[133] He favored a regulation of ecclesiastic benefices.[134]
He discussed such subjects as the administration of justice[135]
and treatment of foreigners.[136] In regard to taxation he recommended that everyone should pay according to his
means.[137] He suggested a merit system for civil service positions and awards for the worthy,[138] projects for the unem-
ployed and the poor,[139] and state encouragement of recreation for the people.[140] Concerning education he wrote:
"Certainly there is nothing of so great importance as the in-
struction of youth. It is the foundation of a State, the support of the tranquility which we are seeking."[141] He devoted
much attention to a study of monetary questions,[142] and he
warned the monarchs not to debase the coinage.[143]

Crucé's sage advice as the Cyneas of a new day went
unheeded by his royal master, and his project to establish

[132] P. 142.   [136] Pp. 283–304.
[133] Pp. 192–98.   [137] Pp. 264–68.
[134] Pp. 232, 234.   [138] Pp. 210–26.
[135] Pp. 178–88, 248–64.   [139] Pp. 244–48.

[140] Pp. 276, 280. He particularly favored music, for he held that "there is
nothing that can more soften men and render them peaceable."

[141] P. 294.

[142] Pp. 304–42.   [143] Pp. 304, 324, 326, 334.

peace went unheeded in the war chambers of their majesties, the kings and princes of Europe. Crucé was wise
enough to realize that his plan would perhaps not material-
ize. The closing words of his book were:

> As for me I can in this only bring wishes and humble remonstrances,
> which perhaps will be useless. I have wished, nevertheless, to leave this
> testimony to posterity. If it serves nothing, patience. It is a small matter,
> to lose paper, and words. I shall protest in that case like Solon of having
> said and done what was possible for me for the public good, and some few
> who read this little book, will be grateful to me for it, and will honor me
> as I hope with their remembrance.[144]

The project of Crucé is particularly noteworthy as being
the earliest completed plan for a world-wide organization
which embraced both Christian and non-Christian nations.
The width of membership in the league is most remarkable
at a time when other plans were built on the conception
of concerted action against the Turks.[145] Of the French thinkers of his age, Butler says that there is not a more daring
speculator in the realm of international relations.[146] In contrast to so many other writers, Crucé sought no special advantage for his own country.[147] He has been termed a fore-
runner of the modern free traders.[148] He laid stress upon
internal peace within each country as a foundation to peace
between countries, whereas other writers either ignored this
or devoted themselves very largely to the relations between
nations. Crucé's work is impressive from the standpoint of
its completeness and grasp of related fields. He included in-

[144] P. 350.

[145] Sir Geoffrey Gilbert Butler, *Studies in Statecraft, Being Chapters, Biographical and Bibliographical, Mainly on the Sixteenth Century* (Cambridge, England,
1920), p. 103.

[146] *Ibid.*, p. 92.   [147] Tansill, *op. cit.*, p. 324.

[148] Franziskus Stratmann, *The Church and War: A Catholic Study* (New York,
1929), p. 98.

teresting reflections and recommendations on such diverse subjects as currency laws, administration of justice, and the nature of sovereignty. To Crucé the foundations were as important as the means of preserving peace.

It has often been said that the most celebrated of all the peace plans of history is the *Grand dessein*, attributed to Henry IV of France.[149] James Brown Scott has said that it

is without question the most famous of the many projects advocating a federation of states in order to secure and to maintain peace between nations. The project is in very truth the classical project of international organization, and it has been both the inspiration and the foundation upon which well-wishers of their kind have, consciously or unconsciously, raised their humbler structures.[150]

Maximilien de Béthune, duc de Sully, minister of finance, confidant and friend to Henry IV, would have us believe that the plan was conceived by the monarch himself, perhaps at the instigation of Queen Elizabeth. Sully stated that, if the plan did not originate with Queen Elizabeth, she had at least thought of it previously as a means of revenge for the whole of Europe on the common enemy, the House of Habsburg. After correspondence with the queen, an attempt was made to arrange an interview in 1601, when the queen went to Dover and Henry was at Calais. Ceremony did not permit the meeting, but Sully broached the subject of the peace project when he went to see her.[151] She favored

[149] Henry IV was born in 1553, came to the throne in 1589, and died in 1610.

[150] James Brown Scott, Introduction to William Ladd, *An Essay on a Congress of Nations for the Adjustment of International Disputes without Resort to Arms* (New York, 1916), pp. xiv, xv.

[151] "The Conference between Sully and Queen Elizabeth at Dover in 1601," the text taken from the Twelfth Book of Sully's *Memoirs*, is given on pp. 54–63, and "The Conference between Sully and James I at London in 1603," the text taken from the Fifteenth Book of Sully's *Memoirs*, is given on

the plan, although she saw certain difficulties in the religious provisions and the attempt to secure equality of the powers. She objected to carrying out the project by force, but she agreed that at least a beginning could be made in that way. Sully said that many of the articles and arrangements were due to the queen, which showed that for wisdom and other mental qualities she was equal to the worthiest of kings.[152]

Modern research has thrown the gravest doubt on Sully's purported visit to England in 1601. Pfister says it was an invention of Sully's.[153] Butler believes that the letter of Elizabeth to the king suggesting a conference is probably a forgery, as Sully himself in later passages credits the king with the initiative. It is more significant, Butler points out, that no reference to Sully's visit has been found in any English or French state papers or in private documents.[154] Moreover, Queen Elizabeth was not in Dover at the time, and Sully's account of the visit contains other chronological impossibilities.[155] Sully also related a visit he made to England in 1603, which Ogg says is "more imaginative than historical."[156]

Whether the "Grand Design" was actually conceived by Henry IV, perhaps at the instigation of Queen Elizabeth, or was the work of his minister Sully, was a question which puzzled historians. Pfister, who made a thorough study of the manuscripts and printed editions of Sully, maintains

---

pp. 63–76 in Sully, " *The Great Design of Henry IV from the Memoirs of the Duke of Sully*," and " *The United States of Europe by Edward Everett Hale*," with an Introduction by Edwin D. Mead (Boston, 1909).

[152] *Sully's Grand Design of Henry IV*, with an Introduction by David Ogg (London, 1921), p. 28; also Mead ed., p. 16.

[153] Christian Pfister, "Les 'Economies royales' de Sully et le Grand dessein de Henri IV," *Revue historique*, LVI (1894), 326.

[154] Butler, *op. cit.*, pp. 82–83.

[155] *Ibid.*, p. 83.   [156] Ogg ed. of Sully, Intro., p. 6.

that the idea of the Grand Design "never entered the head of Henry IV" but was the creation of his minister Sully, who conceived the idea in his retirement from public life under the reign of Louis XIII between 1620 and 1635.[157] Pfister shows that the passages concerning the Grand Design were not in the original draft of Sully's *Memoirs*, and he says that it appears that the passages were added from time to time.[158] All evidence, Pfister states, shows that the passages on the Grand Design, introduced into the printed editions but absent from the manuscript, were created in Sully's mind and therefore do not have historical validity.[159] The original draft, in place of containing a great plan to guarantee European peace, merely reflected the dynastic ambitions of the French king to destroy the power of the House of Habsburg.

Says Pfister:

The clean cut policy followed by Henry IV, aimed at the reduction of the House of Austria was, if I may dare say so, the actual foundation of all these combinations. By a first exaggeration, Sully maintained that his master desired to strip Austria of its possessions in Germany, in Bohemia and in Hungary, and to reduce Spain to the territory of the Spanish Peninsula (the version of the manuscript of the *Economies Royales*). Then he recasts the map of Europe and assigns to one or the other of the states the provinces taken from the Spanish faction. Obsessed by these hallucinations, he composes a Christian Europe of fifteen absolutely equal powers, and completely carried away by his fantasies, he finally dreams that universal peace might reign upon this earth. The Great Project was therefore not conceived by him at one and the same time, but was formed, as it were, of successive layers reared one upon the other.[160]

Ogg, in speaking of Sully's revision of the *Memoirs*, declares:

Imagination now freely supplements fact, documentary evidence is carefully forged wherever it might help to give an appearance of verisimilitude, and, quite unconscious of discrepancies and inconsistencies, a far

[157] *Op. cit.*, pp. 326–29.
[158] *Ibid.*, pp. 336–37.
[159] *Ibid.*, p. 328.
[160] *Ibid.*, p. 318.

more wonderful Grand Design is evolved. To complete the illusion, Henry IV is declared its author as the scheme seems more befitting a great monarch than a cautious financier.[161]

It is this revised version that was published in two volumes in the year 1638. The third and fourth volumes were edited by his secretaries after his death and printed in Paris in 1662.

If the Grand Design was the work of Sully,[162] as it is today generally believed, why did he attribute it to Henry? Two possible reasons may serve as an explanation: first, the desire of Sully to glorify his friend and, second, the prestige which royal authorship would lend the scheme. The question is perhaps of not too great significance, and with Scott's opinion there will be little disagreement: "The im-

[161] Ogg ed. of Sully, Intro., p. 9.

[162] Miss York believes that the Grand Design was the work of Henry IV. She says it must be to Henry's genius that we owe the Grand Design, and not to the brain of Sully, for she doubts if Sully had sufficient imagination to form such a "magnificent plan" (*op. cit.*, p. 93). Miss York, however, does not substantiate her statement that Sully lacked imagination, and she offers no evidence to support her contention on the authorship of the Grand Design. Pyle opines that a man like Sully would not invent a plan for world peace out of whole cloth, as this would seem to be out of keeping with his character, historically and psychologically (Joseph Gilpin Pyle, "An Earlier League To Enforce Peace," *Unpopular Review*, X, No. 20 [1918], 247). In contrast to this and in addition to the authorities already cited who are convinced that Henry was not the author of the Grand Design may be mentioned: Jacob ter Meulen, *Der Gedanke der internationalen Organisation in seiner Entwicklung* (The Hague, 1917), Vol. I; Jacques Hodé, *L'Idée de fédération internationale dans l'histoire;* Butler, *op. cit.;* Sylvester John Hemleben, "Henry Fourth's Plan for a League of Nations," *Alumnae News of the College of New Rochelle*, Vol. IX, No. 2 (April, 1932); Theodor Kükelhaus, "Der Ursprung des Planes vom ewigen Frieden in den Memoiren des Herzogs von Sully," a doctoral dissertation aimed at solving this question, cited in Souleyman, *op. cit.*, p. 28. Souleyman sums up by saying: "At the present time, after much laborious research, it is generally believed that *Le Grand Dessein de Henri IV* is Sully's plan conceived and written about twenty five years after the King's death" (*loc. cit.*).

portant thing to be considered is not so much that the plan
was not the plan of Henry, but that it ascribed to Henry
views which were agitating the public mind and which had
been voiced by the *New Cineas* of Crucé, which appears to
have served as Sully's model."[163] Crucé's work appeared fifteen years before the publication of Sully's *Memoirs*. In the
opinion of Pfister, Sully probably took the idea of creating a
council to judge all differences from the book of Emeric
Crucé.[164]

The Grand Design[165] proposed "to divide Europe equally
among a certain number of powers, in such a manner that
none of them might have cause either of envy or fear from
the possessions or power of the others."[166] Each of the three
religions—Roman Catholic, Protestant, and Reformed or
Calvinist—were to be so securely established that not any of
them could be destroyed. Each was to be preserved and
strengthened, but this indulgence was not to become an encouragement to the formation of new sects, which were to be
suppressed on their first appearance. There was nothing so
pernicious as religious liberty; therefore, each nation was to
be strengthened in the choice which it made of one of the
religions. Italy, which professed Catholicism, was to adhere
to that religion. Obliging all inhabitants of Catholic Italy
to conform or leave the country would entail no hardship.
The same could be observed in Spain. In such states as
France, where there was a governing religion, whoever
should feel that the subordination of Calvinism to the reli-

[163] Scott, Introduction to Ladd, *op. cit.*, p. xv.

[164] *Op. cit.*, pp. 330–31.

[165] See also Ter Meulen, *op. cit.*, pp. 160–68; *Les Français à la recherche d'une société des nations depuis le roi Henri IV jusqu'aux combattants de 1914* (Paris, 1920), pp. 19–22.

[166] Ogg ed. of Sully, p. 41; Mead ed., p. 33.

gion of the prince was a too severe regulation was to be permitted to quit the country.[167] Princes who refused to conform to any of the Christian religions were to be forced out
of Europe. If the grand duke of Muscovy refused to enter
the association after it was proposed to him, he was to be
treated like the sultan of Turkey, deprived of his European
possessions, and confined to Asia.[168] The association was to
be supported by armed forces contributed by the princes in
proportion to their abilities. The respective quotas were to
be determined by the general council. It was suggested that
the entire force should amount to about 270,000 infantry,
50,000 cavalry, 200 artillery, and 120 ships or galleys
equipped and maintained at the expense of the powers.[169]

With this armament the princes would probably seek to
conquer parts of Asia commodiously situated and particularly the whole coast of Africa, which was too near to Europe for the princes not to be frequently incommoded by it.
One precaution in relation to the conquered countries
would be to form them into new kingdoms, uniting them
with the rest of the Christian powers and bestowing them on
different princes. Care would be taken to exclude those
princes who already held rank among the sovereigns of
Europe.[170] The House of Austria was to be divested of the
empire and of all its possessions in Germany, Italy, and the
Netherlands. In other words, it was to be reduced to the
kingdom of Spain; but, that it might not be in an unequal
position with the other powers of Europe, it was to have
Sardinia, Majorca, Minorca, and the other islands on its
coast; the Canaries, the Azores, Cape Verde, and the posses-

[167] Ogg ed., pp. 32–33; Mead ed., pp. 21–22.

[168] Ogg ed., p. 33; Mead ed., p. 23.

[169] Ogg ed., p. 34; Mead ed., pp. 23–24.

[170] Ogg ed., p. 35; Mead ed., p. 25.

sions in Africa; Mexico and the American islands which belong to it; the Philippines, Goa, the Moluccas, and its other possessions in Asia.[171] This severity was just and necessary because of the ambition of the House of Austria to achieve universal monarchy, which appeared evident from the conduct of Charles V and his son. The division and distribution of the territories taken from the House of Austria were elaborately set forth. France was to receive nothing for itself but the glory of distributing them with equity.[172] The number of European powers were to be reduced to fifteen, of which there were to be three kinds: six great hereditary monarchies, five elective monarchies, and four sovereign republics. The hereditary monarchies were France, Spain, Britain, Denmark, Sweden, and Lombardy. The five elective monarchies were the Roman Empire, the papacy, Poland, Hungary, and Bohemia. The four republics were the Venetian, the Italian, the Swiss, and the Belgian.[173]

As to the laws and ordinances necessary to cement this union of the princes, to maintain harmony and the reciprocal oaths and engagements in regard to religion and policy, and the measures to be taken to insure just partitions, and the freedom of commerce—"all these matters are to be understood, nor is it necessary to say anything of the precaution taken by Henry in regard to them." Trifling difficulties, the most that could arise, were to be settled by the general council, representing all Europe.[174] The general council of Europe was to be formed on the model provided by the ancient Amphictyonies of Greece. It was to consist of a certain number of commissioners or ministers from all the

171 Ogg ed., p. 35; Mead ed., p. 25.

172 Ogg ed., pp. 36–41; Mead ed., pp. 25–33.

173 Ogg ed., pp. 41–42; Mead ed., p. 33.

174 Ogg ed., p. 42; Mead ed., p. 34.

Christian governments, who were to be constantly assembled as a senate. They were to deliberate on any affairs that might arise, discuss the different interests, pacify quarrels, and determine the civil, political, and religious affairs of Europe, "whether within itself or with its neighbours." Henry suggested that the senate be composed of four commissioners from each of the following rulers: the Emperor, the pope, the kings of France, Spain, England, Denmark, Sweden, Lombardy, Poland, and the Republic of Venice, and two only from the other republics and inferior powers. The senate thus was to consist of about sixty-six representatives, to be reappointed every three years.[175]

It remained to be determined whether the council was to be permanent or movable, one or divided into three. If divided into three with about twenty-two members each, then centers which would be most convenient were to be selected, as Paris or Bourges for one, and somewhere about Trente and Cracovia for the two others. If the assembly were not divided but united, the place of meeting was to be as nearly as possible in the center of Europe and fixed in some one of fourteen specified cities.[176] Besides the general councils, Henry thought it would perhaps be suitable to form a certain number of smaller or inferior ones for the particular convenience of different districts. Appeals were to be carried to the great general council. The decisions of the great council, pronounced in a manner equally free and absolute, were to be regarded as final and irrevocable, since

[175] Ogg ed., p. 42; Mead ed., pp. 34–35. "On different pages of his *Mémoires* Sully gives different numbers of the representatives to the Senate: 40, 60, 66, and 70, one of the many contradictions in his work that can be easily explained by the fact that certain parts of it were written by his secretaries. The number 66 is referred to more often than the others" (Souleyman, *op. cit.*, p. 24).

[176] Ogg ed., pp. 42–43; Mead ed., p. 35.

they were to proceed from the united authority of all the sovereigns.[177]

Analyzing the plan of Henry IV, one notes that the peace of Europe was to be established on the foundation of war—a war to destroy the power of the House of Habsburg. The map of Europe was to be arranged to the satisfaction of France and was to insure her position in Europe. The scheme was in accord with the dominant principle of French foreign policy. Henry IV had negotiated alliances and had formed a veritable coalition against the House of Austria.[178] In such a league it was necessary that France appear as pursuing a policy untouched by selfishness. The policy had all the evidences of being successful; and, if King Henry had been spared at the hands of Ravaillac, he might, as Ogg surmises, have lived to see the downfall of his enemy.[179] The Grand Design had certain inherent weaknesses which would have been fatal to its successful execution. It attempted to establish a status quo, despite the fact that change is the universal law. The plan attempted to control the rise and fall of nations in the interests of the France of Henry's day. The ease with which the Near Eastern question was disposed—by thrusting the Turk out of Europe—is amusing in the light of subsequent events. The Herculean task of sending the "Muscovite" out of Europe if he refused to join the federation became a simple procedure in the imagination of Sully. The list of fifteen states which would exist in Europe could never have been anything but meaningless in the light of the history of nationality. The repartition of Europe as proposed in the scheme would have

[177] Ogg ed., p. 43; Mead ed., pp. 35–36.

[178] Ferdinand Dreyfus, *L'Arbitrage international, avec une préface de Frédéric Passy* (Paris, 1892), p. 35; Souleyman, *op. cit.*, p. 23.

[179] Ogg ed., Intro., p. 6.

been the occasion for a great European war, for it is not conceivable that losers in the partition would humbly and graciously relinquish their territories. Even if peace had been achieved, there would have been fertile ground for future struggles, for any plan of political organization must have sufficient elasticity to accommodate future developments and unforeseen exigencies. The Grand Design of Henry IV failed to make this provision.[180]

Dante in his *De monarchia* had made a fervent plea for world unity through the re-establishment of a revived Roman Empire, but the centuries between Dante and Henry of Navarre made it clear that the day of a world-state had passed and that world peace had to be based on the organization of independent states. The Grand Design broke away definitely from the old idea of a world-state. It was an attempt to reconcile the two opposing demands of Europe, national independence and world organization. Sully, of course, could not specifically recognize the national principle, for it had not, as yet, received definite expression. The plan took cognizance of the new international order to which any organization for world peace had to be accommodated.[181] Henry's project was the most influential of all similar plans. The Abbé de Saint-Pierre, William Penn, Rousseau, and others took it for their model. For instance, William Penn was thinking of Henry's suggestions when he wrote in justification of his own scheme: "I will not then fear to be censured for proposing an expedient for the present and the future peace of Europe, when it was not only the design but glory of one of the greatest princes that ever reigned in it." Henry's plan was perhaps the basis of Alexander's idea for a holy alliance.[182]

---

[180] Hemleben, *op. cit.*, p. 9.   [181] *Ibid.*, pp. 9–10.

[182] Shirley G. Patterson, Introduction to Jean Jacques Rousseau, "*L'État de guerre*" and "*Projet de paix perpétuelle*" (New York, 1920), pp. xlvii, xlviii.

Phillips speculates that its influence may have extended to the great Napoleon at St. Helena in the formulation of his plan.[183] Count de Las Cases reported Napoleon as saying:

One of my greatest ideas was the bringing together and the concentration of the peoples forming a geographical unit which revolution and policy had broken up and cut to pieces. Thus, though scattered, there are in Europe more than 30,000,000 Frenchmen, 15,000,000 Spaniards, 15,000,000 Italians, 30,000,000 Germans, and of each of these peoples I would fain have made a separate and distinct nation. . . . . After this summary simplification, it would have been easier to give one's self up to the beautiful dream of civilization; for in such a state of things there would have been a greater chance of bringing about everywhere a unity of codes, of principles, of opinions, of sentiments, of views, and of interests. Then perhaps, under the aegis of universal enlightenment, it would have been possible to conceive of an Amphictyonic Assembly of Greece, or of an American Congress for the European family of nations.[184]

Muir doubts the authenticity of Napoleon's reflections on St. Helena, particularly as recorded by Las Cases. He holds that the object was to create a Napoleonic legend and to justify the great general in the eyes of posterity.[185] Whether the Grand Design actually influenced Napoleon may be left to the field of speculation. Its actual effect, however, upon successive plans is demonstrable, and no project of a league to enforce peace has carried more prestige with later builders of similar projects.

[183] Walter Alison Phillips, *The Confederation of Europe: A Study of the European Alliance, 1813–1823, as an Experiment in the International Organization of Peace* (London, 1920), p. 24.

[184] Comte de Emmanuel Las Cases, *Journal de la vie privée et des conversations de l'Empéreur Napoléon à Sainte Hélène* (London, 1823), IV, Part VII, 125, 126.

[185] Ramsay Muir, *Nationalism and Internationalism* (London, 1916), pp. 144–45.

CHAPTER II

PROJECTS TO THE CLOSE OF THE
EIGHTEENTH CENTURY

SCHEMES advocating conferences to prevent war
seemed to be in the very air during the early seven-
eenth century. Two years after the publication of *Le
Nouveau Cynée* there appeared (1625) the most celebrated of
Hugo Grotius' works, *De jure belli ac pacis*. Its success was
rapid and complete, and in such high esteem was the work
held that Gustavus Adolphus is reputed to have carried a
copy with him on his campaigns. One writer has said: "No
work, according to general testimony, has ever received
more universal approbation or has maintained its reputation to so high a degree as this treatise of Grotius."[1] It has
been called "one of those rare books that cannot die."[2]

On account of his work, *De jure belli ac pacis*, Grotius has
been styled "the Father of International Law." Nys has
pointed out that the illustrious Dominican Francis de Victoria (1480–1546) was perhaps the first to conceive an exact
idea of international law.[3] Scott[4] brings out clearly and

[1] Sir William Rattigan, "Hugo Grotius," in Sir John Macdonnell and
Edward Manson (eds.), *Great Jurists of the World*, with an Introduction by van
Vechten Veeder (Boston, 1914), p. 178.

[2] C. van Vollenhoven, "Grotius and Geneva," *Bibliotheca Visseriana* (Leyden, 1926), VI, Part XIII, 39.

[3] Ernest Nys, *Études de droit international et de droit politique* (Brussels, 1896),
I, 241; C. H. McKenna, *Francis de Vitoria, Founder of International Law* (New
York, 1930), p. 7.

[4] James Brown Scott, *The Spanish Origin of International Law* (Washington,
D.C., 1928); *idem, The Spanish Conception of International Law and of Sanctions*
(Washington, D.C., 1934); *idem, The Catholic Conception of International Law:*

forcefully the significance of Victoria and also of the Jesuit,
Suarez (1548–1617), in the history of international law.[5]
Grotius himself acknowledged that he consulted Victoria
among other theologians and jurists,[6] and we know that he
was familiar with the writings of the famous Jesuit, Suarez,[7]
and that he held these works in high esteem.[8] Grotius has
some four references to Suarez' work in the notes of his
treatise, and in Scott's opinion we can be sure that Suarez'
influence on Grotius was greater than the four references
would suggest.[9] Grotius was in a large way indebted to

---

*Francisco de Vitoria, Founder of the Modern Law of Nations; Francisco Suárez,
Founder of the Modern Philosophy of Law in General and in Particular of the Law of
Nations* (Washington, D.C., 1934); *idem, Law, the State and the International
Community* (New York, 1939), I, 310–23, 558–69.

[5] Lawrence says that "it is to one who was at once a Spaniard, a School-
man, a Theologian and a Jesuit, that we owe the clear enunciation of two
most fruitful principles. The first is that there is really and truly a Society or
Family of Nations, and the second is that the law which must be applied to
this family or society is not so much a law *common* to all nations, as the Classical
Roman Jurist conceived of the *Jus Gentium*, but a law *between* nations, a law
which, as Suarez himself says, all peoples and nations ought to observe between themselves" (T. J. Lawrence, *The Society of Nations: Its Past, Present,
and Possible Future* [New York, 1919], pp. 27–28).

[6] Ernest Nys (ed.), Introduction to Francisci de Victoria, *De Indis et de
iure belli relectiones* (Washington, D.C., 1917), p. 61; William F. Roemer, "The
Scope of This Study Determined by a Christian Philosophy of Peace," in
William F. Roemer and John Tracy Ellis, *The Catholic Church and Peace Efforts*
(New York, 1934), p. 17; McKenna, *op. cit.*, p. 7.

[7] Roemer, in Roemer and Ellis, *op. cit.*, pp. 19–20.

[8] See further: Herbert Francis Wright, *Francisci de Victoria "De iure belli
relectio"* (Washington, D.C., 1916); Coleman Phillipson, "Franciscus a Victoria (1480–1546), 'International Law and War,' " *Society of Comparative
Legislation Journal*, XV (1915), 175–97; Jacques Hodé, *L'Idée de fédération internationale dans l'histoire: les précurseurs de la société des nations* (Paris, 1921), pp.
67–73; Louis Carle Bonnard, *Essai sur la conception d'une société des nations avant
le XXᵉ siècle* (Paris, 1921), pp. 25–35; Francisco Suarez, *De divina gratia*
(Moguntiae . . . . , 1620–51).

[9] Scott, *The Spanish Origin of International Law*, pp. 71–72.

Albericus Gentilis (1552–1608), whose chief work, *De jure belli*, was published in 1598. Grotius owed much of the plan and subject matter of his own work to Gentilis, who furnished, in particular, the framework of the first and third books of Grotius' *De jure belli ac pacis*.[10] It is scarcely accurate, therefore, to call Grotius the founder of international law.[11]

It appears quite certain that Grotius began to gather materials for his book in 1622.[12] The work was published in 1625. Grotius resided for some time in Paris, and some presume that Grotius knew Crucé and was influenced by the monk's work. Nys's supposition was that Grotius' idea of arbitration and a congress of nations may have been drawn from *Le Nouveau Cynée*.[13] Nys's assumption was repeated by Balch,[14] Ter Meulen,[15] and others. However, the evidence

[10] Amos S. Hershey, *The Essentials of International Public Law and Organization* (New York, 1929), p. 66, n. 9; Rattigan, "Hugo Grotius," in Macdonnell and Manson, *op. cit.*, p. 179; Roemer, in Roemer and Ellis, *op. cit.*, pp. 20–21; Lawrence, *op. cit.*, p. 29.

[11] Most of the underlying principles had already been set forth in the works of earlier philosophers, and there can be no doubt that Victoria and Suarez, in turn, were indebted in particular to Augustine and to Thomas Aquinas.

[12] Hamilton Vreeland, *Hugo Grotius, the Father of the Modern Science of International Law* (New York, 1917), p. 164; C. van Vollenhoven, *On the Genesis of "De iure belli ac pacis" (Grotius, 1625)* (Amsterdam, 1924), p. 3.

[13] Nys, *Etudes de droit international et de droit politique*, I, 316.

[14] Thomas Willing Balch (ed. and trans.), Introduction to Éméric Crucé, *The New Cyneas* (Philadelphia, 1909), pp. xxvi, xxvii; Thomas Willing Balch, *Éméric Crucé* (Philadelphia, 1900), pp. 41–42.

[15] Jacob ter Meulen, *Der Gedanke der internationalen Organisation in seiner Entwicklung* (The Hague, 1917), I, 158–59. The supposition is repeated by Elizabeth V. Souleyman, *The Vision of World Peace in Seventeenth and Eighteenth-Century France* (New York, 1941), p. 20.

on Crucé's influence on Grotius is far from conclusive.[16] It
has been advanced that, since Cruce was a man of little
standing, whose literary reputation was questionable, it is
hardly logical to assume that Grotius would have sought
suggestions from him.[17] It is quite probable that Grotius
knew Cruce, for Grotius had a wide acquaintanceship. In
the opinion of Knight it is unlikely that Grotius actually
associated with the monk, since it is difficult to discover the
great Dutch jurist mixing at all with people of no importance except in his earlier days.[18] The idea of a conference
to avoid war had been advocated for a long time, and he
must have been acquainted with many peace plans and, no
doubt, had discussed them at different times. Grotius, in
fact, quoted Lodovicus Molina, a Jesuit priest, who wrote a
book in 1614 recommending the pope as the international
arbitrator.[19] Van Vollenhoven assumes that it was natural
for a Protestant to substitute a conference of princes for the
pope as arbitrator.[20]

"It would be useful, and indeed, it is almost necessary,"
the Dutch jurisconsult said, "that certain Congresses of
Christian Powers should be held, in which the controversies
which arise among some of them may be decided by others
who are not interested; and in which measures may be taken
to compel the parties to accept peace on equitable terms."[21]

[16] Jackson Harvey Ralston, *International Arbitration from Athens to Locarno*
(Stanford, Calif., 1929), p. 118.

[17] W. S. M. Knight, *The Life and Works of Hugo Grotius* (London, 1925),
p. 197; van Vollenhoven, *On the Genesis of "De iure belli ac pacis,"* pp. 11–12.

[18] Knight, *loc. cit.*

[19] Van Vollenhoven, *On the Genesis,* pp. 10–11; Knight, *loc. cit.*

[20] Van Vollenhoven, *On the Genesis,* p. 11.

[21] *Hugonis Grotii, "De jure belli et pacis,"* translated by William Whewell
(Cambridge, 1853), II, art. 4, 406.

There were three ways,[22] Grotius held, by which controversies, dangerous to the peace of Europe, might be settled:

> [ART.] VII. I. The first is, Conference. There are two ways of settling disputed questions, says Cicero; one by discussion, the other by force: and the first being the character of man, the second of brutes, we are to have recourse to the latter, only if the former fails . . . .
>
> [ART.] VIII. 1. Another way is Compromise, or Arbitration, between parties who have no common judge. As Thucydides says, It is wicked to proceed against him as a wrong doer, who is ready to refer the question to an arbitrator . . . .
>
> [ART.] IX. The third way is by Lot; . . . .
>
> 　　1. Closely related to the practice of casting Lots, is the practice of Single Combat.

Grotius did not demand a permanent assemblage like Crucé, nor did Grotius insist upon a permanent tribunal. He was satisfied with periodical conferences in which international difficulties could be adjusted. The development of the principle of the pacific settlement of disputes may be considered one of Grotius' outstanding merits. White said that Grotius' stand on arbitration is the most penetrating of all the doctrines in *De jure belli ac pacis*.[23] In placing a wreath upon the tomb of Grotius at Delft on the Fourth of July, 1899, at the time of the First Hague Conference, Mr. White said on behalf of the American delegation:

---

[22] *Ibid.*, pp. 401–7; *Hugonis Grotii "De jure belli ac pacis," libri tres*, translated with an Introduction by W. S. M. Knight (London, 1922, 1925), pp. 62–63; *Hugonis Grotii "De jure belli ac pacis,"* the translation of Book I by Francis W. Kelsey with the collaboration of A. E. R. Boak *et al.* and an Introduction by James Brown Scott (Oxford, 1925), pp. 560–63.

[23] Andrew Dickinson White, "Grotius *De iure belli ac pacis*," in A. Lysen, *Hugo Grotius, Essays on His Life and Works, Selected for the Occasion of the Tercentenary of His "De iure belli ac pacis," 1625–1925*, with a Preface by Jacob ter Meulen (Leyden, 1925), p. 57.

My Honored Colleagues of the Peace Conference, the germ of this work in which we are all so earnestly engaged, lies in a single sentence of Grotius's great book. Others indeed had proposed plans for the peaceful settlement of differences between nations, and the world remembers them with honor . . . . but the germ of arbitration was planted in modern thought when Grotius, urging arbitration and mediation as preventing war, wrote these solemn words in the De Jure Belli ac Pacis: "maxime autem christiani reges et civitates tenentur hanc inire viam ad arma vitanda."[24]

However, since Grotius' main interest was to humanize warfare, he neglected to suggest any complete plan of international organization.

Some decades later the ambitions of Louis XIV to extend the boundaries of France precipitated the War of Devolution, 1667–68. The Dutch war of 1672 followed, then that of the League of Augsburg, 1688–97, and the rumblings of the War of the Spanish Succession were not far distant. The times prompted renewed interest in plans which sought to prevent war. William Penn made his offering in *An Essay towards the Present and Future Peace of Europe*. The work was written in 1693.[25] "The merit of Penn's plan," says Hicks, "lies in the fact that it was disinterested, and not like Henry's, to be preceded by a political manoeuvre."[26] However, the project in its main outlines was not particularly distinguished from those that preceded it. The scheme was

[24] Reported in James Brown Scott, *The Hague Peace Conferences of 1899 and 1907: A Series of Lectures Delivered before the Johns Hopkins University in the Year 1908* (Baltimore, 1909), I, 740–41.

[25] At the time of writing the essay Penn had already acquired considerable experience in the administration of government. It was in 1681 that the king had signed a charter for the colony of Pennsylvania, where Penn was to try the "holy experiment" of a Quaker colony dominated by Quaker ideas of government and social order (Harold Spender, "The League of Nations: A Voice from the Past," *Contemporary Review*, CXIV [1918], 409).

[26] Frederick Charles Hicks, *The New World Order* (New York, 1920), p. 70.

directly related to the Grand Design, to which Penn expressed his general adherence.[27] Penn first treated of the
desirableness of peace,[28] then the truest means of obtaining
it, to wit, justice, concerning which he said: "Peace is maintained by Justice, which is a Fruit of Government, as Government is from Society, and Society from Consent."[29] In
other words, peace can be secured only through justice, and
government is synonymous with maintaining justice. The
purposes of war, as Penn saw them, are three:[30] to keep, to
recover, and to add. The first is defensive, for it is merely
trying to preserve against invasion what rightfully belongs to
a country. The second is also permissible, although it is offensive, as this is an attempt to recover what has been taken
away through violence. The third is not allowable, as it is
merely the passion of increasing dominion at the expense of
neighboring states which are weaker. The first two causes of
war are suitable for adjudication by the parliament of nations.

Penn recommended that the sovereign princes of Europe
"who represent that Society or Independent State of Men

[27] William Penn, *An Essay towards the Present and Future Peace of Europe*
(Washington, D.C.: American Peace Society, 1912), pp. 20–21; *William
Penn's Plan for the Peace of Europe* ("Old South Leaflets," No. 75 [Boston:
Directors of the Old South Work, 1896]), p. 19; *The Peace of Europe: the Fruits
of Solitude and Other Writings by William Penn*, with an Introduction by Joseph
Besse ("Everyman's Library," No. 724 [New York, n.d.]), p. 21. There were
two sources of inspiration for Penn's plan: one was the Grand Design and
the other was the practical example of the confederation of the Netherlands
(V. J. Lewis, "William Penn," *New Commonwealth*, II, No. 12 [September,
1934], 177).

[28] American Peace Society ed., pp. 1–3; "Everyman's Library" ed., pp.
3–5; "Old South Leaflets," pp. 1–3.

[29] Amer. Peace Soc. ed., p. 4; "Everyman's Lib." ed., p. 6; "Old South
Leaflets," p. 4.

[30] Amer. Peace Soc. ed., pp. 6–7; "Everyman's Lib." ed., pp. 8–9; "Old
South Leaflets," p. 6.

that was previous to the Obligations of Society, would, for the same Reason that engaged Men first into Society, Love of Peace and Order"[31] agree to convene a general parliament. This sovereign assembly was to be called "The Sovereign or Imperial Dyet, Parliament or State of Europe" and was to meet annually or at least every two or three years. The parliament was to formulate rules of justice which the sovereign princes were to observe in their relations with one another. All differences between sovereigns that were not settled privately were to be laid before the parliament. If any power in the league refused to submit its case or refused to abide by the decision of the parliament or delayed compliance with the judgment beyond the time stipulated, all the other powers, "united as one strength," were to compel submission and performance of the sentence. Damages were to be levied. Europe thus would have peace, for no one sovereignty would have the power to dispute the decision of the united nations.[32]

The number of representatives awarded to each power was to be based upon wealth, which was to be estimated through a review of the revenues of land, exports and imports, and taxes paid in support of government. Without any pretense to exactness, but merely for "example's sake," Penn gave the following estimation as to the number of delegates: the empire of Germany, twelve; France, ten; Spain, ten; Italy, eight; England, six; Portugal, three; Sweden, four; Denmark, three; Poland, four; Venice, three; the Seven Provinces, four; the Thirteen Cantons, two; the dukedoms of Holstein and Courland, one. If the Turks and Mus-

[31] Penn's idea of the origin of society is representative of the conception in vogue in certain intellectual circles during what has been styled the "Intellectual Revolution."

[32] Amer. Peace Soc. ed., p. 6; "Everyman's Lib." ed., pp. 7–8; "Old South Leaflets," pp. 5–6.

covites entered the league, they were each to have ten representatives. A central location was to be chosen for the first
meeting, and the parliament was to select places for future
meetings.[33] Penn disposed of the possible question of precedency among delegates in a rather novel fashion. He preferred that the meeting-room be round with a number of
doors, so that the delegates could come and go without any
question of precedency. He recommended that the whole
number of representatives be cast in tens, each choosing one,
and the selected members were to preside in turns. Penn
thought the voting should be done by secret ballot "after the
prudent and commendable method of the Venetians," in
order to avoid bribery. He preferred that measures be
passed by three-quarters vote. Since it would take a considerable amount of money to buy such a large number of
votes, the three-quarter rule would greatly help to do away
with corruption. Penn further provided that all complaints
were to be delivered in writing and were to be accessible to
all powers.[34] He held it to be extremely necessary that every
member should be present under great penalties and that
none leave the meeting without permission before the entire
business was concluded. Either Latin or French were suitable languages in which to carry on the discussions in the
parliament. Latin "would be very well for Civilians," but
French would be "most easie for Men of Quality."[35]

The author then considered possible objections to his
project. The first objection that might be brought forth was

[33] Amer. Peace Soc. ed., pp. 8–9; "Everyman's Lib." ed., pp. 10–11;
"Old South Leaflets," pp. 8–9.

[34] Amer. Peace Soc. ed., pp. 9–10; "Everyman's Lib." ed., pp. 11–12;
"Old South Leaflets," pp. 9–10.

[35] Amer. Peace Soc. ed., p. 11; "Everyman's Lib." ed., p. 12; "Old South
Leaflets," p. 10.

that the strongest and wealthiest power would never agree
to the plan and that, if the recalcitrant nation did, there
would be danger that it would achieve its ends through cor-
rupting the other delegates. If necessary, Penn would compel the reluctant power to enter the league. The others were
to unite to achieve this before the country in question became so powerful as to make such action impossible. As to
the second part of the objection, the matter would not present such a serious aspect if men of honor and substance
were appointed.[36] The second objection was that effeminacy
would result from the disuse of soldiering. Penn answered
that this would be taken care of through proper education of
the youth, which would in particular emphasize mechanical
knowledge and natural philosophy. "This would make
them Men: Neither *Women* nor *Lyons.*"[37] The third objection to his project was that it would cause unemployment
for the younger sons. Penn retorted that the country would
have more merchants, farmers, and scientists if the government was properly solicitous for the education of youth.[38]
The last objection was that the project would destroy the
sovereignty of princes. Penn protested that this was a mis-
take, for princes remained just as sovereign at home as they
ever were, for their power over their own people was not
diminished. True, disarmament would follow, and the
funds generally spent on military preparedness would be
spent to better advantage. But no one prince would have
any sovereignty over another; and, Penn said, if this be con-

[36] Amer. Peace Soc. ed., pp. 11–12; "Everyman's Lib." ed., p. 13; "Old
South Leaflets," pp. 10–11.

[37] Amer. Peace Soc. ed., p. 12; "Everyman's Lib." ed., pp. 13–14; "Old
South Leaflets," p. 11.

[38] Amer. Peace Soc. ed., p. 13; "Everyman's Lib." ed., p. 14; "Old South
Leaflets," p. 12.

sidered a lessening of their power, "it must be only because the great Fish can no longer eat up the little ones. . . . ."[39]

He then enumerated the benefits[40] that would result from his proposals: first, the spilling of so much blood would be prevented; second, the reputation of Christendom would be recovered in the sight of the infidels; third, there would be a great saving in money; fourth, the towns, cities, and countries would be preserved instead of being laid waste; fifth, travel and traffic would be easy and secure; sixth, Christians would be united against the Turkish menace; seventh, the European parliament would beget and increase personal friendship between the princes and states; eighth, princes would be free to take wives of their own choice, which, Penn believed, "should be very moving with Princes."

Penn's whole plan of a peace league was based upon the assumption that "wars are the Duels of Princes."[41] The solution for war was therefore as simple as the causes, and a confederation of princes would secure permanent peace. The parliament of the league was, of course, to be representative of the princes. This congress of nations was, therefore, to be diplomatic, not legal. Diplomats, rather than judges trained in the law, were to settle controversies. Quaker though he was, Penn believed that the decisions of the federation should be enforceable; and he was willing that decrees be backed by military force, if necessary. The project was one of the first to look forward specifically to disarmament. The plan frankly advocated unequal represen-

[39] Amer. Peace Soc. ed., p. 13; "Everyman's Lib." ed., pp. 14-15; "Old South Leaflets," p. 12.

[40] Amer. Peace Soc. ed., pp. 13-19; "Everyman's Lib." ed., pp. 15-20; "Old South Leaflets," pp. 12-17.

[41] Amer. Peace Soc. ed., p. 19; "Everyman's Lib." ed., p. 20; "Old South Leaflets," p. 18.

tation according to wealth for the member-states. Penn did not believe in the doctrine of equality of nations. He envisaged a league which might include the Muscovite and the Turk. Whether it was because the Turk might be included or because the federation would provide for concerted action, Penn cited as one of the benefits of his project that Christians would have great security against the inroads of the Turk. Crucé had taken a broader view, for he not only had made a point of including the Turk in the league but had accorded second place to the emperor of the Turks, putting him even ahead of the Emperor of the Holy Roman Empire. With Penn, one feels, the inclusion of the Turk in the league to enforce peace was merely suggested as a possibility which did not merit serious reflection.

Whereas the question of precedence was a matter of real concern to Crucé and others, Penn dismissed the problem with his round room with many doors. His project was not to be introduced by a preliminary upheaval, nor did it, like the Grand Design aim at the destruction of any one great European power. Penn, like Crucé, saw the benefits to commerce which would be brought about by peace. An interesting point to be observed is that Penn provided that all complaints be put in writing, but he did not provide for full publicity of the proceedings. He was haunted by the idea of the corruption of the functionaries, whereas the authors of other plans did not seem to be burdened with this worry. Yet, oddly enough, he believed that the delegates would be the wisest and the noblest of each country. Penn felt that his plan was far from visionary, for he thought that its practicality was proved by the example of the confederation of the United Provinces.

Penn had at least one disciple in John Bellers, his Quaker friend. Bellers was a philanthropist who had spent years in the advancement of education for the poor, the improvement of prisons, and the care of the sick. In 1710[42] he made a proposal to the British Parliament for a peace league. The plan is generally known by its shortened title, *Some Reasons for an European State.*[43] Bellers' work incuded an analysis of the Grand Design and was in its fundamentals a reproduction of Penn's scheme.[44] Bellers was motivated in offering his plan by the occurrence of the war between France and Holland. The Council of State in Holland in the preamble to their state of war had declared that the power of France was so formidable and the guaranties against the pretensions of that crown were so insufficient that the other nations could not protect themselves without joining a mutual league and union, which they hoped would be established after the peace in imitation of the union between the Emperor and the Republic of Venice against the Turks. Bellers viewed this as highly desirable and felt that such a union should be established at the earliest possible moment by the allies, who should invite the neutral powers to join them.

[42] The work appeared in the midst of the War of the Spanish Succession and therefore was one of many peace plans born of war (V. J. Lewis, "John Bellers," *New Commonwealth*, III, No. 1 [October, 1934], 197).

[43] The complete title is *Some Reasons for an European State, 1710, Proposed to the Powers of Europe by an Universal Guarantee, and an Annual Congress, Senate, Dyet, or Parliament. To Settle Any Disputes about the Bounds and Rights of Princes and States Hereafter. With an Abstract of a Scheme Form'd by King Henry the Fourth of France upon the Same Subject and Also a Proposal for a General Council or Convocation of All the Different Religious Perswasions in Christendom (Not To Dispute What They Differ about, but) To Settle the General Principles They Agree in: By Which It Will Appear that They May Be Good Subjects and Neighbours, tho' of Different Apprehensions of the Way to Heaven. In Order To Prevent Broils and War at Home, When Foreign Wars Are Ended, and above All Things, Have Fervent Charity among Yourselves: for Charity Shall Cover the Multitude of Sins.*

[44] James L. Tryon, "Proposals for an International Court," *Proceedings of the American Society for Judicial Settlement of International Disputes, 1913* (Baltimore, 1914), pp. 99–100.

Peace would thus more quickly be secured and would in-
cline France itself to come into the league.[45]

Bellers urged that at the next general peace there should
be a provision for a universal guaranty and an annual parliament of nations. All the states were to be joined together
as one state. There was to be a general renunciation of all
claims of states against each other, and there was to be an
agreement on what might be considered necessary for "a
standing European law." The league was to provide the
means for friendly debate and was to prevent any dispute
from bringing about a war "in this age or the ages to come."
Bellers planned to preserve the status quo as determined by
the next peace treaty, for he said that all princes and states
were to "have all the strength of Europe to protect them in
the possession of what they shall enjoy by the next peace."[46]
The scheme divided Europe into one hundred equal provinces, and each province was to supply to the league one
thousand soldiers or an equal value in ships or money. A
state was privileged to send one representative to the international parliament for every one thousand troops furnished.[47] The parliament was to hear disputes; and, since
most of the delegates would not be directly concerned with
the case, it might well be expected that the parliament would
be "more inclined to that side which hath more reason with
it."[48] Bellers then envisioned disarmament when Europe
might be considered as one government. If states were limited in troops and ships of war, they would be unable to in-

[45] Taro Terasaki, *William Penn et la Paix* (Paris, 1926), pp. 142–43; A. Ruth
Fry, *John Bellers, 1654–1725, Quaker, Economist and Social Reformer*, his writings
reprinted with a memoir by A. Ruth Fry (London, 1935), p. 91.

[46] Terasaki, *op. cit.*, pp. 144–45; Fry, *op. cit.*, p. 92.

[47] Terasaki, *op. cit.*, p. 145; Fry, *op. cit.*, p. 93.

[48] Terasaki, *op. cit.*, p. 146; Fry, *op. cit.*, pp. 93–94.

vade their neighbors. Without disarmament, Bellers held,
"Peace may be little better than a truce."[49]

Men like Penn and Bellers might make their pleas for
peace, but wars continued. The ambition of Louis XIV had
not been dulled. He hoped to dominate Europe, to make
France supreme among the nations of the earth. His attempt was contested in the War of the Spanish Succession,
1702–13; and, when Louis was forced to accept defeat by the
Treaty of Utrecht, France was paralyzed. The time was
propitious for another scheme to guarantee peace. In 1712
Charles Irénée Castel de Saint-Pierre published a small volume at Cologne to which he gave the title *Mémoires pour
rendre la paix perpétuelle en Europe.*[50] The first sketch was followed by a two-volume edition published in 1713 under the
title *Projet pour rendre la paix perpétuelle en Europe.*[51] An English
translation was published in 1714 and entitled *A Project for
Settling an Everlasting Peace in Europe, First Proposed by Henry IV
of France, and Approved of by Queen Elizabeth, and Most of the
Then Princes of Europe, and Now Discussed at Large, and Made
Practicable.*[52] The relation to the project of Henry IV was
made clear. Saint-Pierre wrote:

It falls out happily for this Project, that I am not the Author of it; 'twas
Henry the Great was the first Inventor of it; 'twas that *European Solon*
whom God first of all inspired with the means to make the Sovereigns of
Europe desirous to establish among them an equitable Polity. I
have by dint of Thought, hit upon a Plan in the main like that of that
excellent Prince, my having hit upon it too, does not in any wise diminish
the Glory of Invention due to him. . . . .[53]

[49] Terasaki, *op. cit.*, p. 146; Fry, *op. cit.*, p. 94.

[50] Paul Collinet, Introduction to *Selections from the Second Edition of the
"Abrégé du projet de paix perpétuelle." By C. I. Castel de Saint-Pierre, 1738,* translated by H. Hale Bellot (London, 1927), pp. 1, 4.

[51] 2 vols. Utrecht, 1713.   [52] London, 1714.

[53] *Ibid.*, p. 46. See also Preface to the French ed. of 1713, pp. viii–ix, and
Preface to the English ed. of 1714, pp. iv–v.

Several editions followed. In 1717 the work was completed by the publication of a third volume, *Le Projet de traité pour rendre la paix perpétuelle entre souverains chrétiens*, and in 1729 the first issue was made of the *Abrégé du projet de paix perpétuelle*. The latter appeared in a new edition in 1738.[54] Saint-Pierre said that the work falls into two parts. In the first he attempted to prove five important propositions, and in the second he tried to answer objections to the plan. The abridgment was intended, he said, for those who had already read the larger work or who, "on account of their superior enlightenment," had no need to read it.[55] Saint-Pierre hoped to obtain a hearing for his project by ascribing it to Henry IV as Sully had done before him. The imposing authority of this great name was expected to recommend the scheme to Europe as nothing else possibly could.

Saint-Pierre[56] had been present at the conferences at Utrecht as the secretary to the abbé and future cardinal, Polignac, one of the three French plenipotentiaries.[57] There Saint-Pierre witnessed the difficulties attendant upon the settlement of the terms of peace, and this caused him to draw up the project of a treaty in the hope of rendering peace perpetual. Perhaps it was from the Treaty of Utrecht that Saint-Pierre copied the word "perpetual" which appears in his title. The treaty signed between England and Spain stated: "That there be a Christian Universal Peace, and a

[54] Available in the Bellot translation, *op. cit.*   [55] *Ibid.*, p. 15.

[56] He was described by the bookseller in the Advertisement to the London ed. (1714) as "an eminent *French* Abbot, and of the first Quality for Birth: He is Brother to the Marquiss *de* Saint-Pierre; his Mother was Aunt to the late Mareschal de Bellefond, and to the present Mareschal de Villars; he has been about Twenty Years a member of the *French* Academy, and is now about Fifty Years old. He is said to be extremely studious, though of a very tender Constitution of Body."

[57] Collinet, Introduction to Saint-Pierre, *op. cit.*, p. 1.

perpetual and true friendship between the most Serene and
most Mighty Princess Anne, Queen of Great Britain, and
the most Serene and most Mighty Prince Philip V, Catholic
King of Spain, and their heirs and successors, etc."[58] The
title *La paix perpétuelle* was adopted by many authors of
peace designs after Saint-Pierre. Lorimer thought that it
was an unfortunate title, as it did much, he felt, to prejudice
otherwise well-disposed readers, who thereupon concluded
that the aim of the project was irrational.[59]

Saint-Pierre purposely limited his confederation to Europe because he feared that his earlier idea of including all
the kingdoms of the world "would cast an air of impossibility upon the whole project."[60] He felt that the union of
Europe would anyhow suffice to preserve its peace. He
looked mainly to the German diet as the model for his
European assembly, which was to preserve Europe from
war "as the German diet has actually secured the Peoples of Germany for so many centuries."[61] Saint-Pierre
asserted that the means previously used for maintaining
peace were wholly ineffectual. Europe would have nothing
but almost continual war, because there never was sufficient
security for the execution of treaties. The equilibrium of
power between France and Austria would never offer security for their dominions or commerce.[62] Saint-Pierre

[58] Casimir Freschot, *The Compleat History of the Treaty of Utrecht,* . . . . (London, 1715), I, 237–38.

[59] James Lorimer, *The Institutes of the Law of Nations: A Treatise of the Jural
Relations of Separate Political Communities* (Edinburgh and London, 1884), II,
220.

[60] Preface of Saint-Pierre's French ed. of 1713, pp. xix–xx; Preface, English
ed. of 1714, p. viii.

[61] *Abrégé du projet,* trans. Bellot, p. 24, and see also pp. 53, 56; Preface,
English ed. of 1714, p. iv; English ed. of 1714, pp. 22, 47–48.

[62] "First Discourse," French ed. of 1713, I, 1–59; English ed. of 1714,
pp. 1–23.

hoped that the same motives and the same means which
prompted the German states to form a permanent society
would suffice for the states of Christendom to form a similar
organization. The approbation given by the sovereigns of
Europe to the proposal of Henry IV was an encouraging in-
dication.[63] None of the princes would decline to join the
league if they were able to obtain the security of peace within and without their dominions,[64] and the European society
would offer this security.[65]

Saint-Pierre's plan to pacify Europe was drawn up in the
form of a treaty ready for the signatures of the European
powers. The treaty was divided into "Fundamental Articles," "Important Articles," and "Useful Articles." The
Fundamental Articles laid the framework for the European
society, which was to be a permanent and perpetual union.
The Fundamental Articles opened with the hope that all the
Christian sovereigns of Europe would become members.
The union was to make, if possible, treaties with the Mohammedan sovereigns to keep each within the bounds of his
territory. The sovereigns were to be "perpetually represented" by their deputies in a "perpetual Congress or Senate."[66] The federation was not to be interested in the form of
government of any state; but, if need be, it was to give
speedy assistance to any government that had to contend
with sedition or rebellion.[67] The union was to exert its full

[63] "Second Discourse," French ed. of 1713, I, 60–151; English ed. of 1714,
pp. 23–56.

[64] "Third Discourse," French ed. of 1713, I, 152–278; English ed. of 1714,
pp. 56–103.

[65] "Fourth Discourse," French ed. of 1713, I, 279–84; English ed. of 1714,
pp. 104–5.

[66] Art. I of Fundamental Articles, French ed. of 1713, I, 284–85; English
ed. of 1714, p. 106.

[67] Art. II of Fundamental Articles, French ed. of 1713, I, 290–91; English
ed. of 1714, p. 108.

strength to prevent any harm being done either the royal
personage or the royal prerogative during regencies, minorities, or weak reigns. If violence was done, the union was to
send commissioners into the state to investigate the facts, and
at the same time the union was to send in troops to punish
the guilty.[68] Saint-Pierre believed that the status quo should
endure forever, and he demanded that every sovereign be
contented with the territories he possessed or was to possess
when the treaty was signed. No sovereign was to make an
exchange of territory or sign a treaty without the consent
and under the guaranty of the union by a three-fourths
vote.[69] A significant article which aimed at preventing any
one state from becoming too powerful provided that no sovereign was to possess two sovereignties, except the electors of
the Holy Roman Empire, who might be elected Emperor.[70]
The kingdom of Spain was not to go out of the House of
Bourbon.[71]

The deputies were to labor incessantly "to digest all the
Articles of Commerce in general, and of the different Com-
merces between particular Nations"; and the laws were to
be equal and reciprocal and founded upon equity. The articles passed by a plurality of the deputies were to be executed provisionally until they were amended by a three-
quarters vote when more members signed the general alliance. The union was to establish in different towns
"Chambers for maintaining Commerce," consisting of dep-

[68] Art. III of Fundamental Articles, French ed. of 1713, I, 293–94; English
ed. of 1714, p. 109.

[69] Art. IV of Fundamental Articles, French ed. of 1713, I, 297–99; English
ed. of 1714, pp. 110–11.

[70] Art. V of Fundamental Articles, French ed. of 1713, I, 319; English ed.
of 1714, p. 119.

[71] Art. VI of Fundamental Articles, French ed. of 1713, I, 319–20; English
ed. of 1714, p. 119.

uties who were to reconcile disputes arising over commerce
or other matters involving a value over ten thousand livres.
Their judgment was to be without appeal. Each monarch
was to consider the judgments of the chambers of commerce
as if they were his own. Each sovereign was expected to
extirpate robbery and piracy upon pain of making reparation. If he needed help in this matter, the union was to assist him.[72]

After the society of Europe was once formed to the number of fourteen states, any sovereign who refused to enter the
union was to be declared an enemy to the rest of Europe,
and the league was to make war upon him until he was
willing to join; but, if he persisted in his refusal, he was to be
entirely dispossessed. War was to be renounced as an instrument of national policy, for a sovereign was to take up
arms only against a country which the union had declared
an enemy to European society. If a monarch had a complaint or a demand to make against another, he was "to give
a Memorial to the Senate in the City of Peace," and the
senate was to reconcile the differences by its mediating commissioners. If the controversy was still unsettled, the senate
was to judge the case by a plurality of votes provisionally
and by a three-fourths final vote. The judgment was not to
be pronounced until each deputy learned the orders of his
sovereign and communicated them to the senate. Saint-
Pierre planned a strong federation in which all the member-
states were to make war upon a member which did not live
up to its covenant.

The Sovereign who shall take up Arms before the Union has declared
War, or who shall refuse to execute a Regulation of the Society, or a
Judgment of the Senate, shall be declared an Enemy to the Society, and
It shall make War upon him, 'till he be disarmed, and 'till the Judgment

[72] Art. VII of Fundamental Articles, French ed. of 1713, I, 321–23; English
ed. of 1714, p. 120.

and Regulations be executed; and he shall even pay the Charges of the War, and the Country that shall be conquered from him at the time of the Suspension of Arms, shall be for ever separated from his Dominions.[73]

The senate was to represent twenty-four specified powers. There was to be equality of the powers, for each was to have but one deputy and one vote.[74] The members and associates of the union of Europe were to contribute to the league expenses, each in proportion to its revenues.[75] Any matter considered of first importance to the security of the society was to be decided by a plurality of votes provisionally.[76] None of the eleven Fundamental Articles were to be altered in any way without the unanimous consent of all members. The other articles could be amended by a three-fourths vote.[77] The twelve Fundamental Articles were to be signed by the rulers, whereas the Important Articles were offered for the convenience of those who wished to examine the work and especially to lessen the troubles of ministers of state.[78]

In the Important Articles, Saint-Pierre began by suggest-

[73] Art. VIII of Fundamental Articles, French ed. of 1713, I, 326–28; English ed. of 1714, p. 122.

[74] Saint-Pierre stipulated that the following were to be accorded representation in the senate of Europe: France, Spain, England, Holland, Savoy, Portugal, Bavaria and associates, Venice, Genoa and associates, Florence and associates, Switzerland and associates, Lorraine and associates, Sweden, Denmark, Poland, the pope, Muscovy, Austria, Courland and associates, Prussia, Saxony, Palatine and associates, Hanover and associates, ecclesiastical electors and associates (Art. IX of Fundamental Articles, French ed. of 1713, I, p. 343; English ed. of 1714, p. 128).

[75] Art. X of Fundamental Articles, French ed. of 1713, I, 345–46; English ed. of 1714, p. 129.

[76] Art. XI of Fundamental Articles, French ed. of 1713, I, 348–49; English ed. of 1714, p. 130.

[77] Art. XII of Fundamental Articles, French ed. of 1713, I, 350; English ed. of 1714, p. 131.

[78] English ed. of 1714, p. 134.

ing the city of Utrecht as a suitable provisional place for the senate to meet.[79] The association was to maintain an ambassador at the court of each of the league members. The organization was also to maintain "a resident" in each great province of two million inhabitants, who was to act in the capacity of a witness to the other sovereigns that the prince in whose land he was residing had no intention of disturbing the common peace.[80] When the alliance was engaged in armed conflict with an enemy, no nation was allowed to furnish a larger number of soldiers than another. To enable a weak country to support a sufficiently large contingent, the league was required to furnish the necessary funds, which, incidentally, were to be paid into the treasury by the most powerful sovereign.[81] That a king might not be easily tempted to break the peace of Europe with impunity, Saint-Pierre would threaten him with a loss of part of his dominions in case they rose in revolt in favor of the alliance.[82] The society was to give suitable rewards to anyone who discovered a conspiracy against it.[83] Every year, on the same day, every state was to hold a ceremony in the capital city in which the sovereign, the princes of the blood, and fifty of the principal ministers and officers were to renew their oaths to the union before all the people.[84] In order to avoid occa-

[79] Art. I of Important Articles, French ed. of 1713, I, 358–59; English ed. of 1714, p. 134.

[80] Art. II of Important Articles, French ed. of 1713, I, 364–65; English ed. of 1714, p. 136.

[81] Art. III of Important Articles, French ed. of 1713, I, 373; English ed. of 1714, p. 139.

[82] Art. IV of Important Articles, French ed. of 1713, I, 375; English ed. of 1714, p. 140.

[83] Art. V of Important Articles, French ed. of 1713, I, 379; English ed. of 1714, p. 142.

[84] Art. VI of Important Articles, French ed. of 1713, I, pp. 379–80; English ed. of 1714, p. 142.

sions of war arising out of colonial claims, the association was to appoint commissioners, who were to act as a fact-finding commission in the disputed territory. After hearing the report the union was to give its verdict by a three-fourths vote.[85] In the event that there was no lawful successor to the throne of one of the member-states, the association was obliged to nominate a successor, or turn the government into a republic if the sovereign had been opposed to having a successor.[86]

While Henry's plan was to be preceded by a political maneuver and by remaking Europe by force, the Abbé de Saint-Pierre contemplated no such upheaval. Force was the keynote of Henry's Grand Design, but Saint-Pierre believed that it was not necessary to initiate the reign of peace through the use of force. The union could be established by a treaty of alliance to be signed by the sovereigns of Europe. "Peace was thus to be ushered in by a stroke of the pen."[87] Dreyfus points out that what Henry IV wanted to obtain with the aid of all the resources of diplomacy, with alliances and with all his military forces, the Abbé de Saint-Pierre

[85] Art. VII of Important Articles, French ed. of 1713, I, 380–81; English ed. of 1714, pp. 142–43. In an "Explication" on Article VII Saint-Pierre showed himself opposed to emigration to the colonies. "Those lands, so Remote, Uncultivated, Uninhabited, are but of little Importance. . . . . Nay we may say, that tho' there may be some little Profit to a few poor families, who may go and settle there; yet it is, opening a Door for the common People to Desert the State by; and 'tis a considerable loss of Trade, when those who should Traffick together are dispersed and at a distance from each other; and commerce is never greater, more frequent, more rich in a State, than when the People are all gathered together in a small compass" (French ed. of 1713, I, 381–82; English ed. of 1714, p. 143).

[86] Art. VIII of Important Articles, French ed. of 1713, I, 383–84; English ed. of 1714, pp. 143–44.

[87] James Brown Scott, Introduction to William Ladd, *An Essay on a Congress of Nations for the Adjustment of International Disputes without Resort to Arms* (New York, 1916), p. xxii.

hoped to accomplish by a book.[88] While Saint-Pierre expected a league to be formed upon the signatures of monarchs, it was certain that those who refused to join the association after it was formed were to be treated as declared
enemies of European peace. Like Henry's plan, and also like
Penn's, the Abbé's scheme represented a strong federation.
It was not possible for a nation to withdraw any time at its
own pleasure without being treated as the common enemy
of the general alliance. The council was given real strength
in the power to levy taxes, to pass laws that were binding,
and to punish recalcitrant or offending members. In some
respects, Saint-Pierre's plan was less liberal than Penn's.[89]
The latter's plan provided that the delegates to the congress
were to be selected by each nation for their wisdom and justice, and Penn planned that the congress was to be more of a
deliberative body. The Abbé, however, left great powers in
the hands of the sovereigns, for the delegates were merely to
act as agents who would be responsible to, and would take
their commands from, their royal masters.[90]

Saint-Pierre's plan, like the Grand Design, was based on
the idea of confederating kings, not peoples, and of leaguing
together state governments, not nations. He was not aware
of the national idea or the doctrine of popular rights,[91] but it

[88] Ferdinand Dreyfus, L'Arbitrage international, avec une préface de Frédéric Passy (Paris, 1892), p. 56.

[89] John Spencer Bassett, The Lost Fruits of Waterloo (New York, 1918), p. 29.

[90] It is not to be gathered from this that Saint-Pierre believed in the divine-right-of-king's theory. He explicitly stated that it is not true that a sovereign has only to account to God for what he does. The king must also account to the public upon whom his reputation depends (Abrégé du projet, trans. Bellot, p. 57).

[91] Camille Seroux d'Agincourt, Exposé des projets de paix perpétuelle de l'Abbé de Saint-Pierre, de Bentham et de Kant (Paris, 1905), p. 487; Ramsay Muir, Nationalism and Internationalism (London, 1916), p. 142.

must be remembered that he was of the eighteenth century and that he thought in terms of eighteenth-century political conceptions. A European league to Saint-Pierre and his fellow-intellectuals could mean only one thing—a league of princes. As long as nations were ruled by monarchs, often irresponsible, regarding states as their personal property to do with as they saw fit and taking a selfish interest in the aggrandizement of their kingdoms, there was little prospect of securing a real league to enforce peace. Cardinal Fleury obviously saw this, for he said to the Abbé de Saint-Pierre: "You must begin by sending a troop of missionaries to prepare the hearts and minds of the contracting sovereigns."[92]

Leibnitz wrote a letter to Saint-Pierre in 1715 in which he pointed out to the Abbé what he considered the most glaring defects of the plan. The system of the Empire, Leibnitz stated, was superior in two respects to that proposed by Saint-Pierre.[93] In the Empire the tribunal of the imperial chamber was composed of judges and assessors, who were at liberty to act freely and were not bound by the dictates of a prince; whereas, according to Saint-Pierre's plan, the delegates were bound by the instructions of their sovereign. In the Empire, subjects could make their complaints to the chamber and could plead against their princes or magistrates, whereas no such provision was made in the Abbé's scheme.[94] At another time, Leibnitz showed that he consid-

[92] Cited in A. F. Pollard, *The League of Nations in History* (London, 1918), p. 6; Sir Austen Chamberlain, *The League of Nations* (Glasgow, 1926), p. 10.

[93] Walter Alison Phillips, "Historical Survey of Projects of Universal Peace," in Edith M. Phelps (comp.), *A League of Nations* (New York, 1919), pp. 19–20.

[94] Leibnitz' own plan, published under the pseudonym of Caesarinus Furstenerius, called for a reorganization of medieval Christianity under the supreme temporal direction of the Emperor and the spiritual direction of the pope. Leibnitz sought, above all, to develop the power of the Holy Roman

ered Saint-Pierre's idea of maintaining everlasting peace through decisions of a senate as utopian. "It reminds me," he said, "of a motto on a grave, *pax perpetua;* for the dead fight not; but the living are of another temper, and the most powerful have little respect for courts."[95]

Lorimer saw in Saint-Pierre's plan three errors of particular significance:[96] First, like the doctrine of the balance of power, which it was an attempt to embody in a positive institution, it aimed at finality, always impossible of realization, and an object not just in its nature if it were possible. Second, it established an equality of votes between states which were not equal, thus separating law from fact. Third, for certain purposes it required unanimous consent, impossible of attainment in a deliberative body. Another writer said that

the project was a serious, high-minded and wholly disinterested attempt to establish a permanent peace by means of a European society or union based upon the maintenance of the then existing status. Therein lay its strength and its weakness—its strength, because the sovereigns of Europe would be more inclined to sign a treaty guaranteeing them their thrones, their possessions and the rights of their successors against war from without and rebellion from within; its weakness, because it precluded the possibility of change, and change is apparently the one constant factor in the world's history. It closed the door to the ambition of the sovereign who might wish to increase his dominions, and it blighted the hope of the people who might wish to change their sovereigns or their forms of government, and by so doing better their own condition.[97]

Empire to embrace a hegemony of Europe. The Empire, to Leibnitz, was a model for the Christian society (Hodé, *op. cit.*, pp. 93–97; V. J. Lewis, "Leibnitz," *New Commonwealth*, III, No. 5 [February, 1935], 276). For Latin text: Ter Meulen, *op. cit.*, p. 207.

[95] Cited in Collinet, Introduction to Saint-Pierre, *op. cit.*, pp. 7–8.

[96] *Op. cit.*, pp. 222–23.

[97] Scott, Introduction to Ladd, *op. cit.*, p. xxviii.

There are those who hold that it can hardly be said that the Abbé's peace proposal was unworkable. Wheaton[98] held that the main provisions of Saint-Pierre's plan were incorporated in the Germanic Confederation of 1815, and Phillips[99] showed that the Abbé's scheme was, in its main principles, carried out in the Holy Alliance.[100] Saint-Pierre, at least, formulated his plan "in full Expectation to see it one Day executed."[101] In some respects Saint-Pierre may be said to have been distinctly modern, for he advocated proposals that have found vogue in more recent years. In other particulars his recommendations have not found favor, even today. He foresaw general renunciation of war and a league of states with a preliminary guaranty of existing boundaries.[102] The member-states were to agree to obligatory mediation of any dispute by the senate. If a state refused to abide by the decision or made preparations for war, the grand alliance was to proceed against the offending state.

[98] Henry Wheaton, *History of the Law of Nations in Europe and America* (New York, 1845), p. 263.

[99] Walter Alison Phillips, *The Confederation of Europe: A Study of the European Alliance, 1813–1823, as an Experiment in the International Organization of Peace* (London and New York, 1914, 1920), pp. 24, 27, 29, 34–35.

[100] One writer sees the influence of the Abbé affecting Necker, Napoleon, Metternich, and the Holy Alliance (Vera Telfer, "Catholic Projects for a League of Nations," *Catholic World*, CXX [October, 1924], 80).

[101] Preface to Saint-Pierre's French ed. of 1713, p. xxiv; Preface to the English ed. of 1714, p. x.

[102] Paul Vaucher, "The Abbé de Saint-Pierre," in F. J. C. Hearnshaw (ed.), *The Social and Political Ideas of Some Great French Thinkers of the Age of Reason* (London, 1930), p. 111. Concerning Saint-Pierre's progressive ideas in general, Souleyman says: "Most of his ideas were in advance of his age; they were directed toward the betterment of government, the amelioration of the lot of the lower classes, reforms in educational methods, the abolition of privileges and hereditary titles. Like Dubois, the Abbé saw the necessity of a universal law for all the different parts of France. There was hardly a field of social or political life which he had not observed and studied" (*op. cit.*, p. 77).

Saint-Pierre went a step further than modern writers would generally be willing to go. The Abbé wanted to use the league to interfere in the internal conditions of a member-state which faced revolt or civil war. He believed that the use of the armed forces of the whole of Europe to put down insurrection would effectively do away with civil war, since, knowing the odds against him, no man would be so rash as to attempt to overthrow the government.[103] Saint-Pierre thus did not distinguish between domestic and foreign affairs when these were related to the problem of securing peace.[104] The Abbé felt that disarmament was of primary importance.[105] Unlike proposals contemporaneous to our own day, which have generally permitted the great powers to have larger armaments, Saint-Pierre asked that all states, large or small, should have the same armies numerically.[106] The commissioners of the European alliance, were to review the troops of each power twice a year and thus prevent all new armament except by the order of the union.[107] Saint-Pierre held that, while it was not right for one prince to have more soldiers than another, nevertheless, in case federated Europe was obliged to undertake a war, the more powerful and wealthier countries were to contribute more to the maintenance of the armies than the less powerful.[108]

[103] *Abrégé du projet*, trans. Bellot, p. 32.

[104] Baron David Davies, *The Problem of the Twentieth Century: A Study in International Relationships* (London, 1930), p. 79.

[105] English ed. of 1714, p. 90.

[106] John Bassett Moore, *The Peace Problem: Address on the Peace Problem, Delivered at the Twentieth Celebration of Founders' Day, Held at Carnegie Institute, in Pittsburgh, Pa., on April 27, 1916* (Washington, D.C., 1917), p. 8.

[107] *Abrégé du projet*, trans. Bellot, p. 35.

[108] French ed. of 1713, Explication, Art. X, p. 347; English ed. of 1714, Explication, Art. X, p. 130.

Saint-Pierre declared that, in addition to rendering war impossible, his project would "make commerce between Christian Nations perfectly secure, free, and constant."[109] This was of the greatest importance, Saint-Pierre maintained, for "nothing enriches a State more than the Subjects applying themselves to Commerce."[110] It was of the utmost significance in his plan, he thought, that all sovereigns were to agree that the articles of foreign commerce were to be regulated by the senate. Saint-Pierre stressed that no one nation was to be preferred to another, that all were to be free equally to buy and sell, and that no sovereign was to lay a duty of import or export upon either foreigner or subject.[111] Saint-Pierre expressed a disbelief in the current notion that, when countries increased their trade, it was done at the expense of the other commercial nations. He was convinced that the commerce of all nations would be augmented by the increase in commerce of one.[112]

Saint-Pierre went even further than the League of Nations erected after World War I in the prohibition of secret treaties, for he demanded that there were to be no treaties made between nations except "with the Advice and Consent of the rest of the Union."[113] Among the blessings of peace which would result from his project, Saint-Pierre held, would be an improvement in education.[114] Another blessing would be that some monarchs would not need to abstain from a second marriage out of fear of the divisions between

[109] *Abrégé du projet*, trans. Bellot, p. 34.

[110] English ed. of 1714, p. 89.

[111] French ed. of 1713, Explication, Art. VII, p. 323; English ed. of 1714, Explication, Art. VII, pp. 120–21.

[112] English ed. of 1714, p. 99.

[113] French ed. of 1713, Explication, Art. IV, p. 315; English ed. of 1714, Explication, Art. IV, p. 117.

[114] English ed. of 1714, p. 81.

the children of different wives. Because of the powerful protection afforded by the union to all states, "no Sovereign
will be hindered by such a Fear from marrying a new Wife,
one of an Age to have Children."[115] It will be noted that the
benefits of the plan were to be conferred largely on Europe,
for this was a European federation. The Mohammedan sovereigns, however, were to have representatives at the city of
peace. They were not to be members of the union with the
prerogative of arbiters but only associates with the advantage of having its full protection.[116] It will be noted that this
plan did not provide for the pre-eminence of the Emperor.
As Phillips says: "From this vision of perpetual peace the
venerable phantom of the Holy Empire has vanished all but
completely."[117] The work is far more detailed and far more
elaborate than many plans, such as those of Penn and
Bellers.

While Saint-Pierre's project attracted considerably more
attention in its time than the plan of William Penn, and influenced subsequent thought[118] to a much greater extent

[115] *Ibid.*, p. 93.

[116] French ed. of 1713, Explication, Art. IX, pp. 344–45; English ed. of
1714, Explication, Art. IX, p. 129.

[117] Phillips, *The Confederation of Europe*, p. 27.

[118] An illustration of the influence of Saint-Pierre on subsequent thought
can be seen in the *Anonymous Peace Project* of 1745, summarized by Souleyman
(*op. cit.*, pp. 92–95). One of the plans based on Henry IV and Saint-Pierre is
the interesting work of a former galley slave, Pierre-André Gargaz: *A Project
of Universal and Perpetual Peace* (printed by Benjamin Franklin, 1782, at Passy;
reprinted by George Simpson Eddy, New York, 1922). See also Souleyman,
op. cit., pp. 176–81. Also based on the projects of Henry IV and Saint-Pierre
was the plan of Cardinal Alberoni for "reducing the Turkish Empire to the
obedience of Christian princes: and for a partition of the conquest together
with a scheme of perpetual dyet for establishing the public tranquillity."
Alberoni's plan is given in the *American Journal of International Law*, VII (1913),
83–107, translated by Theodore Henckels. For an account of Cardinal Al-

than most other schemes for world peace,[119] the arguments
of the good Abbé failed to impress the sovereigns of his day,
and it was upon these sovereigns that the success of the plan
depended.[120] For one thing, he was unpopular in court circles. In 1718 he was expelled from the French Academy because he refused the title of "Great" to Louis XIV.[121] If
Saint-Pierre had used a more attractive style of writing, his
works would perhaps have had a wider contemporary reading public.[122] Even if Saint-Pierre had been given a more
favorable official hearing or wider public acclaim, it is to be
greatly doubted if his plan would have had a chance of being
applied. "If the Abbé's plan was not accepted and made
operative at once if was not because it was impractical but
because it was not practicable then. . . . . Great ideas, like
great men, are sometimes born into the world before the
world is ready for them."[123]

Europe enjoyed a brief period of peace after the Treaty of

---

beroni see "An Italian Precursor of Pacifism and International Arbitration"
by Mil. R. Vesnitch, contained in the same volume, pp. 51–83. In 1857 De
Molinari published a work on Saint-Pierre to which he prefixed an Introduction giving his own plan (Gustave de Molinari, *L'Abbé de Saint-Pierre, etc.*
[Paris, 1857]).

[119] V. J. Lewis says it exercised "a profound effect" on the political thought
of subsequent centuries. Lewis suggests that Saint-Pierre's work "probably
led Immanuel Kant to write his treatise on Perpetual Peace" (V. J. Lewis,
"Saint-Pierre," *New Commonwealth*, III, No. 3 [December, 1934], 235).

[120] See further: Saint-Pierre, *Der Traktat vom ewigen Frieden, 1713, herausgegeben
und mit einer Einleitung versehen von Wolfgang Michael* (Berlin, 1922); Gilberte
Derocque, *Le Projet de paix perpétuelle de l'Abbé de Saint-Pierre comparé au pacte
de la Société des nations* (Paris, 1929).

[121] Souleyman, *op. cit.*, p. 78.

[122] Vaucher considers Saint-Pierre's peace tract very long and confusing
("The Abbé de Saint-Pierre," in Hearnshaw, *op. cit.*, p. 111).

[123] Robert Goldsmith, *A League To Enforce Peace*, with an Introduction by
A. Lawrence Lowell (New York, 1917), p. 91.

Utrecht, but it was not due to the work of the Abbé. Rather it was due to the fact that Europe was so worn out from the struggle that it had neither the strength nor the desire to repeat such an undertaking.[124] The period, too, was one of great industrial prosperity. Walpole dominated England and was careful not to rouse the dogs of war. Fleury guided the destinies of France and appreciated the value of peace. Prussia was directed by Frederick William I with his sure sense of economy and efficient use of resources. Austria was ruled by Charles VI, who, besides being a peaceful monarch, had many domestic difficulties which excluded any thought of foreign wars. But, when a new generation had grown up, a generation which had not tasted the bitterness of war, Europe was ready for another catastrophe. It was precipitated in 1740 by the young Prussian king, who could not resist the temptation of trying out the splendid military resources which he had inherited. Out of the struggle which now ensued came the proposition of Rousseau.

It was in 1761 that the work of Saint-Pierre was revived by Jean Jacques Rousseau in *A Project for Perpetual Peace*, which was published as a summary of Saint-Pierre's plan. In a letter dated 1760[125] Rousseau said that he had received the manuscripts six years before and that they had been committed to him by a nephew of the Abbé's, the Comte de Saint-Pierre. He therefore began to abridge the writings[126]

[124] Bassett, *op. cit.*, pp. 29–30.

[125] A letter from Jean Jacques Rousseau to M. de Bastide, at Montmorency, December 5, 1760, given in *A Project of Perpetual Peace, Rousseau's Essay*, translated by Edith M. Nuttall with an Introduction by G. Lowes Dickinson (London, 1927), p. xxv.

[126] He was engaged in writing at least as early as 1756, for at that time D'Argenson wrote: "Rousseau is busily engaged in the analysis of the political works of Saint-Pierre" (cited in G. Lowes Dickinson, Introduction to *ibid.*, p. vii.

so that they might be more conveniently read and their value more widely appreciated.[127] Rousseau's work was translated into English in the same year and published in London[128] with a second edition in 1767. His plan was purportedly the work of Saint-Pierre. Disclaiming originality, Rousseau clarified, condensed, and criticized the work of Saint-Pierre; and in his abridgment of the plan Rousseau restated the project in his own words. Vaughan holds: "There is, in fact, much more of Rousseau than of Saint-Pierre in the whole performance."[129] To this abstract of Saint-Pierre's project Rousseau later added *Jugement sur la paix perpétuelle*, his criticism of the scheme of Saint-Pierre. This was avowedly an independent work and was not published until 1782, six years after Rousseau's death.

Rousseau opened his *A Project for Perpetual Peace* with the statement: "As a more noble, useful, and delightful Project never engaged the human mind, than that of establishing a perpetual peace among the contending nations of Europe, never did a writer lay a better claim to the attention of the public than he who points out the means to carry such a design into execution."[130] Rousseau advocated a federation of Europe, as did Saint-Pierre, and presented the following arguments in support of his scheme: first, the misery and waste

---

[127] In his childhood Rousseau had known the Abbé. He was familiar with the chaotic condition of the Abbé's papers when he sought permission to edit them (V. J. Lewis, "Rousseau," *New Commonwealth*, IV, No. 2 [November, 1935], 438).

[128] Jean Jacques Rousseau, *A Project for Perpetual Peace* (London, 1761).

[129] C. E. Vaughan, Introduction to Rousseau, *A Lasting Peace through the Federation of Europe and the State of War*, translated by C. E. Vaughan (London, 1917), p. 7.

[130] Jean Jacques Rousseau, *A Treatise on the Social Compact, or the Principles of Political Law: A Project for a Perpetual Peace* (London, 1795), p. 184; Nuttall ed., p. 3.

of war necessitated some plan to secure a lasting peace; second, the continuous recurrence of war was inevitable so long as each state retained its absolute independence, and therefore all were to be placed in a state of mutual dependence; third, the establishment of a federation of peoples with a court or parliament to arbitrate all disputes between the member-states was a *sine qua non*. The decisions of the parliament were to be enforced by a federal army, if necessary.

Rousseau outlined his plan for a constitution of the federation of Europe in five articles. The first article[131] called for a perpetual and irrevocable alliance to be contracted between the sovereigns. These were to appoint their plenipotentiaries in a permanent diet in which all disputes were to be settled by arbitration or by judicial pronouncement. The second article[132] suggested that the sovereigns were to be specified whose delegates were to be entitled to vote in the diet, those who were to be invited to adhere to the federation, the order, date, and manner in which each was to be awarded the presidency for an equal period of time, and, finally, the quota of contributions and the methods of assessing them to meet the common expenses. The third provision[133] stated that the members of the confederation were to guarantee to one another the possession and government of their territories according to actual possession at the time and in accordance with the treaties then in effect. The members were to agree to submit their differences to the

[131] Art. I, ed. of 1761, p. 19; ed. of 1795, p. 202; Vaughan ed., p. 61; Nuttall ed., pp. 44–45; Rousseau, "*L'Etat de guerre*" and "*Projet de paix perpétuelle*," with Introduction and notes by Shirley G. Patterson and Foreword by George Haven Putnam (New York, 1920), p. 41.

[132] Art. II, ed. of 1761, p. 19; ed. of 1795, p. 202; Vaughan ed., p. 62; Nuttall ed., pp. 45–46; Patterson ed., p. 41.

[133] Art. III, ed. of 1761, pp. 19–20; ed. of 1795, pp. 202–3; Vaughan ed., pp. 62–63; Nuttall ed., pp. 46–47; Patterson ed., pp. 41–42.

diet, renouncing the right to settle their disputes by force.
They were also to renounce the right to make war on
one another under any pretext whatsoever. The fourth
article[134] stipulated that a contracting power which violated the treaty was to be placed under the ban of Europe and treated as a common enemy if it refused to execute the judgments of the grand alliance, prepared for
war, made a treaty hostile to the end of the federation, or
took up arms against any member-state, in which case the
others were to proceed against it and reduce it to obedience.
Lastly,[135] the provisional decisions of the diet were to be
passed by a majority vote, and the final decisions were to
require a three-fourths majority of the members of the diet
acting under instructions from their governments. The diet
or congress was to legislate for the well-being of Europe but
was not permitted to change any of the fundamental articles
without the unanimous consent of the powers adhering to
the treaty.

Of the powers that were to constitute the commonwealth
of Europe, Rousseau offered a suggested list of nineteen sovereigns who were to have an equal voice in the deliberations
of the diet.[136] The motives which prompt disputes and lead

[134] Art. IV, ed. of 1761, p. 20; ed. of 1795, p. 203; Vaughan ed., p. 63;
Nuttall ed., pp. 46–47; Patterson ed., p. 42.

[135] Art. V, ed. of 1761, pp. 20–21; ed. of 1795, pp. 203–4; Vaughan ed.,
p. 64; Nuttall ed., pp. 48–49; Patterson ed., pp. 42–43.

[136] Rousseau included the following in his list of sovereigns, each of whom
was to have one vote: the Emperor of the Romans; the emperor of Russia; the
kings of France, Spain, and England; the States-General; the kings of Denmark, Sweden, Poland, and Portugal; the pope; the king of Prussia; the
elector of Bavaria and his associates; the Elector Palatine and his associates;
the Swiss and their associates; the ecclesiastical electors and their associates;
the Republic of Venice and her associates; the King of Naples and the King
of Sardinia (ed. of 1761, pp. 22–23; ed. of 1795, pp. 205–6; Vaughan ed.,
pp. 66–67; Patterson ed., pp. 44–45).

to war would no longer have any significance, Rousseau thought, if his plan were put into operation. He saw the motives for war as the desire of princes to make conquests, to protect themselves from aggression, to weaken a too powerful neighbor, to maintain their rights against attack, to settle a difference which has defied friendly negotiations, or to fulfil some treaty obligation. He maintained that every one of these motives would disappear under the new order which he was proposing.[137] Rousseau enumerated the following advantages which his peace design would confer upon the princes who adopted it: first, absolute certainty of the settlement of all disputes without recourse to war; second, security for the prince through the abolition of all existing claims; third, guaranty of the person of the prince and the integrity of his dominions against both outside aggression and internal rebellions; fourth, execution of all engagements between princes, under the guaranty of the commonwealth of Europe; fifth, freedom of trade for all states; sixth, elimination of extraordinary military expenditures in time of war and their reduction in time of peace; seventh, increase of population, public wealth, and revenue of the prince; eighth, "an open door for all useful foundations, calculated to increase the power and glory of the Sovereign, the public wealth and the happiness of the subject."[138]

The following is Rousseau's argument in summary:

If our reasoning has been sound in the exposition of this Project, it has been proved: firstly, that the establishment of a lasting peace depends solely upon the consent of the Sovereigns concerned and offers no obstacle except what may be expected from their opposition; secondly, that the establishment of such a peace would be profitable to them in all manner of ways, and that, even from their point of view, there is no comparison

[137] Ed. of 1761, pp. 24–26; ed. of 1795, pp. 207–9; Vaughan ed., pp. 69–72.

[138] Ed. of 1761, pp. 38–39; ed. of 1795, pp. 221–22; Vaughan ed., pp. 88–90; Nuttall ed., pp. 90–93; Patterson ed., pp. 60–61.

between its drawbacks and advantages; thirdly, that it is reasonable to expect their decision in this matter will coincide with their plain interest; and lastly, that such a peace, once established on the proposed basis, will be solid and lasting and will completely fulfil the purpose with which it was concluded.[139]

Rousseau said that he would not venture to say with the Abbé that the true glory of princes lies in their serving the people and their highest interest is a good reputation. Such a statement merely heaped ridicule on Saint-Pierre in all the council chambers of Europe; so Rousseau would confine himself to what he considered the real interests of princes. Actual possession of territory has a much greater value to princes than a possible gain in the future—a sort of a "bird in the hand is worth two in the bush" idea. Rousseau concluded that, since the more powerful have no motive for taking chances on what they have and the weaker have no chance of gaining, both would find it to their advantage to renounce what they would like to win in order to feel sure of what they already have. Rousseau called attention to the terrible waste in men and money and strength of every form that even a most successful war entails. If the losses were compared with the profits, it would be found that the losses are greater than the gain. The only consolation the conqueror has is the knowledge that his enemy is more enfeebled than he, but even this advantage is more in the appearance of things than in reality. The strength gained against the enemy is more than balanced by the greater relative strength of the neutrals who have retained all their resources while the warring nations dissipated theirs. Wars, therefore, frequently cost more than they are worth. But even graver than the cost of war, even more serious than the lives lost, are the losses of those who are not born, the losses due to the interruption of trade, the desertion of the fields, the increase

[139] Vaughan ed., pp. 90–91; Nuttall ed., pp. 92–95.

of taxes. This evil, which, Rousseau said, no one sees at first, makes itself felt cruelly at the end. "And then the king is astonished to find himself so weak, as the result of making himself so strong."[140]

Rousseau in his second part, or "Criticism on Perpetual Peace," emphasized what he believed was the simplicity of the good Abbé in imagining that kings and princes would do the right thing if it were shown them, as though men were guided by their lights rather than by their passions.[141] Of course, Rousseau believed that the plan of a league to enforce peace was undeniably beneficent, practicable, and certainly not utopian. He pointed to Henry IV as proof of the practicality of such a proposal. "To prove that the Project of the Christian Commonwealth is not utopian, I need do no more than name its original author. For no one will say that Henry IV was a madman, or Sully a dreamer."[142] Yet Rousseau feared that the plan would never be adopted for the selfishness of kings and that of ministers would prevent its realization.[143] "As for disputes between prince and prince," Rousseau queried, "is it reasonable to hope that we can force before a higher tribunal men who boast that they hold their power only by the sword? . . . ."[144] Rousseau roundly

[140] Ed. of 1761, pp. 27 ff.; ed. of 1795, pp. 210–13; Vaughan ed., pp. 73–77.

[141] John Morley, *Rousseau* (New York, 1878), pp. 164–65.

[142] Vaughan ed., p. 102.

[143] Rousseau asked "whether there is in the whole world a single Sovereign who, finding himself thus bridled for ever in his most cherished designs, would endure without indignation the very thought of seeing himself forced to be just not only with the foreigner, but even with his own subjects?" (Vaughan ed., p. 96). Rousseau, unlike Saint-Pierre, does not place his hope in monarchs. Rousseau did not believe in divine right and did not expect to see peace actually made permanent until the downfall of monarchs had been effected (Souleyman, *op. cit.*, p. 142).

[144] Vaughan ed., p. 97; Nuttall ed., pp. 104–5.

denounced the influence of ministers in state decisions. If
kings would reject this peace when they weigh their interests
themselves, what can be expected when the calculation is
made for them by ministers, whose interests are always contrary to those of the people and generally to the princes as
well. Ministers are in perpetual need of war to make themselves indispensable, so that the king cannot extricate himself without their help. They would ruin the state to keep
their places.[145]

Rousseau did not believe with Saint-Pierre that, even
with men of good will, it would be easy to find a favorable
moment to carry the plan into effect. It would be necessary
in such a case, Rousseau held, that the sum of private interests would not outweigh the common interest, that each
should see in the well-being of all the greatest good to be
hoped for himself. But, Rousseau said, "this demands a union of wisdom in so many heads and a union of relations in
so many interests" that there would hardly come about such
a fortuitous union of all the necessary circumstances. "However, if this agreement does not happen," he declared,
"there is only force to take its place, in which event it is no
longer a question of persuading but of compelling, and instead of writing books we must raise troops."[146] While Rousseau looked upon Saint-Pierre's project as very wise, he
thought the Abbé naïve in imagining that all that was necessary was to assemble a congress and propose therein his
plan, that the princes would sign it and all would be over.
Saint-Pierre's judgment in putting the plan into effect was,
in Rousseau's eyes, childlike.

The value of Rousseau's work lay primarily in his justification of the good Abbé's purpose—he made clear the need

---

[145] Vaughan ed., p. 100; Nuttall ed., pp. 108–11.

[146] Vaughan ed., pp. 101–2; Nuttall ed., pp. 110–13.

of an international organization for the negotiation of treaties and the pacific settlement of disputes.[147] According to
Rousseau's experience, war was a matter between kings and
cabinets, not between nations. His scheme retained the
weaknesses of the Abbé's plan; and, where the Abbé would
initiate his grand alliance by persuasion, Rousseau would
apparently initiate his by force, which reminds one strongly
of the Grand Design. Yet, in seeming contradiction, Rousseau wrote of Henry's plan: "While we admire so fair a
scheme, let us console ourselves for the fact that it was not
carried into execution, by the reflection that it could only
have been done by violent means which would have stag-
gered humanity."[148] Nevertheless, in an apparent about-
face, he spoke of the execution of Henry's plan in a highly
pleased way. With a decidedly modern ring he wrote: "A
war, destined to be the end of all wars, was about to usher in
eternal peace."[149] How ambitious and warlike monarchs
could be persuaded to undertake a plan like that of the
Abbé's is, of course, difficult to imagine; but it may be just
as difficult to see how peace could be secured through war,
such as that inferred by the Grand Design and by Rousseau.
Rousseau had no faith in the efficacy of moral restraint or
reason; his appeal was to self-interest, and his remedy was
force. "With him and the ideas derived from his philosophy," one writer states, "the notion of an organised international society, according to nature, may be said to have
shed the Christian guardianship which had evolved it and
indeed its whole relation to the supernatural."[150]

[147] Scott, Introduction to Ladd, *op. cit.*, p. xxxiv.

[148] Nuttall ed., pp. 128–29.   [149] Vaughan ed., p. 110.

[150] John Eppstein (comp.), *Ten Years' Life of the League of Nations: A History
of the Origins of the League and of Its Development from A.D. 1919 to 1929*, with an
Introduction by Viscount Cecil of Chelwood and an Epilogue by Gilbert
Murray (London, 1929), p. 18.

With Rousseau we come to "a prophet of international peace"[151] who saw Europe as a real community with a religion and a moral code, with customs and laws of its own, "which none of the component nations can renounce without causing a shock to the whole frame."[152] War has made a bitter irony of this community of interests; but, Rousseau believed, peace would restore the brotherhood of enlightened humanity. Dickinson in a comparison between the plans of Saint-Pierre and Rousseau, on the one hand, and the League of Nations established after World War I, on the other hand, holds that the League of Nations is less absolute and uncompromising. The federation of Saint-Pierre and Rousseau was to be perpetual, whereas the members of the League of Nations may withdraw. "Our League is thus more tentative and experimental."[153] It is to be noted that their league was not a league of all nations and did not comprise as many powers as the modern League. Their conception of a league included what modern nations are unwilling to permit, namely, interference by the League in the internal affairs of member-states. Stawell says this is precisely the point taken up by the European alliance after Waterloo.[154]

A plan which differed from Rousseau's in many respects was the project of Jeremy Bentham entitled "A Plan for an Universal and Perpetual Peace." The work was not published during his lifetime; it was not until 1843 that his plan was given to the world in Bowring's great edition.[155] In Vol-

[151] Alfred Bert Carter Cobban, *Rousseau and the Modern State* (London, 1934), p. 178.

[152] Vaughan ed., pp. 44–45.

[153] Dickinson, Introduction to Nuttall ed., p. xviii.

[154] F. Melian Stawell, *The Growth of International Thought* (London, 1929), p. 162.

[155] *The Works of Jeremy Bentham*, published under the superintendence of his executor, John Bowring (11 vols.; Edinburgh, 1843).

ume II, pages 535–60, appear four essays on international law published from Bentham's original manuscripts dated from 1786 to 1789. The fourth essay is devoted to the peace project. In justification of his plan Bentham wrote: "The happiest of mankind are sufferers by war; and the wisest, even the least wise, are wise enough to ascribe the chief of their sufferings to that cause."[156] The work was dedicated to the common welfare of all civilized nations but especially to Great Britain and France.

Bentham proposed the establishment of a world court whose decrees were to be enforced by public opinion, through the press and printed manifestoes, and, if necessary, by putting the offending state "under the ban of Europe." It is difficult to see how Bentham, who had such a low opinion of international morality,[157] could have trusted so benignly in the magic of public opinion, especially when he was face to face with the reality of how little public opinion yielded in the national affairs of his day. He was the first of a series of eminent peace advocates to rely solely upon public opinion to coerce individual states which have broken their pledges. He was also one of the first to stress the necessity of disarmament[158] as a requisite for international peace.[159] Bentham rested his argument on morality, not force. He stated:

. . . . for constituting esteem force is not the instrument, but justice. The sentiment really relied upon for security is fear. By respect then is meant, in plain English, fear. But in a case like this fear is much more

---

[156] *Ibid.*, II, 546.   [157] Lorimer, *op. cit.*, p. 222.

[158] Wehberg credits him with being likewise one of the first to throw "full light" upon the difficulties of an agreement with respect to armaments (Hans Wehberg, *The Limitation of Armaments*, translated by Edwin H. Zeydel [Washington, D.C., 1921], p. 6).

[159] One writer on Bentham seems to think that this was a singularly inopportune time to propose a reduction in armaments (John Maxcy Zane, "Jeremy Bentham," in Macdonnell and Manson, *op. cit.*, p. 541).

adverse than favourable to security. So many as fear you join against you till they think they are too strong for you, and then they are afraid of you no longer. Meanwhile they all hate you, and jointly and severally they do you as much mischief as they can. You, on your part, are not behind-hand with them. Conscious or not conscious of your own bad intentions, you suspect theirs to be still worse. Their notions of your intentions is the same. Measures of mere self-defence are naturally taken for projects of aggression. The same causes produce, on both sides, the same effects; each makes haste to begin for fear of being forestalled. In this stage of things, if on either side there happens to be a Minister, or a would-be Minister, who has a fancy for war, the stroke is struck, and the tinder catches fire.[160]

Certainly Bentham's advice is as sound and as applicable to our own time as to his.

Bentham's plan never had the slightest chance of being undertaken, for it was nullified in its entirety by two pre-requisite and fundamental aims: first, that nations were to renounce their colonies, a thing which states are as yet unwilling to do; and, second, that countries were to disarm, a proposal as little acceptable in Bentham's day as in our own times.[161] His first proposition[162] concerning the renunciation of colonies was based upon his belief that colonies were unprofitable to the mother-country and, in addition, provided a fruitful cause for involving her in wars. Then, too, the mother-country would no longer be burdened with the expense of administering and protecting the dependencies. This proposition was directed mainly to Great Britain and France. It was likewise to the interest of the colonies to be freed from the connection with the mother-country, which governed them for her own benefit. Furthermore, the colonies were better able to govern themselves, since the great

[160] Bowring ed., II, 559; Jeremy Bentham, *Plan for an Universal and Perpetual Peace*, with an Introduction by C. John Colombos (London, 1927), pp. 42–43.

[161] Bowring ed., II, 546; Colombos ed., p. 11.

[162] Proposition I, Bowring ed., II, 548; Colombos ed., pp. 13–14.

distance made colonial administration ineffective.[163] As to
the second aim, which called for disarmament, Bentham
declared that Great Britain was not to maintain a naval
force beyond that needed to defend its commerce against
pirates.[164] Neither was Great Britain to have any treaty of
alliance, defensive or offensive,[165] nor was she to conclude
any treaties to obtain commercial advantages over other
nations.[166] It was not to the interest of Great Britain to make
any long-term preparations for the increase of its naval
force through the navigation act, bounties on the Greenland
trade, and other trades regarded as nurseries for seamen.[167]
All the advantages resulting from his recommendations,
Bentham pointed out, would accrue to France as well as to
Great Britain.[168]

If the two fundamental propositions were adhered to by
Great Britain and France, Bentham believed that the principal obstacles to the establishment of general peace for all
Europe would be removed.[169] For the maintenance of such
a pacification, general and perpetual treaties might be made
limiting the number of troops each power was to maintain.[170]
In this condition of general tranquillity there was to be no
secret diplomacy, which Bentham believed was repugnant
to the interests of peace.[171] On the evils of secret diplomacy
Bentham wrote:

[163] Bowring ed., II, 548; Colombos ed., p. 17.

[164] Proposition IV, Bowring ed., II, 550; Colombos ed., p. 21.

[165] Proposition II, Bowring ed., II, 549; Colombos ed., p. 18.

[166] Proposition III, Bowring ed., II, 549; Colombos ed., pp. 18–21.

[167] Proposition V, Bowring ed., II, 550; Colombos ed., p. 21.

[168] Proposition VI–X, Bowring ed., II, 550; Colombos ed., p. 21.

[169] Proposition XI, Bowring ed., II, 550; Colombos ed., p. 21.

[170] Proposition XII, Bowring ed., II, 550; Colombos ed., pp. 22–26.

[171] Proposition XIV, Bowring ed., II, 554; Colombos ed., pp. 31–44.

What, then, is the veil of secrecy that enwraps the proceedings of the Cabinet? A mere cloak for wickedness and folly; a dispensation to Ministers to save them from the trouble of thinking; a warrant for playing all manner of mad and silly pranks, unseen and uncontrolled; a licence to play at hazard with their fellows abroad, staking our lives and fortunes upon the throw.[172]

Bentham, "with characteristic predilection for legal processes,"[173] laid emphasis upon the establishment of a tribunal.[174] He hoped that the court would not need to be armed with coercive powers.[175] With the establishment of a common tribunal, he believed, "the necessity for war no longer exists from differences of opinion. Just or unjust, the decision of the arbiters will save the credit, the honour of the contending party."[176] The common congress or court was to be constituted by each power sending two deputies—one the principal, the other an occasional substitute. The meetings of the congress, open to the public, were to be concerned with deciding controversies, circulating in all states the opinion reached, and "after a certain time, in putting the refractory State under the ban of Europe."[177] Concerning the execution of the decisions of the court, Bentham wrote:

There might, perhaps, be no harm in regulating, as a last resource, the contingent to be furnished by the several States for enforcing the decrees of the Court. But the necessity for the employment of this resource would, in all human probability, be superseded for ever by having recourse to the much more simple and less burthensome expedient of introducing into the instrument by which such Court was instituted a clause guaranteeing the liberty of the Press in each State, in such sort that the Diet might find

172 Bowring ed., II, 558; Colombos ed., p. 40.

173 Moore, *op. cit.*, p. 5.

174 Proposition XIII, Bowring ed., II, 552; Colombos ed., pp. 26–31.

175 Bowring ed., II, 552; Colombos ed., p. 26.

176 Bowring ed., II, 552; Colombos ed., p. 27.

177 Bowring ed., II, 554.

no obstacle to its giving, in every State, to its decrees and to every paper whatever, which it might think proper to sanction with its signature, the most extensive and unlimited circulation.[178]

Since the plan[179] remained in unpublished form for so many years, it had no influence upon passing events and remained practically unnoticed. Bentham's plan deserves close study, particularly for his confidence in the power of public opinion and his strong advocacy of the international court of judicature. One writer remarks that Bentham's sketch "makes several suggestive proposals which even after a century may still be of value to those interested in the problem of preserving society from further wars."[180]

But the work of another thinker, Immanuel Kant, attracted immediate attention. In 1793 England began her great war with France, which was already involved with Austria and Prussia. In 1795 the Peace of Basel terminated for a time the struggle between Prussia and France. The philosopher Immanuel Kant was doubtlessly influenced by the treaty, concluded at Basel,[181] just as Saint-Pierre was moved by the Congress of Utrecht to formulate his peace project. It was in 1795 that Kant published at Königsberg his tract *Zum ewigen Frieden*. The plans of Kant and Saint-Pierre were both in the form of treaties, ready for the signatures of the nations. Kant's work proved of tremendous

[178] *Ibid.*

[179] See further: Edgard Briout, *L'Idée de paix perpétuelle de Jérémie Bentham* (Paris, 1905); Seroux d'Agincourt, *op. cit.*, pp. 319–409.

[180] J. O. M., "Jeremy Bentham," *New Commonwealth*, V, No. 3 (December, 1936), 41.

[181] In the separate treaty of Basel, 1795, Prussia gave France a free hand on the left bank of the Rhine, and Prussia turned her attention to the partition of Poland. Kant was indignant and drew up his plan as a just treaty which would provide a proper foundation for peace in Europe (Dickinson, Introduction to Rousseau, "*A Project of Perpetual Peace*," *Rousseau's Essay*, Nuttall ed., p. xii).

interest to his day; fifteen hundred copies of his tract were sold in a few weeks, and a second edition was published the next year (1796).[182] An English edition was published in London at the same time, and a French edition in Königsberg.[183] "Edition followed edition, and critical comment piled up a voluminous literature. In fact, from a bibliographical standpoint, Kant's little work holds place along with Sully's Memoirs and Saint-Pierre's Projet."[184] Of *Zum ewigen Frieden*, Nicholas Murray Butler says: "Every page of this precious essay will bear reading and rereading in the light not only of the times in which it was written, but also in the light of all that has happened since and of all that is going on at this very moment."[185]

The plan proposed by the philosopher of Königsberg was based on the same idea as that held successively by Saint-Pierre, Penn, Rousseau, and Bentham—a general confederation of European states. Less exact in its proposals than the work of Saint-Pierre or Penn, the general proposition was, nevertheless, made most clear, and the essay of the German philosopher became a classic of international government. The preliminary articles provided:[186] first, that no secret

[182] Victor Delbos, "Les Idées de Kant sur la paix perpétuelle," *Nouvelle revue*, CXIX (August, 1899), 410; Edwin D. Mead, "Immanuel Kant's Internationalism," *Contemporary Review*, CVII (February, 1915), 228.

[183] Concerning the manuscripts and early editions see *Zum ewigen Frieden: Ein philosophischer Entwurf von Immanuel Kant. Text der Ausgabe A (1795) unter Berücksichtigung des Manuscriptes, der Ausgaben A a (1795) und B (1796)*, hrsg. von Karl Kehrbach (Leipzig, 1905), pp. liv, lv.

[184] Hicks, *op. cit.*, p. 73.

[185] Nicholas Murray Butler, Introduction to Immanuel Kant, *Perpetual Peace* (New York, 1939), p. viii.

[186] Kant, *Perpetual Peace*, translated by Benjamin F. Trueblood (Boston, 1897), pp. 5–10; Butler ed., pp. 2–10; *Perpetual Peace, a Philosophical Proposal*, translated by Helen O'Brien with an Introduction by Jessie H. Buckland (London, 1927), pp. 19–23; *Eternal Peace and Other International Essays*, trans-

reservations were to be included in treaties; second, that no independent state was to be acquired by another; third, that standing armies were to be abolished; fourth, that no national debts were to be contracted for the external affairs of the state; fifth, that no state was to interfere by force with the internal affairs of another state; sixth, that no state at war was to commit such acts of hostility as would render future confidence impossible.[187]

The second section of Kant's essay contained the three definitive articles of a perpetual peace with a running commentary for each:

First, the civil constitution of each state was to be republican. Kant believed that perpetual peace was to be achieved only under a republican constitution, since under such a constitution the consent of the subjects was needed to go to war. Otherwise, the decision of war was left to the whim of the ruler, who "can, therefore, decide on war for the most trifling reasons, as if it were a kind of pleasure party. . . . ." Kant distinguished between a republican and a democratic constitution as follows: "Republicanism is the political principle of severing the executive power of the government from the legislature. Despotism is that principle in pursuance of which the state arbitrarily puts into effect laws which it has itself made . . . ."; and "democracy in the proper sense of the word, is of necessity despotism, because it establishes an executive power. . . . . Therefore the 'whole people,' so-

---

lated by W. Hastie (Edinburgh, 1891), pp. 79–87; *Perpetual Peace*, translated with an Introduction by M. Campbell Smith (New York and London, 1903, 1915), pp. 107–16; Kehrbach ed., pp. 5–10; *Zum ewigen Frieden*, mit Ergänzungen aus Kants übrigen Schriften und einer ausführlichen Einleitung über die entwicklung des Friedensgedankens herausgegeben von Karl Vorländer (Leipzig, 1914), pp. 4–10.

[187] From this last preliminary article we understand that Kant did not expect an immediate cessation of warfare.

called, who carry their measure are really not all, but only a majority: so that the universal will is in contradiction with itself and with the principle of freedom. . . . ."[188]

Second, the law of nations was to be founded on a federation of free states. Kant believed that peace was to be achieved only if states resolved to give up their lawless freedom and yield to the coercion of public laws. He proposed that "they [the states] can form a State of Nations, one, too, which will be ever increasing and would finally embrace all the peoples of the earth. . . . ." He realized the impossibility of establishing a world republic and proposed a "negative substitute for it, a federation averting war, maintaining its ground and ever extending over the world [which] may stop this tendency to war and shrinking from the control of law. . . . ."[189]

Third, the rights of men, as citizens of the world, were to be limited to the conditions of universal hospitality.[190] Here Kant showed that the relation of the federated states to one another and to the whole was to be determined by cosmopolitan law.[191]

To his plan Kant added two "Supplements." The first[192]

[188] Trueblood ed., pp. 11–14; Butler ed., pp. 12–17; O'Brien ed., pp. 25–29; Hastie ed., pp. 89–93; Smith ed., pp. 120–28; Kehrbach ed., pp. 12–17; Vorländer ed., pp. 12–16.

[189] Trueblood ed., pp. 14–19; Butler ed., pp. 18–23; O'Brien ed., pp. 29–32; Hastie ed., pp. 94–100; Smith ed., pp. 128–37; Kehrbach ed., pp. 17–21; Vorländer ed., pp. 16–21.

[190] Trueblood ed., pp. 19–21; Butler ed., pp. 23–27; O'Brien ed., pp. 33–34; Hastie ed., pp. 100–104; Smith ed., pp. 137–42; Kehrbach ed., pp. 22–25; Vorländer ed., pp. 21–25.

[191] One writer discerns in this a similarity to the idea of Bentham that one of the causes of war is the existence of colonies. Kant opposed colonization by right of conquest (Seroux d'Agincourt, *op. cit.*, p. 493).

[192] Trueblood ed., pp. 21–29; Butler ed., pp. 27–37; O'Brien ed., pp. 34–41; Hastie ed., pp. 105–15; Smith ed., pp. 143–57; Kehrbach ed., pp. 25–34; Vorländer ed., pp. 25–34.

treated the topic "Of the Guarantee of Perpetual Peace." Kant began this Supplement with the statement: "The guarantee of this treaty is nothing less than the great and ingenious artist, nature (*natura daedala rerum*). Her mechanical march evidently announces the grand aim of producing among men, against their intention, harmony from the very bosom of their discords." To accomplish this, nature has made three preparatory arrangements. First, she has made it possible for man to exist in all parts of the earth. Second, she has, by means of war, dispersed men in order that the most inhospitable regions be inhabited. Third, nature has, by the same means, compelled men to enter into relations more or less in accordance with right. Kant then examined what is most essential to a perpetual peace, that is, what nature has done in promoting this aim, how she favors the moral purpose of man and guarantees the execution of the laws reason prescribes to him, so that whatever man ought to do as a free agent according to the civil, public, and cosmopolitical right, and does not do, shall be accomplished by the compulsion of nature without prejudice to his liberty. Kant stated that, when nature wills that this or that arrive, it does not mean that she makes it a duty to us. It is practical reason alone that can prescribe laws to free beings without constraining them. It means, Kant said, that nature does it herself, whether we will it or not. Even if men were not compelled through discord to submit to the constraint of laws, war from without would compel them to do this. Nature has arranged that every people finds at its side another people crowding upon it.

Therefore, it must form itself into a state capable of opposing hostile enterprises. The republican constitution is the only one which is completely in accord with the rights of man. But it is the most difficult to found and maintain. Indeed, it has been asserted that it required angels to realize "a form of government so sublime." So nature comes to the aid of the general will by employing these selfish inclinations, so that it requires a good state organization, and this is certainly not beyond the power of mortals. The question is to so organize the state that the forces of selfishness are so arrayed against one another that the one will check the other or destroy its disturbing influence. In this way man is forced to be, if not a good moral being, at least a good citizen. The idea of the law of nations presupposes a number of independent neighboring states. This situation is in itself a state of war; but reason prefers this coexistence of states to a union that might end in universal monarchy. The ruler of every state, however, desires to secure to himself a constant state of peace by the conquest of the whole world, if possible. But nature wills otherwise. She employs two means to prevent a fusion of peoples—a difference of language and religion. If nature wisely separates nations, it, on the other hand, brings together, through their mutual self-interest, peoples whom the idea of the cosmopolitical right alone would never have secured against violence and war. The spirit of commerce, here meant, sooner or later takes hold of every nation and is incompatible with war. It is in this manner that nature guarantees a perpetual peace. It prevents us from regarding permanent peace as a chimerical aim and makes it thereby a duty in us to contribute toward it.

The second Supplement[193] Kant called "Secret Article for Securing Peace." The article declared: "The maxims of philosophers, on the conditions which render a perpetual peace possible, shall be consulted by those states armed for war." In an appendix to the plan, Kant dealt with "On the

[193] Trueblood ed., pp. 29–31; Butler ed., pp. 37–40; O'Brien ed., pp. 42–43; Hastie ed., pp. 116–18; Smith ed., pp. 158–60; Kehrbach ed., pp. 34–36; Vorländer ed., pp. 34–36.

Disagreement between Morality and Politics in Reference to Perpetual Peace" and "Of the Agreement between Politics and Morality According to the Transcendent Idea of Public Rights."[194]

Kant's recommendations differed from many of his predecessors in that Kant struck at the roots of war. His principles were supported by arguments drawn from "nature," long realized as being philosophically untenable. Yet his plan involved ideas that are strictly modern.[195] Hughan pointed out that at least six of the Fourteen Points were anticipated and that Kant's proposals in regard to absolutism, armaments, war loans, secret diplomacy, self-determination, intervention, methods of warfare, and a league of nations, if carried out, would have made the war of 1914 an impossibility.[196] Kant did not think that immediate peace was possible. That is why he analyzed the causes of war, for he was convinced that permanent peace was not attainable without sufficient preparation. "But he did see clearly the distant goal; and, more than that, he marked out the toilsome pathway which the world must travel before it can ever reach that goal."[197]

Kant's plan was less detailed and pretentious than Henry's or Saint-Pierre's. The German philosopher failed to work out in detail the idea of a congress applying the principles of international law, and he failed to suggest an

[194] Trueblood ed., pp. 31–53; Butler ed., pp. 41–67; Hastie ed., pp. 119–48; Smith ed., pp. 161–96; Kehrbach ed., pp. 37–56; Vorländer ed., pp. 37–55.

[195] Kehrbach's Preface to *Zum ewigen Frieden* (1905), p. xvii; Patterson Introduction to Rousseau, "*L'Etat de guerre*" and "*Projet de paix perpétuelle*," p. lii.

[196] Jessie Wallace Hughan, *A Study of International Government* (New York, 1923), pp. 155–56.

[197] Dwight Whitney Morrow, *The Society of Free States* (New York, 1919), p. 139.

international court to administer the law of nations. His union of states was not an indissoluble one; and he guarded
himself, as if by anticipation, against the imputation of desiring to establish a universal state. Kant explicitly said:
"This alliance does not tend to any dominion over a state,
but solely to the certain maintenance of the liberty of each
particular state, partaking of this association, without being
therefore obliged to submit, like men in a state of nature, to
the legal constraint of public force."[198] In Kant's opposition
to a stricter bond of union, Lorimer saw a reverting to the
opinion of Grotius.[199]

Kant demanded the abolition of standing armies; but he
did not, of course, discuss conscription, the development of
which he could not very well foresee. He insisted that no
national debts were to be contracted for the external affairs
of the state. It is surprising to find Kant emphasizing national indebtedness at a time when the international credit
system was still in its infancy.[200] The essay by Kant was particularly unusual in that it was a direct attack on imperialism, which was not to develop fully for nearly a century.
Kant held that the rights of men in foreign countries should
be limited to the privileges accorded by hospitality. Kant's
proposal that all states should have constitutional governments must have appeared quite radical, for, with the exception of England and France after the Revolution, every European country was ruled by a despot. Kant was anxious to
have constitutional government established in all states, for
then, he assumed, the consent of subjects would be needed
to go to war. He was convinced that the people would not

[198] Butler ed., p. 21; O'Brien ed., p. 31.

[199] Lorimer, *op. cit.*, II, 226–27.

[200] Austin Harrison, "Kant on the League of Nations," *English Review*,
XXIX (November, 1919), 458.

decide on war so lightly as princes.[201] His work included philosophical arguments which appear, at times, strange and illogical. For example, man, according to Kant, could be a good citizen but not necessarily would he be a good moral being. Kant recognized no law among states in practice, because he admitted no superior to make and enforce law. Kant's recommendations, closely akin to Rousseau's, which he obviously had given careful reading,[202] were unproductive at the time. His proposals seem to carry even greater weight today, and some of them seem even more suited to the present than to his own age. In the application of means for the preservation of peace, we have not only never followed Kant, but it can be said that the world is no better off today than it was after Kant wrote his treatise.[203]

[201] Friedrich Paulsen, *Immanuel Kant: His Life and Doctrine*, translated by J. E. Creighton and Albert Lefevre (New York, 1902), p. 358.

[202] We know that Kant held Rousseau in high esteem; the only picture in his frugal home was a portrait of Rousseau. Kant was also greatly indebted in the field of politics to Hobbes, Locke, and Montesquieu (Smith, Introduction to Kant, *Perpetual Peace*, Smith ed., pp. 46–57). In earlier works he made admiring references to Rousseau. Through Rousseau's work he must have been acquainted with Saint-Pierre (Dickinson, Introduction to Rousseau, *A Project of Perpetual Peace*, Nuttall ed., pp. xi–xii).

[203] On Kant's conceptions on peace see further: Arturo Orzábal Quintana, "Kant y la paz perpetua," *Nosotros*, Año 18, XLVI, No. 179 (April, 1924), 441–57; J. Declareuil, "Kant, le droit public et la société des nations," *Revue générale de droit international public*, XXV (1918), 113–43; A. Aulard, *La Paix future d'après la Révolution Française et Kant* (Paris, 1915).

CHAPTER III

PLANS OF THE NINETEENTH CENTURY

IN THE early part of the nineteenth century, toward the close of the Napoleonic wars, Claude Henri, comte de Saint-Simon, in collaboration with Augustin Thierry,[1] published in Paris a brochure of one hundred and twelve pages, dated October, 1814.[2] The work was entitled, *De la réorganisation de la société européenne ou de la nécessité et des moyens de rassembler les peuples de l'Europe en un seul corps politique en conservant à chacun son indépendance nationale.* His proposal called for a parliament for each nation[3] and a general parliament for all Europe which was to be given the power of judging international differences and examining all questions of European interest.[4] There was also to be a king,[5] although Saint-Simon did not say how he was to be designated. The general parliament, consisting of two hundred and forty members,[6] was to be fashioned on the English Parliament,

---

[1] C. Bouglé, Introduction to *L'Œuvre d'Henri de Saint-Simon*, textes choisis par C. Bouglé, notice bibliographique de Alfred Pereire (Paris, 1925), p. xiii; Louis Carle Bonnard, *Essai sur la conception d'une société des nations avant le XXᵉ siècle* (Paris, 1921), p. 125; Jacques Hodé, *L'Idée de fédération internationale dans l'histoire: les précurseurs de la société des nations* (Paris, 1921), pp. 187–95.

[2] Alfred Pereire, Introduction to *De la réorganisation de la société européenne ou de la nécessité et des moyens de rassembler les peuples de l'Europe en un seul corps politique en conservant à chacun son indépendance nationale, par M. le comte de Saint-Simon et par A. Thierry, son élève (Octobre 1814)* (Paris, 1925), p. xxxvii; Bouglé, Introduction to Bouglé ed., p. xiii.

[3] Pereire ed., p. 58.

[4] Bouglé ed., p. 96; Pereire ed., p. 51.

[5] Pereire ed., p. 50.

[6] Bouglé ed., p. 95; Pereire ed., p. 47.

having two chambers, a house of deputies, and a house of peers. The deputies were to hold office for a term of ten years and were to be elected by the literates.[7] The peers were to be appointed by the king.[8] This common parliament[9] was to be undertaken immediately by the French and the English, who already had a representative system. Europe would have the best organization possible,[10] Saint-Simon thought, if his project were put into effect.[11]

It was on the eve of the great assemblage at Vienna that Saint-Simon's work was published. During the years 1814 and 1815 the Congress of Vienna met to reconstruct Europe. Tsar Alexander I of Russia had felt the need of a spiritual basis for the preservation of peace. On September 26, 1815, Emperor Alexander of Russia announced to the world the scheme of the Holy Alliance. The idea of the Holy Alliance likely was the outcome of his early training. His tutor, La Harpe, a fervent disciple of Rousseau,[12] had made him familiar with Saint-Pierre's project and Henry Fourth's Grand Design.[13] Now at this propitious time Alexander perhaps

[7] Bouglé ed., p. 95; Pereire ed., p. 47.   [8] Pereire ed., p. 49.

[9] *Ibid.*, pp. 57 ff. Power was given into the hands of the wealthy in preference to the learned. To sit in the house of peers a man had to have £20,000 a year in land, and to sit in the house of commons £1,000 a year in land (Arthur John Booth, *Saint-Simon and Saint-Simonism: A Chapter in the History of Socialism in France* [London, 1871], p. 55).

[10] Bouglé ed., p. 92; Pereire ed., pp. 43–44; Hodé, *op. cit.*, p. 192.

[11] See further: J. L. Puech, "La Société des nations et ses précurseurs socialistes," *Revue politique et littéraire, Revue bleue*, LIX, No. 3 (February 5, 1921), 82–85, No. 5 (March 5, 1921), 147–51; Ferdinand Dreyfus, *L'Arbitrage international, avec une préface de Frédéric Passy* (Paris, 1892), pp. 91–100; Alfred Pereire, "Bibliographie" in Pereire ed., pp. xli–xlvi; *idem*, "Notice bibliographique," Bouglé ed., pp. xxx–xxxii.

[12] J. O. M., "Alexander I and the Holy Alliance," *New Commonwealth*, V, No. 4 (January, 1937), 58.

[13] J. A. R. Marriott, *The European Commonwealth* (Oxford, 1918), p. 341.

felt called by Providence to carry out the great plan of King Henry. Credit for the conception of the project is, however, sometimes given to Baroness Krüdener.[14] This remarkable woman was a religious enthusiast who believed that she had revelations from God and that she was divinely called to induce the tsar to initiate a regime of peace. At first Alexander refused to see her, but finally an interview was arranged. He was deeply impressed with her; and when he went to Paris after the second defeat of Napoleon, he gave her quarters near his palace; and there, it has been said, the plan of the Holy Alliance was formulated.[15] But the tsar himself informed Castlereagh that the idea of a holy alliance came to him when Castlereagh, in the closing days of the Congress of Vienna, proposed a general alliance to guarantee the European status quo.[16]

The tsar felt that the great Christian principles of peace and mutual good will, solemnly avowed by all the European monarchs, would provide the basis for the administration of their respective states. The reciprocal relations of the powers were henceforth to be based "upon the sublime truths which the holy religion of our Savior teaches." The Alliance stipulated that "the precepts of Justice, Christian

[14] As to the originator of the idea of the Holy Alliance, the claim has also been made on behalf of Frank Bader, who in 1814 wrote a letter to the monarchs of Russia, Austria, and Prussia suggesting a Christian alliance founded on universal love and brotherhood. An upholder of the Bader claim declares with some eloquence: "Many things conspired to make Bader's plan bear fruit in Alexander's heart" (Homer L. Boyle, *History of Peace, Compiled from Governmental Records, Official Reports, Treaties, Conventions, Peace Conferences and Arbitrations* [Grand Rapids, Mich., 1902], p. 8).

[15] John Spencer Bassett, *The Lost Fruits of Waterloo* (New York, 1918), pp. 60–61.

[16] Charles C. Tansill, "The European Background of the Monroe Doctrine," in Alva Curtis Wilgus (ed.), *Modern Hispanic America* (Washington, D.C., 1933), I, 495–96.

Charity and Peace . . . . must have an immediate influence on the councils of Princes, and guide all their steps"; that the monarchs would, accordingly, "remain united by the bonds of a true and indissoluble fraternity and considering each other as fellow countrymen, they will, on all occasions and in all places, lend each other aid and assistance" while "regarding themselves towards their subjects and armies as fathers of families"; that governments and their subjects should consider themselves as "members of one and the same Christian nation." The powers who should "choose solemnly to avow the sacred principles which have dictated the present Act" were invited to join "this Holy Alliance."[17]

Of all the princes who signed the Holy Alliance, probably only Alexander himself did so with conviction. Cardinal Fleury had remarked to Saint-Pierre that it would be necessary to send very persuasive missionaries to touch the hearts of the monarchs to convert them to the peace project. "Here," observes one writer, "was the Tsar of all the Russias volunteering for the office."[18] Nevertheless, all the European monarchs appended their signatures except the sovereign of Great Britain, the pope, and the sultan. Great Britain's refusal to sign was due to Castlereagh, who considered the tsar as mentally unbalanced.[19] He found a loophole of escape in the constitutional objection that the prince-regent, ruling in place of his insane father, had no authority to sign. The powerful indorsement of Great Britain was thus lacking, although Castlereagh promised to support the prin-

[17] The text of the Holy Alliance: Walter Alison Phillips, *The Confederation of Europe: A Study of the European Alliance, 1813–1823, as an Experiment in the International Organization of Peace* (London, 1920), pp. 305–6; Stephen Pierce Duggan (ed.), *The League of Nations: The Principle and the Practice* (Boston, 1919), pp. 318–20.

[18] Ramsay Muir, *Nationalism and Internationalism* (London, 1916), p. 160.

[19] Bassett, *op. cit.*, p. 61.

ciples of the Alliance. As it was to be a union of Christian states, the sultan was not invited to join. The pope presumably felt that he did not need the tsar of Russia to explain to him the Christian principles of government, and he doubtlessly would have refused the invitation if it had been proffered.

It is significant, as Tansill points out, that Alexander did not intend to limit the Holy Alliance to a European membership. From 1816 on he persistently endeavored to get the United States to join. From 1809 to 1812 he had done what he could to protect American shipping in the Baltic, and during the War of 1812 he had sought to mediate between Great Britain and the United States. At the close of that war many Americans considered Russia as the only friend the United States had in Europe. The news of the signing of the treaty of the Holy Alliance was quite favorably received in the United States. "It was not then," Tansill says, "the fearsome bogy that in the passage of a very few years Americans were so wont to regard it; it was merely a plan for world peace, and as such, awakened a responsive chord in certain circles in the United States."[20]

The undemocratic nature of the Holy Alliance was, no doubt, one of the most important contributing factors leading to American disapproval of it as a league to enforce peace. Former President John Quincy Adams perhaps voiced the objections of many of his contemporaries to the Holy Alliance in his letter to William Ladd:

The Holy Alliance itself was a tribute from the mightiest men of the European world to the purity of your principles and the practicability of your system for the general preservation of peace. The poisonous ingredient in that league was the *unlimited* sovereignty of the parties to it. The league was *autocratic*, and so peculiar was this feature in its composi-

[20] In Wilgus, *op. cit.*, pp. 496–97.

tion, that the prince regent of Great Britain, when invited to become a party to it, because the constitution of that country did not recognize treaties as national, under the personal signature of the monarch, [declined]. The professed principles of the Holy Alliance were the perpetual preservation of peace, and the sovereigns who signed the treaty, declared that they considered the Christian principles of benevolence, mutual forbearance and charity, as obligatory upon them as *sovereigns* equally as upon individuals. But they bound themselves to support each other against all wrong-doers (they themselves to be the judges of the wrong), not only of foreigners, but of their own subjects.[21]

In popular parlance the Holy Alliance became synonymous with the Quadruple (later Quintuple) Alliance by which Europe was ruled for some years after 1815 and which became associated with the policy of reaction and suppression.[22] A clear distinction should be drawn between the Holy Alliance and the Quadruple Alliance. The former was a general treaty embodying vague principles, while the latter was established on definite treaties to preserve peace on the basis of the settlement of 1815. The Holy Alliance presented many obvious weaknesses. It had no executive and no legislative body; it contained no specific organization. It was merely a loose league of kings. It even failed to provide means for the settlement of international disputes. The Holy Alliance was a league of sovereigns, not a league of nations in the modern understanding of the term. Beneath its defects, however, was the idea of a unified Europe, in which justice and good will would take the place of suspicion and intrigue. Certainly this was a noble conception. Marriott

[21] Extract of letter from President John Quincy Adams to William Ladd in Ladd, *An Essay on a Congress of Nations for the Adjustment of International Disputes without Resort to Arms*, with an Introduction by James Brown Scott (New York, 1916), pp. 46–47 n.

[22] Boyce shows that no distinction seems to have been made in the minds of statesmen of the period (Myrna Boyce, *The Diplomatic Relations of England with the Quadruple Alliance, 1815–1830* [Iowa City, Iowa, 1918], p. 11).

goes so far as to call it "the only practical attempt ever made
to apply the principles of Christianity to the regulation of
international politics."[23] The Holy Alliance exercised a
powerful influence. It shaped the policy of Nicholas I of
Russia in regard to the Convention of Berlin in 1833 and
inspired the tsar's intervention in 1849 to crush the Hun-
garian insurrection. It perhaps motivated Nicholas II to
call the first international peace conference at The Hague in
1899.[24]

The Holy Alliance did not do the practical work of maintaining peace. That was left to the Quadruple Alliance.
The year 1815, like the year 1919, was marked by the victory of allied arms over what was felt to be the menace to
European security and by the attempt of the victorious nations to maintain peace through a rearrangement of the
map of Europe in accordance with their own political
standards. The Quadruple Alliance was formulated at
Chaumont in March, 1814, by Great Britain, Russia, Prussia, and Austria and received its final shape at the Second
Treaty of Paris, November 20, 1815. The Alliance was not
to be merely defensive but a genuine league of nations,
bound not "by a vague confession of Legitimist faith, but by
specific agreements. . . . . "[25] France was admitted at the first
congress held at Aix-la-Chapelle in 1818, and the Quadruple
Alliance thus became the Quintuple Alliance. The assembled powers at the Congress declared: "The object of the
union is as simple as it is great and salutary. It does not
tend to any new political combination—to any change in

[23] Marriott, *op. cit.*, p. 338.

[24] York holds that the calling of the first Hague Conference was the "chief
practical effect of the Holy Alliance" (Elizabeth York, *Leagues of Nations:
Ancient, Mediaeval and Modern* [London, 1919], p. 315).

[25] A. F. Pollard, *The League of Nations in History* (London, 1918), p. 9.

the relations sanctioned by existing treaties; . . . . it has no other object than the maintenance of peace. . . . ."[26]

Castlereagh was enthusiastic over the system of periodic conferences, which he hailed as "a new discovery" in the art of government, "at once extinguishing the cobwebs with which diplomacy obscures the horizon, bringing the whole bearing of the system into its true light, and giving to the counsels of the Great Powers the efficiency and almost the simplicity of a single State."[27] Differences arose among the allies;[28] England severed her relations definitely in 1822.[29] The disposition of the Alliance to win back for Spain her colonies in the New World led to the promulgation of the Monroe Doctrine.[30] France later withdrew from the Alliance, leaving Austria, Russia, and Prussia in a triple alliance, which continued to repress reform until the revolutions of 1848.

While the Quintuple Alliance eventually broke up, the principle of association was not lost and continued in what is known as the "Concert of Europe," "in which new garb the European system, based upon and regulated by treaties, and

[26] Phillips, *op. cit.*, p. 178.

[27] Pollard, *loc. cit.;* for the foreign policy of Castlereagh in this period see also Charles Kingsley Webster, *The Foreign Policy of Castlereagh, 1815–1822: Britain and the European Alliance* (London, 1925).

[28] John Bassett Moore, *The Peace Problem: Address on the Peace Problem, Delivered at the Twentieth Celebration of Founders' Day, Held at Carnegie Institute in Pittsburgh, Pa., on April 27, 1916* (Washington, D.C., 1917), p. 7.

[29] On the basis of the diplomatic correspondence Boyce concludes that neither Castlereagh nor Canning countenanced the Quadruple Alliance in its later development. Boyce shows that Castlereagh's stand was negative, a policy of nonagreement, whereas Canning was more effective in his opposition to the other powers (Boyce, *op. cit.*, p. 16).

[30] William Penn Cresson, *The Holy Alliance: The European Background of the Monroe Doctrine* (New York, 1922); J. Reuben Clark, *Memorandum on the Monroe Doctrine* (Washington, D.C., 1930).

constituting a league of nations for the preservation of peace, continued to carry on the work."[31] In 1856 Turkey was admitted to the Concert of Europe, and in 1878 the Concert was remodeled by the Treaty of Berlin. Perhaps the most valuable contribution of the Concert of Europe was the establishment of "the tradition of that sense of common interests among nations which has been, and will be, the strongest influence making for peace." The Concert of Europe further provided "a new sanction to international law, ... and so made possible the developments which led to the Conferences at The Hague. . . . ."[32]

The desire for peace was not limited to Europe. It found expression in the United States in the formation of peace societies,[33] such as the American Peace Society, founded in 1828 by William Ladd.[34] The first American organizations were limited largely to the New England states; but, after a long series of lectures delivered in New England and the middle states, Ladd succeeded in establishing a national organization at New York, the American Peace Society.[35] He had been converted to the peace movement through reading a pamphlet by a clergyman, Noah Worcester, *A Solemn Review of the Custom of War, Showing That War Is the Effect of Popular Delusion, and Proposing a Remedy.*[36] The au-

[31] John Bassett Moore, "Some Essentials of a League for Peace," in Duggan, *op. cit.*, p. 68.

[32] Phillips, *op. cit.*, p. 275.

[33] Merle Eugene Curti, *The American Peace Crusade, 1815–1860* (Durham, N.C., 1929).

[34] James Brown Scott, *Peace through Justice* (New York, 1917), pp. 8–16; George C. Beckwith, *Eulogy on William Ladd, Late President of the American Peace Society* (Boston, 1841).

[35] Elihu Burritt, Introduction to John Hemmenway, *The Apostle of Peace: Memoir of William Ladd* (Boston, 1872), p. 11.

[36] Philo Pacificus (pseud.) (n.p., n.d.).

thor was the founder of the Massachusetts Peace Society.[37] He had experienced great difficulty in finding a publisher for the tract, and it was published in 1814 only on the condition that it be issued anonymously.[38] Ladd himself credited the essay with riveting his attention in such a way that he henceforth devoted himself fully to the cause of peace.[39]

It was the American Peace Society which was responsible for one of the most celebrated and influential schemes for peace ever propounded, that of William Ladd in 1840.[40] Ladd, in the Advertisement to his work, *An Essay on a Congress of Nations*, rested his claim to originality upon the separation of his subject into two distinct parts: first, a congress of ambassadors from all those Christian and civilized nations who should choose to send them for the purpose of settling the principles of international law by compact and agreement in the nature of a mutual treaty and of devising and promoting plans for the preservation of peace; and, second, a court of nations, composed of the most able civilians in the world, to arbitrate or judge such cases as should be brought before it by the mutual consent of two or more contending nations. He thus separated the diplomatic body from the judicial branch, which, he maintained, required such different characters in the exercise of their functions.

[37] George C. Wing, "William Ladd, the Apostle of Peace," *Sprague's Journal of Maine History*, XI, No. 2 (1923), 55–56.

[38] Arthur D. Call, "The Will To End War," *Advocate of Peace*, LXXXVI, No. 4 (April, 1924), 233.

[39] James Brown Scott, Preface to Georg Schwarzenberger, *William Ladd: An Examination of an American Proposal for an International Equity Tribunal* (London, 1935), p. xii.

[40] *Prize Essays on a Congress of Nations, for the Adjustment of International Disputes, and for the Promotion of Universal Peace without Resort to Arms, Together with a Sixth Essay Comprising the Substance of the Rejected Essays* (Boston, 1840). Ladd's essay appears on pp. 509–638.

He considered the congress as the legislature, the court as
the judiciary, leaving the functions of the executive with
public opinion, "the queen of the world."[41]

Ladd retained some features of previous projects as essential to his own plan, and some he definitely rejected. He
stated that, while the pacific principle of other plans was
only of secondary consideration to their authors, the fulfilment of this principle was his chief aim. "Ought we not to
suppose," he asked,

that in this enlightened age of the world, this chief motive would be sufficient to induce Christian nations to make the safe and cheap attempt,
when the good to be obtained by success is commensurate only with the
extent and duration of the world? Is it too much to hope that, in this age
of reason and philanthropy, the preservation of peace, equity, and justice,
and the avoidance of all the sins and horrors of war may be a sufficient
motive to induce Christian nations to try the experiment recommended
in these Essays?[42]

Elsewhere Ladd wrote that "the spirit of peace, when fairly
put in practice, has never failed of its object; but has proved
the best security of nations, the surest preservation of their
honor and interests, and the greatest source of national happiness and prosperity."[43]

He claimed for his plan that it would not change essentially, by any direct influence, the existing relations of nations toward each other with respect to peace and war. His
plan was only a general treaty to be entered into by all the

[41] William Ladd, *An Essay on a Congress of Nations for the Adjustment of Inter-
national Disputes without Resort to Arms, Together with a Sixth Essay Comprising the
Substance of the Rejected Essays* (Boston, 1840), Advertisement, pp. iii, iv; *idem,
An Essay on a Congress of Nations for the Adjustment of International Disputes without
Resort to Arms,* Advertisement, Scott ed., pp. xlix, l.

[42] 1840 ed., pp. 579–80; Scott ed., p. 59.

[43] William Ladd (Philanthropos [pseud.]), *A Brief Illustration of the Principles
of War and Peace* (Albany, 1831), pp. 110–11.

nations, so that henceforth they would endeavor to settle their disputes by the law of reason, "as becomes rational creatures, and not by the law of violence which becomes only brutes."[44] Ladd felt that, if war were necessary in the nature of things and men must fight, they should mutually agree that they would give up some of the most barbarous features of war and protect the peaceful. Therefore he said that the American Peace Society plan

has nothing to do with physical force and leagues offensive and defensive, which at the commencement of the . . . . councils, leagues, diets, alliances, and congresses, sowed the seeds of their dissolution; but our plan depends entirely on the influence of moral power for the good it will do to the world, but it retains the expectation of settling the principles of international law, by compact and agreement, in a general treaty, to which the nations of Christendom will be parties; and it also retains the principle and practice of peaceful mediation between contending factions or nations, and the promotion of every plan for bettering the moral, intellectual, and physical condition of man.[45]

Careful to respect the theory of the equality of states, Ladd provided that a nation might send as many delegates to the congress as it chose but that each delegation was to be considered as a separate college and entitled to only one vote and to only one turn to speak in the discussions, "so as to be considered as but one person." He stated that his plan differed in this respect from previous schemes, which gave an uneven number of delegates to the various powers.[46] Ladd saw a difference between his congress and the previous diets or congresses, such as those of Greece, the Hanse towns, and the Italian cities. He believed that their utility was eventually destroyed because they admitted two principles

[44] 1840 ed., p. 580; Scott ed., p. 59.

[45] 1840 ed., pp. 580–81; Scott ed., pp. 59–60.

[46] 1840 ed., p. 581; Scott ed., p. 60.

of which his plan was free. The first was the enforcement of their decrees by the power of the sword, instead of depending upon moral power alone. The other was the union of the legislative, judicial, and executive powers in one body, which introduced intrigue, ambition, and many other baneful practices. Nevertheless, he said, with all these disadvantages they continued to preserve peace for centuries with but little interruption, proving adequately the force of the principle which he advocated.[47] Of all previous unions, Ladd had the greatest respect for the Helvetic Union, because he considered the civil part of the institution—the diet and the court of judges or arbitrators—as the nearest working model of his proposed congress and court of nations which ever existed.[48]

An Essay on a Congress of Nations by William Ladd consisted of fifteen chapters, and the essential part of the plan was treated in two divisions: first, the organization of the proposed congress of nations and, second, the court of nations for the peaceful adjudication of cases of international difficulty. In his exposition on the congress of nations[49] Ladd took up the initial steps in organizing such a body. He proposed assembling a convention composed of ambassadors of all the Christian or civilized nations that were willing to send representatives. Each nation was to have one vote. The convention was to organize itself into a congress of nations, and those who could not approve the character of the organization were free to withdraw. The congress of nations was then to choose its officers and clerks. It was empowered to admit new members, providing they assented to the rules already adopted and the laws of nations already

[47] 1840 ed., p. 610; Scott ed., pp. 85–86.

[48] 1840 ed., p. 562; Scott ed., p. 44.

[49] 1840 ed., pp. 521–24; Scott ed., pp. 8–11.

enacted by the congress. One of the first labors of the congress was to consider the principles of the law of nations. No principle was to be established unless it had the unanimous consent of all the nations represented and was ratified by the governments of all the member-states. In that way, every principle of international law would resemble a treaty. Ladd admitted that the progress which the congress would make might very well be slow, but he held that this would be more likely to produce permanent results. The congress was also to turn its attention at an early date to the establishment of the court of nations. The assembly was forbidden to intervene in the domestic affairs of nations. It was to limit itself to the relations between nations. Ladd explained that the congress was to concentrate on four main efforts: first, to define the rights of belligerents toward one another and to endeavor to abate the horrors of war, lessen its frequency, and promote its termination; second, to settle the rights of neutrals; third, to agree on measures useful to mankind in a state of peace; and, fourth, to organize a court of nations.

In the second part of the plan Ladd dealt with the court of nations.[50] The court was to be composed of as many members as the congress decided. Ladd suggested two members from each of the powers represented at the congress. The court was to be merely advisory. It was to act as a high court of admiralty. It was to take cognizance only of such cases as were referred to it by the mutual consent of the parties involved. The court was to have no power to enforce its decisions. The members of the court were to be appointed by the congress and were to enjoy tenure as agreed upon by the congress. Ladd suggested tenure on good behavior. The manner by which they were to be paid salaries was left to the congress. The court was to organize itself by

[50] 1840 ed., pp. 550–54; Scott ed., pp. 34–37.

choosing a president, vice-presidents, and the necessary secretaries and clerks. It was to hear counsel of both sides of the questions to be judged. The court was to meet once a year for the transaction of business. Ladd advised that it should not meet in a country which had a case on trial. The members of the court were to enjoy the same immunities as ambassadors. Decisions were to be made by a majority, which was to appoint one of its number to write up its verdict. Cases were to be judged by the "true interpretation" of existing treaties and by the laws passed by the congress of nations. Where treaties and laws failed to establish the point at issue, the case was to be decided by the principles of equity and justice. In cases involving a boundary dispute the court was empowered to send surveyors to the disputed region to collect facts. The court was also authorized to offer its mediation where war already existed or in any difficulty arising between nations which threatened the peace of the world. Indeed, the members of the court were to act as conservators of the peace of Christendom and to watch over the welfare of mankind. If the court was appealed to in a case concerning an internal dispute, such as a matter of succession to the throne, the opinion was to be rendered in accordance with the laws and usages of the country asking advice. From time to time it was the duty of the court to suggest to the congress topics involving new or unsettled principles favorable to the peace of the world. Ladd said that there were many other cases besides those mentioned in which the court would either prevent war or end it.

For the operation of his project Ladd depended upon the force of public opinion, in which he had great confidence.

If an Alexander, a Caesar, a Napoleon, have bowed down to public opinion, what may we not expect of better men, when public opinion becomes more enlightened? . . . . Already there is no civilized nation that can withstand the frown of public opinion. It is therefore necessary, only to enlighten public opinion still farther, to insure the success of our plan.[51]

He was convinced, as he said in an address before the Massachusetts Peace Society, that "a revolution of public opinion has commenced; and revolutions do not go back. The time will come, and that shortly, when nations will settle their disputes by amicable adjustment or arbitration, and will look back on war with as much amazement, as we do on the ordeal by battle and the burning of heretics. . . . ."[52]

As Ladd himself pointed out, his plan differed from the others in that he provided for a court of nations, distinct from a congress of nations. Other writers had proposed a congress in which the diplomatic and judicial functions were merged, but Ladd separated the two. He looked upon the congress as the legislature, the court as the judiciary; and he left the function of the executive to public opinion. Bentham had, it is true, proposed one body with both functions and had relied upon public opinion in much the same way as Ladd; but, since Bentham's work was not published until 1843, it cannot be considered as Ladd's pattern. Moreover, as Hicks indicates,[53] Ladd's independent thinking can be seen in his earlier essays under the pseudonym "Philanthropos."[54] For example, in his tract of 1832, *A Dissertation on a Congress of Nations*, can be seen the nucleus of the plan which

[51] 1840 ed., pp. 600–601; Scott ed., p. 77.

[52] William Ladd, *Address Delivered at the Tenth Anniversary of the Massachusetts Peace Society, December 25, 1825* (Boston, 1826), p. 17.

[53] Frederick Charles Hicks, *The New World Order* (New York, 1920), p. 74.

[54] William Ladd (Philanthropos [pseud.]), *A Brief Illustration of the Principles of War and Peace; idem, A Dissertation on a Congress of Nations* (n.p., 1832); *idem, A Solemn Appeal to Christians of All Denominations in Favor of the Cause of Permanent and Universal Peace* (New York, 1834).

Ladd later developed. In this essay he discussed the abolition of war through two means: spontaneous public opinion
and a congress of nations. After tracing in history the instances of nations banding together to insure peace and
showing the feasibility of his plan, he took up the question:
"Why do not all the nations of Christendom unite in so
beneficial a measure?" It may also be said that Ladd's
scheme was more in accord with the newer democratic principles than its predecessors; it was modeled on American institutions and American ideals of democracy.

Former projects had made but a limited appeal and, in
general, had little influence upon the public at large.
Ladd's plan, on the other hand, was widely circulated in the
United States, where it was granted much favorable comment. It was published in England,[55] where it exercised considerable influence on the peace movement there. The project was introduced by Ladd's disciple, Elihu Burritt, in the
peace conferences of Brussels (1848), Paris (1849), Frank-
fort (1850), and London (1851).[56] Ladd's predecessors had
generally contemplated changes in the family of nations
which were unwelcome at the time, as they would have
jeopardized the independence of nations. Scott says:

> They disregarded systematically the equality of nations. For the most
> part they advocated either a perpetual and forcible union, or at least a
> voluntary federation, and they required for their operation a change of
> thought as well as a change in the standard of conduct. They were op-
> posed to existing conditions, and for that reason they lacked a substantial
> basis on which to rear permanent structures. Mr. Ladd, on the contrary,
> accepted nations as actually constituted, proposed a Congress of such

[55] William Ladd, *An Essay on a Congress of Nations, for the Adjustment of International Disputes without Resort to Arms* (London, 1840).

[56] Scott, Introduction to Ladd, *An Essay on a Congress of Nations*, pp. xliii-
xliv.

nations, in which each would be represented with an equal vote, and the establishment of a court of justice for the settlement of disputes between them.[57]

Another American plan, entitled *War and Peace*, was offered in 1842 by Jay.[58] The project provided for an agreement in future treaties not to resort to war but to submit controversies to arbitration and to abide by the decisions rendered.[59] Jay held that war itself may be eliminated by the gradual growth of a public opinion against it and by the creation of agencies which nations can create and use just as individuals have created and used them. He favored the establishment of a court to decide differences between nations, which, although impossible of fulfilment at the moment, due to existing unfavorable conditions, could be reached by degrees. He proposed to insert an article in the next American treaty with France providing that, if any controversy were to arise in the future, neither nation was to resort to hostilities, and the controversy was to be submitted to arbitrament of one or more friendly powers, the award to be considered as binding.[60] Each treaty thus made would be an incentive to the formation of similar treaties, and Jay trusted that it was not the vain hope of idle credulity that at last a union might be formed of every Christian nation for guaranteeing the

[57] *Ibid.*, p. xxxviii.

[58] William Jay, *War and Peace: The Evils of the First and a Plan for Preserving the Last* (New York, 1842); *idem, War and Peace: The Evils of the First and a Plan for Preserving the Last*, with introductory note by James Brown Scott (New York, 1919).

[59] This plan of arbitration was proposed later in more definite form as a petition by the American Peace Society to the Senate of the United States (George Barrell Cheever, *The True Christian Patriot: A Discourse on the Virtues and Public Services of the Late Judge Jay*, delivered before the American Peace Society [Boston, 1860], pp. 9–10).

[60] 1842 ed., pp. 79–82.

peace of Christendom by establishing a tribunal for the adjustment of national differences and by preventing all forcible resistance to its decrees. He thought that it was unnecessary to discuss the character with which such a tribunal was to be invested.

Whenever it shall be seriously desired, but little difficulty will be experienced in placing it on a stable and satisfactory basis. That such a court, formed by a congress of nations in obedience to the general wish, would, next to Christianity, be the richest gift ever bestowed by Heaven upon a suffering world, will scarcely be questioned by any who have patiently and candidly investigated the subject.[61]

Jay was also aware of the problem of disarmament,[62] and he questioned the necessity of such a system of military preparations which impose "such onerous burthens on human industry" and exact "such cruel sacrifices of human happiness, comfort and virtue. . . . ."[63]

Some years later the Crimean War was waged and occasioned another project for peace. Gustave de Molinari was greatly stirred by that struggle. He saw the destruction and suffering which the war caused, the baneful consequences for commerce and industry; and he noticed the harmful effects upon neutrals. In 1857, shortly after the Crimean War, he wrote a book[64] on Saint-Pierre and prefixed to it an Intro-

[61] *Ibid.*, p. 96.

[62] William Jay, "Inefficacy of War," in *Views of War and Peace, Designed Especially for the Consideration of Statesmen* (Boston, n.d.), p. 11.

[63] William Jay, *An Address Delivered before the American Peace Society at Its Annual Meeting, May 26, 1845* (Boston, 1845), p. 31.

[64] Gustave de Molinari, *L'Abbé de Saint-Pierre, membre exclu de l'Académie française: sa vie et ses œuvres, précédées d'une appréciation et d'un précis historique de l'idée de la paix perpétuelle, suivies du jugement de Rousseau sur le projet de paix perpétuelle et la polysynodie ainsi que du projet attribué à Henri IV, et du plan d'Emmanuel Kant pour rendre la paix universelle, etc., etc., avec des notes et des éclaircissements* (Paris, 1857).

duction which presented his own views. In this work, *L'Abbé de Saint-Pierre, etc.*, he maintained that wars were the concern of all nations and not only of belligerents. He proposed that all nations were to act in concert when a dispute arose and were to prevent a conflict from ensuing, using force, if need be.[65] In fact, he urged the substitution of "collective justice" in place of the claim of each individual government to be the judge of its own rights.[66]

Just as an individual was incapable of resisting the combined power of all other individuals in the state, so one nation was not in a position to contest the concerted action of the others. Therefore, a union of states, a "concert universel," was to be established with the power to interpret laws and decide disputes instead of allowing each state to interpret its own "droit de guerre" and execute its own judgments.[67] Disarmament would then follow inevitably[68] and would allow the reduction of armed forces to a minimum. This would save millions for the people, who were bowed beneath the load of armed peace.[69] Two-thirds of European budgets were apportioned to war purposes and war debts, and De Molinari said dryly that the premium paid for insuring "security" exceeds the risk.[70] He noted that, since 1815, five great European powers actually dictated the political destinies of Europe; and he cited as cases in point the inter-

[65] *Ibid.*, pp. 52–55.

[66] Hodgson Pratt, Introduction to Gustave de Molinari, *The Society of Tomorrow: A Forecast of Its Political and Economic Organisation*, translated by P. H. Lee Warner (New York and London, 1904), p. xiv.

[67] De Molinari, *L'Abbé de Saint-Pierre*, pp. 55–56.

[68] *Ibid.*, pp. 57–58; *idem, The Society of Tomorrow*, p. 45.

[69] De Molinari, *L'Abbé de Saint-Pierre*, pp. 57–58; *idem, The Society of Tomorrow*, p. 42.

[70] Pratt, Introduction to De Molinari, *The Society of Tomorrow*, pp. xiii–xiv.

ference in the state of affairs in Greece and in Belgium and the waging of the Crimean War.[71] He believed that, if this system were enlarged to include all powers, the peace of Europe would not be seriously troubled. De Molinari realized that it would take time to establish the "concert universel" and to remove the risks of war, but he looked forward to ultimate achievement.[72]

About two decades later Johann Caspar Bluntschli presented a peace project to which he gave the title, "Europa als Statenbund." The plan forms the third part of chapter xii, "Die Organisation des europäischen Statenvereines," in his *Gesammelte kleine Schriften*.[73] The plan was first published in a popular journal, *Gegenwart*, in 1878.[74] In Bluntschli's opinion his work bore a close relationship to the Grand Design of Henry IV, which, he thought, distinguished it from other plans.[75] The Heidelberg professor contended that previous schemes resolved themselves into the establishment of universal monarchies or universal republics. He objected to these plans on the ground that the "fundamental condition of the solution of the problem of European organisation is the preservation of the independence and freedom of the confederated States."[76]

Bluntschli's confederation was to consist of eighteen specified states[77] whose independence and freedom were to be

[71] *L'Abbé de Saint-Pierre*, p. 56.   [72] *Ibid.*, pp. 56, 59.

[73] *Gesammelte kleine Schriften: Aufsätze über Recht und Staat* (Nördlingen, 1879), Vol. I.

[74] His last article was likewise published in this journal, September 10, 1881. See also Herbert Baxter Adams, *Bluntschli's Life-Work* (Baltimore, 1884), p. 18.

[75] *Op. cit.*, pp. 311–12.

[76] Cited in James Lorimer, *The Institutes of the Law of Nations* (Edinburgh and London, 1884), II, 271.

[77] *Op. cit.*, p. 300.

carefully preserved. The project called for the establishment of a code of international law and an international legislature. The latter was to consist of two houses: first, a united council, consisting of the representatives of the associated powers, the six great powers to have two votes each, the remaining twelve states to have one vote each;[78] and, second, a senate, representing the various European peoples and elected by the national parliaments. In the senate the great powers were to have eight or ten votes each; the minor states, four or five votes each.[79] The members of the council were to vote in accordance with the wishes of their governments. The members of the senate were to be free to vote as they saw fit. The presidency of the council was to rotate annually among the great powers.[80] One function of the senate was to act as a check on the council. Rules agreed upon by a majority of both houses were to be promulgated as international law. The enactment of a code of international law was to be the chief work of the council and the senate.

Questions relating to peace and higher politics, such as involved the independence and freedom of nations, were to be intrusted to the council,[81] whose decision, if by majority only, was not to be binding unless assented to by the senate. Questions of lesser importance, such as those dealing with boundaries or with the interpretation of treaties, were to be laid before administrative bureaus under the direction of the council. The executive power was to be placed in an administrative bureau of the council under the direction of the president.[82] In exceptional cases, where compulsion was needed in the execution of a decision, resort was to be had to the great powers acting as a college of the council. In ordinary cases the execution of the decision could be left to the individual states themselves. To prevent oppression by

[78] *Ibid.*, p. 303.   [79] *Ibid.*   [80] *Ibid.*, p. 305.   [81] *Ibid*, p. 306.   [82] *Ibid.*

the great powers and to insure justice, only those decisions were to be carried out by armed force which received a majority of votes in the senate and a two-thirds majority of the council and the college of the great powers.[83] Bluntschli offered detailed suggestions with regard to the settlement of disputes by arbitration.[84]

The preponderance of authority given to the great powers in Bluntschli's federation was criticized by Lorimer as follows:

For the central executive and the smaller Powers to retire from the scene on all great occasions, and to intrust the solution of international questions to the great Powers exclusively, is simply to abandon the international factor altogether. It is to go back to the "European Concert," which is held together by no permanent bond of union, and acts, if at all, only after the event.[85]

Bluntschli frankly admitted that his scheme would not do away altogether with wars and that disarmament and the abolition of standing armies would by no means be immediate results.[86]

A few years after the publication of Bluntschli's work there appeared the project of James Lorimer of Edinburgh. Lorimer's scheme, written in 1884, is the most noteworthy plan in the latter part of the nineteenth century. The project was given in his work *The Institutes of the Law of Nations*.[87] He designed an international government with a separate

---

[83] William Menzies Alexander, *League of Nations in History* (London, 1918), pp. 5–6; Henry S. Fraser, "A Sketch of the History of International Arbitration," *Cornell Law Quarterly*, XI, No. 2 (February, 1926), 184–85.

[84] William Evans Darby, *International Tribunals* (London, 1899), pp. 236–38.

[85] Lorimer, *op. cit.*, pp. 274–75.

[86] Baron Walter G. F. Phillimore, *Schemes for Maintaining General Peace* (London, 1920), p. 11.

[87] Vol. II. The plan appears in chap. xiv, pp. 279–87.

executive. Lorimer said that he thought he was the first to enunciate the idea of an executive, the functions of which were to be exclusively international. His object, he said, was to keep the international government apart from the national governments. In order that the international government may act as "the guardian of the freedom of all national governments," it must have a separate freedom, and that, he held, can be best achieved by means of a separate executive.[88] Lorimer stated that the closest parallels to the functions of his proposed international government were to be found in those assigned to the Delegatiops in the Austro-Hungarian Empire, the international executive corresponding to the central Ministry of War.[89] He also proposed a reduction of armaments.[90] "The risk of War," according to Lorimer, "would be diminished by the limitation upon the combustible matter in each community, while the relief from taxation and compulsory service would increase wealth and furthermore direct the attention of each generation toward occupations of civil life."[91]

Lorimer felt that a spirit of mutual concession would be gradually evoked by the new reciprocal duties and the new international interest which would result from closer association. This spirit would, as time went on, add to the stability of the institution. An international profession composed of dignified and powerful officials, which would also aid in the preservation of the international structure, was to be created. The diminution of national forces would afford prodigious relief from taxation, which, alone, would offer a strong

[88] *Ibid.*, p. 273.   [89] *Ibid.*, p. 276.   [90] *Ibid.*, pp. 245 ff.

[91] "Opinion of Mr. Lorimer, Professor in the University of Edinburgh, on the Question of Disarmament," in *Documents respecting the Limitation of Armaments, Laid before the First Hague Peace Conference of 1899 by the Government of the Netherlands* (Washington, D.C., 1916), p. 9.

guaranty for the permanence of the new arrangement. Lorimer thought that the military class would contend violently against any arrangement of disarmament which would so greatly reduce the importance of their profession, and he saw in this the most formidable difficulty in the way of national development and international organization. He likewise expected opposition from the old-school diplomatists, but he felt that their opposition would not be persistent, as they would find more honorable occupation as officials of the international government.[92]

His project called for a treaty to which all states were to be invited to become a party. The treaty was to be negotiated in two parts:

I. An undertaking by the parties to reduce, simultaneously and proportionally, their national forces to the limit which they may reciprocally recognise as necessary for municipal purposes, but so as to preserve the *relative* power of each State unchanged.

II. An undertaking to establish a government for international purposes exclusively, consisting of a legislature, judicature, executive, and exchequer.[93]

The legislative department of this international government was to consist of a senate and a chamber of deputies. Each of the six great states—Germany, France, Russia, Austria, Italy, and England—was to send five senators and fifteen deputies; each of the smaller states was to send a number proportional to its international importance as determined by the great powers. The senators, appointed for life, were not to receive remuneration for their services, as they were to be chosen from those who had already attained high position and fortune. However, they were to enjoy international titles. Such a title was to descend to the son or nearest male relative. Each senator was to have only one vote. The

[92] *Op. cit.*, pp. 276–78.   [93] *Ibid.*, p. 279.

senators were to be chosen by the crown or chief executive in concert with the upper house of the legislature. In states in which there was no upper house, the appointment was to be made by the chief central authority of the state. The deputies were to receive about one thousand pounds for each session but were not to have hereditary rank. They were to be appointed as their states determined, and each deputy was to have one vote.[94]

There was to be a bureau or ministry of fifteen members—five senators chosen by the senate and ten deputies chosen by the chamber of deputies, including at least one representative from each of the great powers. Each member was to receive about one thousand pounds. The elections were to be annual, and a member could be re-elected. The bureau was to elect the president of the international government from among its own members. The president, with a salary of about ten thousand pounds for each session, was to hold office for one session but was to be re-eligible each alternate session.[95] The ultimate place of meeting, failing Constantinople, was to be the canton of Geneva, which was to be declared international property. Meetings were to be held in the autumn of each year between the sessions of the national legislatures.[96] The president's assent was to be requisite to any measure adopted by a majority of both houses. In the event of his twice refusing assent, the measure was to be submitted to the bureau and was to become law if adopted by a majority of its members. All national questions were to be excluded from the deliberations of the international assembly, as well as all colonial and extra-Euro-

[94] *Ibid.*, pp. 279–81.

[95] *Ibid.*, pp. 281–82.

[96] *Ibid.*, p. 282. See also chap. xi, "Want of an International Locality," pp. 264–67.

pean problems not involving questions of peace and war between European states. Civil wars were to be within the jurisdiction of the assembly. Claims for territorial changes within Europe were to be competent to the assembly. Debts contracted by any state were to be enforced by the international government, but bankrupt states were to be excluded from sitting or voting in the international legislature.[97]

The judicial tribunal was to consist of two branches: the one civil, the other criminal. The judges were to be appointed by the bureau. There were to be fourteen judges and a president, six of whom, at least, were to be chosen from the six great powers. The judges were to be appointed for life, and paid. They were to have rank and hereditary title of senators. In civil cases all the judges were to constitute a single court, and their judgment was to be determined by majority vote. All questions of public international law or the legislative enactments of the international government were to be competent to the civil tribunal. Questions of private international law were to be competent to it only on appeal from a state tribunal. The bureau was to appoint an attorney-general, by whom civil suits might be instituted in the name of the government. The attorney-general was to be the public prosecutor of international crimes, at whose instance or with whose concurrence all prosecutions before the criminal court were to be instituted. There was to be an international bar, to which the members of the bars of the several states or persons who held the highest legal degrees in state universities were to be admitted by the court.[98]

Each state, when called upon, was to supply a contingent of men, or an equivalent in money, of such extent as the legislative department determined. By this means the inter-

[97] *Ibid.*, pp. 283–84.   [98] *Ibid.*, pp. 284–85.

national government was to be enabled to enforce the enactments of the international legislature and the decrees of the international courts. An act of war by any state without consent of the international government or the levying of troops beyond the force assigned to it by the treaty of proportional disarmament was to be treated as an act of international rebellion.[99] Disarmament, Lorimer held, was difficult to achieve but not impossible. His plan required a general treaty of proportional disarmament which aimed to reduce the national forces of individual states "to the limit requisite for national purposes." Otherwise, he said, it was obvious that any one of the great states that was outvoted in the international legislature might break up the whole organization.[100] Said Lorimer: "For a time we should, no doubt, have panics and relapses into partial re-armaments; but I believe there is no prediction that may be made with greater safety than that, if national forces were once reduced to the limit required for the preservation of national order, that step would be irrevocable."[101] There was to be a small standing force at the seat of the international government, supplied by the separate states, for the purpose of enforcing order and averting sudden danger. This force was to be under the orders of the president, responsible to the legislature. The standing army was to be paid by the international government; and each international contingent, when in the field, was to be paid by the state to which it belonged. The expenses of the international government were to be defrayed by an international tax, levied by the government of each state upon its citizens; and the extent of the tax imposed upon each state was to be in proportion to its number of representatives in the international legislature. The finan-

[99] *Ibid.*, p. 286.
[100] *Ibid.*, p. 245.   [101] *Ibid.*, p. 277.

cial affairs of the international organization were to be under the management of the bureau.[102]

Lorimer's plan caught a vision of an international government with its own officials to serve it. He required an international tax to support the proposed government. Lorimer called for a separate executive, which, he thought, distinguished his project from others. He anticipated Bluntschli's objection that the executive would be a menace to national freedom. To diminish such a risk, he provided that the chief of the executive should be elected by the international bureau.[103] Bluntschli concurred with Lorimer in recognizing that other plans had failed because they aimed at two impossible objectives: first, the establishment of a federation of equal states politically and, second, the setting-up of an arrangement which was to be permanent and immutable.[104] The first, these two writers agreed, aimed at putting into practice that which did not agree with fact. As to the second, Lorimer himself, in referring to Sully's pages, said: "Such words as 'irrévocable' and 'irréformable' are as meaningless in the mouths of princes as of other people."[105] In appreciation of Lorimer's plan, one writer states:

> This scheme shews that Lorimer was a man of vision, and its elaboration is not the work of a mere dreamer, but arose from a desire to put his ideas into concrete shape. . . . . The world has moved a long way in the direction pointed out by Lorimer, but there are still lacking some of the institutions which he predicated as necessary for a complete system of international organisation.[106]

While various peace programs were presented during the nineteenth century, lovers of world peace drew their great-

[102] *Ibid.*, pp. 286–87.   [103] *Ibid.*, p. 273.

[104] Andrew Wishart, "A Scottish Jurist and the League Idea," *Juridical Review*, XXXIV (December, 1922), 334.

[105] *Op. cit.*, p. 219.

[106] A. Pearce Higgins, "James Lorimer," *Juridical Review*, XLV, No. 3 (September, 1933), 254.

est encouragement from two endeavors made in the actual
political order, namely, the creation of the Permanent
Court of Arbitration at The Hague and the Central American Court of Justice. In the strict sense of the term, these
cannot be called projects to guarantee peace. They were
not attempts to inaugurate leagues to enforce peace in the
way of establishing an international government. They were
restricted to what was but one part of most plans for organizing peace, the pacific settlement of disputes through recourse
to a court. They were not attempts to view the problem of
securing world peace from the standpoint of a solution in its
entirety. It was not expected that these projects would abolish all war or usher in permanent peace. A world organization to preserve peace among all nations at all times and
under all circumstances did not ensue from the labors of the
Hague conferences of 1899 and 1907 or the Washington
Conference of 1907. The latter, furthermore, was limited to
a few states. While the Hague Court and the Central American Court cannot be called "projects of international government" in any complete meaning of the term, nevertheless, due to their relationship with successive plans for the
organization of world peace, some attention, even if that
must be most brief, may properly be given to them here. A
more detailed presentation is hardly fitting, but the relationship of the Hague Court and the Central American Court to
the general subject can, at least, be indicated.

On August 24, 1898, Tsar Nicholas II of Russia issued a
call to the nations to send representatives to The Hague to
promote international understanding and peace. In the
Russian circular note[107] proposing the peace conference the

[107] The tsar's proposal was presented by Count Mouraviev, the Russian
minister of foreign affairs, to the foreign representatives at Saint Petersburg
("Russian Note Proposing the First Conference," in James Brown Scott [ed.],
The Hague Conventions and Declarations of 1899 and 1907, Accompanied by Tables of

nations were asked to consider "a possible reduction of the excessive armaments which weigh upon all nations." The note declared that the maintenance of general peace and the reduction of armaments was the ideal toward which the endeavors of all governments should be directed. What the tsar's motives[108] were in calling the conference will perhaps always be disputed. It may well be that the government wished to limit armaments because Russia was unable, for financial reasons, to follow the pace set by the other powers. A second circular was handed, January 11, 1899, to the diplomatic representatives at Saint Petersburg, and this note proposed a program for the conference.[109] The invitation sent from The Hague[110] was accepted by all the twenty-six governments to whom it was addressed;[111] and the confer-

---

Signatures, Ratifications and Adhesions of the Various Powers and Texts of Reservations [New York, 1915], pp. xv–xvi). Call (*op. cit.*, No. 5 [May, 1924], p. 302) credits Grotius' work and some others as being "evidences of that public sentiment" which made the tsar's letter possible.

[108] Some writers believe that Nicholas II was inspired by the example of Alexander I (e.g., Joseph Hodges Choate, *The Two Hague Conferences*, with an Introduction by J. B. Scott [Princeton, 1913], p. 4).

[109] "Russian Note Proposing the Program of the First Conference" in Scott (ed.), *The Hague Conventions and Declarations*, pp. xvii–xix; A. Pearce Higgins, *The Hague Peace Conferences and Other International Conferences concerning the Laws and Usages of War: Texts of Conventions with Commentaries* (Cambridge, England, 1909), pp. 39–40.

[110] "Netherland's Invitation to the First Conference," Scott (ed.), *The Hague Conventions and Declarations*, pp. xix–xx; *Documents Relating to the Program of the First Hague Peace Conference Laid before the Conference by the Netherland Government* (Oxford, 1921), p. 4.

[111] "Liste des gouvernements représentés à la Haye et de leurs délégués," in *Conférence internationale de la paix, La Haye, 18 Mai–29 Juillet 1899* (La Haye, 1899), pp. 3–8. The United States was represented by the Hon. Andrew D. White, ambassador to Berlin, the Hon. Seth Low, president of Columbia University, the Hon. Stanford Newel, envoy extraordinary to The Hague, Captain Alfred T. Mahan, U.S.N., Captain William Crozier, U.S.A., and the

ence, by a delicate compliment, opened on the Tsar's birthday, May 18, 1899.[112] The conference elected M. de Staal, Russian ambassador, to preside.

Three committees were formed to deal with disarmament, regulations in warfare, and mediation and arbitration. Russia's proposal that there should be no increase of armies or military expenditures for a period of five years was declined because of the opposition of Germany. As a result, Germany was usually blamed, in large part, for the failure of the proposal.[113] Evidence is abundant that none of the powers seriously contemplated the limitation of armaments.[114] The difficulties involved in the reduction of armaments appeared to statesmen as unsurmountable.

Three momentous conventions were adopted relating to (1) the pacific settlement of international conflicts, (2) the laws and customs of war by land, and (3) the adaptation to maritime warfare of the principles of the Geneva convention of August 22, 1864. Three declarations on the following matters were also adopted, prohibiting (1) the launching of projectiles and explosives from balloons or by other similar new methods; (2) the use of projectiles the only object of which is the diffusion of asphyxiating or deleterious gases; and (3) the use of bullets which expand or flatten easily in the human body, such as bullets with a hard envelope, of which the

---

Hon. Frederick W. Holls, of New York. See James Brown Scott (ed.), *Instructions to the American Delegates to the Hague Peace Conferences and Their Official Reports*, with an Introduction by James Brown Scott (New York, 1916), pp. 6–58.

[112] The date of adjournment was July 29, 1899.

[113] James T. Shotwell, *Plans and Protocols To End War: Historical Outline and Guide* (New York, 1925), p. 85.

[114] Sidney Bradshaw Fay, *The Origins of the World War* (New York, 1930), I, 123; G. Lowes Dickinson, *The International Anarchy, 1904–1914* (New York, 1926), pp. 347–51.

envelope does not entirely cover the core, or is pierced with incisions. The conference unanimously adopted a resolution that the restriction of expenditures on armaments was desirable.

An important achievement in the work of the conference was its attempts to humanize the conduct of war,[115] but the creation of the Permanent Court of Arbitration[116] may be said to be the most significant accomplishment. The Hague Court, as it came to be called, was not, in a strict sense, a real or permanent court.[117] The misnomer was partly responsible for a deception of public opinion which led expectations to be entertained which could not possibly be fulfilled.[118] Provision was made for permanent lists or panels of judges to act as arbitrators, and this meant that the court was formed anew for every case. Another defect was the strong national character of the court, since each party to the dispute proposed two judges, and the four selected a fifth. Very serious was the lack of obligatory jurisdiction, for difficulties involving honor or vital interests were exempt from the jurisdiction of the court, and there was no way of compelling a nation to submit its grievances. "Not a single power," wrote Mr. White, the American delegate, "was willing to bind itself by a hard and fast rule to submit all questions to ar-

[115] *Conférence internationale de la paix, La Haye, 1899*, annexes III–VII, pp. 235 ff.

[116] *Ibid.*, pp. 224 ff. In the convention for the pacific settlement of international disputes provision was made in Title II for good offices and mediation and in Title III for international commissions of inquiry.

[117] Philip C. Jessup, *The United States and Treaties for the Avoidance of War* (New York, 1928), p. 187; N. Politis, "The Work of the Hague Court," *Judicial Settlement of International Disputes*, No. 6 (November, 1911), p. 4; Manley O. Hudson, *The World Court, 1921–1938* (Boston, 1938), p. 2.

[118] Manley O. Hudson, "The Permanent Court of Arbitration," *American Journal of International Law*, XXVII, No. 3 (July, 1933), 445.

bitration, and least of all the United States. A few nations were willing to accept it in regard to minor matters—as, for example postal or monetary difficulties and the like."[119]

Although the achievements[120] of the conference were considerable, it is, of course, true that the conference failed to effect the purpose for which it was called, namely, a reduction of armaments. It may properly be said:

> But failure in this respect, a failure which had been foreseen from the first, did not mean that 26 Powers had assembled for two months for naught. Idealists had expected too much, and were dissatisfied with the results; but the solid work of the Conference as attested by the three Conventions, two of which were completions of work which previous gatherings had failed to accomplish, cannot but be viewed as marking an important epoch in the development of international law.[121]

Scott has said that the convention for the settlement of disputes "alone would have justified any Conference." He states that "the Conference itself was more important than its labors, because it showed the possibility of twenty-six nations meeting in conference and agreeing upon measures of interest to the world's welfare. An idea is generally greater than its realization."[122] If the idea was not wholly realized, it must be added that it was due in part to

[119] Cited in Dickinson, *op. cit.*, p. 352.

[120] The several conventions, declarations, and recommendations agreed upon for submission to the governments represented were summarized in the "Final Act," which was signed by all ("The Final Acts of the First and Second Conferences," in Scott [ed.], *The Hague Conventions and Declarations*, pp. 1–40; "Tables of Signatures to the Conventions of the First Peace Conference, 1899," in James Brown Scott, *The Hague Peace Conferences of 1899 and 1907: A Series of Lectures Delivered before the Johns Hopkins University in the Year 1908* [Baltimore, 1909], II, 63–167; Higgins, *The Hague Peace Conferences*, pp. 95–526).

[121] Higgins, *The Hague Peace Conferences*, pp. 42–43.

[122] James Brown Scott, Introduction to *The Hague Conventions and Declarations*, pp. vi–vii.

the attitude of statesmen and officials, to "blunt indifference," and to the "sarcastic derision" which was levied at it
in many quarters.[123] The value of the work of the conference
was attested by the fact that four cases were taken to The
Hague from 1899 to 1907.[124]

The First Hague Conference had made no definite provision for a subsequent meeting. President Roosevelt suggested the assemblage of another conference,[125] and the tsar
formally proposed a second meeting.[126] A program was
drafted by Russia,[127] and the invitation was extended by the
Netherlands government in April, 1907.[128] The Second
Conference assembled at The Hague, June 15.[129] Forty-four

[123] *A League of Nations* (New York, 1919), p. 56.

[124] Fraser, *op. cit.*, p. 204; Politis, *op. cit.*, p. 6; Higgins, *The Hague Peace Conferences*, pp. 44–50.

[125] "American Note of October 21, 1904, regarding the Second Conference" and "American Note of December 16, 1904, regarding the Second
Conference," in Scott (ed.), *The Hague Conventions and Declarations*, pp. xx–
xxvi.

[126] "Russian Memorandum of September 13, 1905, Proposing the Second
Conference," *ibid.*, p. xxvii.

[127] "Russian Note Proposing the Program of the Second Conference,"
ibid., pp. xxix–xxxi.

[128] "Netherland Invitation to the Second Conference," *ibid.*, pp. xxxi–xxxii.

[129] The date of adjournment was October 18, 1907. The delegation of the
United States to the conference was composed of the following members:
Commissioners plenipotentiary with the rank of ambassador extraordinary:
Joseph H. Choate, of New York; Horace Porter, of New York; Uriah M.
Rose, of Arkansas. Commissioner plenipotentiary: David Jayne Hill, of New
York, envoy extraordinary and minister plenipotentiary of the United States
to the Netherlands. Commissioners plenipotentiary with rank of minister
plenipotentiary: Brigadier General George B. Davis, judge-advocate-general,
U.S.A.; Rear Admiral Charles S. Sperry, U.S.N.; William I. Buchanan, of
New York. Technical delegate and expert in international law: James Brown
Scott, of California. Technical delegate and expert attaché to the commis-
sion: Charles Henry Butler, of New York. Secretary to the commission:
Chandler Hale, of Maine. Assistant secretaries to the commission: A. Bailly-

states were represented; and the Latin-American republics, which incidentally had not been invited to the First Conference, sent delegates with few exceptions. Russia, after her defeat by Japan, had changed her attitude toward disarmament and now declined to discuss the subject. England attempted to include the question of limitation of armaments, but Germany regarded this as a scheme to arrest her naval development and to prevent her from catching up in strength with England, who enjoyed a marked naval superiority. Germany's opposition to the limitation of armaments was shared tacitly by France and Russia; and, since it was left to Germany to voice the opposition, she received the blame for thwarting the proposals.[130]

Important conventions were adopted in relation to the following: (1) the pacific settlement of international disputes, (2) the restriction of the employment of force for the recovery of contract debts, (3) the commencement of hostilities, (4) the laws and customs of land warfare, (5) the

Blanchard, of Louisiana; William M. Malloy, of Illinois. On their instructions see Scott, *Instructions to the American Delegates to the Hague Peace Conferences and Their Official Reports*, pp. 69–85.

[130] Fay, *op. cit.*, p. 123. A member of the American delegation commented as follows: "The fact that no provision could be made looking to disarmament or the limitation of armaments by the powers was not unexpected. It was known before the conference convened that some of the powers would not even consent to debate such a question. This was not very surprising, as nations, like individuals, object to abandoning their sole means of defense until some competent, impartial tribunal enjoying their entire confidence is established for the settlement of their differences. In past endeavors there has been an effort to put the cart before the horse in expecting nations to disarm before a satisfactory international court of justice is established to take the place of force" (Horace Porter, "The Second Hague Conference," in James Brown Scott [ed.], *American Addresses at the Second Hague Peace Conference Delivered by Joseph H. Choate, General Horace Porter, James Brown Scott* [Boston, 1910], pp. xxviii–xxix).

rights and duties of neutral powers and persons in war on land, (6) the status of enemy merchant ships at the outbreak of hostilities, (7) the transformation of merchant ships into warships, (8) the laying of automatic submarine contact mines, (9) bombardment by naval forces in time of war, (10) the adaptation of the principles of the Geneva convention of 1906 to maritime war, (11) restrictions in the exercise of the right of capture in maritime war, (12) the establishment of an international court of prize, (13) the rights and duties of neutral powers in maritime war, and (14) declaration prohibiting discharge of projectiles and explosives from balloons. In addition to these conventions a draft convention relative to the creation of a judicial arbitration court was also drawn up.

The Second Hague Conference confirmed the resolution adopted by the First Conference in regard to the limitation of military expenditures and declared that, "inasmuch as military expenditure has considerably increased in almost every country . . . . it is eminently desirable that the Governments should resume the serious examination of this question."[131] Compulsory arbitration[132] was not adopted; and after deliberations extending over a period of three months[133] a resolution was unanimously passed recognizing the principle of compulsory arbitration.[134] The Second Hague Conference revised the provisions which the First

[131] Scott (ed.), *The Hague Conventions and Declarations*, p. 28.

[132] Scott, *The Hague Peace Conferences of 1899 and 1907*, I, 330–85.

[133] *Ibid.*, p. 384.

[134] Art. XXXVIII, "Convention for the Pacific Settlement of International Disputes, October 18, 1907," in George Grafton Wilson, *The Hague Arbitration Cases: Compromis and Awards with Maps in Cases Decided under the Provisions of the Hague Conventions of 1899 and 1907 for the Pacific Settlement of International Disputes and Texts of the Conventions* (Boston, 1915), pp. 489–90. For the entire convention, *ibid.*, pp. 473–513.

Conference had made in regard to mediation and good offices. The contracting powers agreed to have recourse "as far as circumstances allow" to good offices or mediation of one or more friendly powers. As to the Hague Tribunal, there was some improvement made, inasmuch as the choice of judges was restricted to a single national of each contesting party. Certain changes in the matter of procedure were also made.

The achievements[135] of the Second Hague Conference were significant. The main accomplishments of the conference of 1907, as seen by Scott, were: (1) the revision of the convention for the pacific settlement of international conflicts so as to make it more comprehensive and more adequate, (2) the unanimous agreement to renounce force and submit international differences over contract indebtedness to arbitration, (3) the establishment of an international court of prize, (4) the unanimous recognition of the principle of obligatory arbitration, (5) the establishment of a court of arbitral justice, (6) the provision that a Third International Conference of Peace meet in approximately eight years after the Second Conference.[136]

The Hague Court prior to World War I handled fifteen cases[137] submitted to it for arbitration. We can appreciate

---

[135] The results of the conference of 1907 were embodied in the fourteen conventions referred to above and a "Final Act" in which certain principles were declared "unanimously admitted" (Higgins, *The Hague Peace Conferences*, pp. 95–526; Scott [ed.], *The Hague Conventions and Declarations*, pp. 1–259).

[136] James Brown Scott, "The Second Hague Conference: A Peace Conference," in Scott (ed.), *American Addresses to the Second Hague Peace Conference*, pp. xlvii–xlviii.

[137] The compromise and award of each case may be obtained in Wilson, *op. cit.* Up to 1932 twenty-one cases were settled (Hudson, "The Permanent Court of Arbitration," *American Journal of International Law*, XXVII, No. 3 [July, 1933], 446–60).

the Court when we realize that all the cases represented problems that diplomacy was unable to solve.[138] Indeed, a great jurist wrote:

> The day was past when a Permanent Court was of interest only to isolated writers, living at different times and in different lands, sometimes read and sometimes forgotten, dreaming, in their libraries or in their more or less official positions, of helping to make the world's future brighter by their proposals. . . . . Now it was the nations themselves, acting through their diplomatic representatives and meeting in a sort of universal parliament, that had brought the question up for discussion, that had considered it and had voted on it, and, in the very midst of their conflict of opinions as to how it should be organized, had gone on record as being convinced that the time for solving this question had come.[139]

The Hague conferences may be considered to be of particular importance in that they represented the conception of a continuous handling of international problems through successive conferences. They resulted in the adoption of a number of international conventions by many nations and proved themselves to be a good means of initiating such measures. They pointed the way to further international agreements. There resulted a restatement of the laws of war and maritime neutrality. The Hague conferences prepared the ground for the later League of Nations and the Permanent Court of International Justice. The conferences represented a united effort of the nations to deal with the questions which led to World War I. One of our best authorities on the Hague conferences, writes: "The Peace Conferences held at The Hague were the first truly international assemblies meeting in time of peace for the purpose of preserving

---

[138] Denys P. Myers, "The Origin of the Hague Arbitral Courts," *American Journal of International Law*, VIII (October, 1914), 799.

[139] Antonio Sanchez de Bustamante, *The World Court*, translated by Elizabeth F. Read (New York, 1926), pp. 66–67.

peace, not of concluding a war then in progress. They marked an epoch in the history of international relations."[140]

The five Central American states, Costa Rica, Guatemala, Honduras, Nicaragua, and Salvador, at the Washington Conference, November 14–December 20, 1907, with the co-operation of the United States and Mexico,[141] established the Central American Court of Justice. To this court all disputes were to be submitted, including, for the first time in history, questions involving "national honor and vital interests." The contracting states, in addition, concluded the following treaties and conventions: a general treaty of peace and amity, additional convention to the general treaty of peace and amity, extradition, future conferences, communications, an International Central American Bureau, and a Central American Pedagogical Institute.[142]

It was provided that the Court of Justice have its seat in the city of Cartago in the republic of Costa Rica, although it could sit elsewhere if deemed advisable. The inaugural session opened on May 25, 1908. The Court consisted of five justices, one justice and two substitutes being appointed by the legislative power of each republic for five years. They enjoyed the privileges and immunities of diplomatic agents. The justices were not permitted to exercise their profession or hold office. The Court elected its own president and vice-president and organized the personnel of its office. The at-

[140] James Brown Scott, Prefatory Note, *The Proceedings of the Hague Peace Conferences, Translation of the Official Texts* (New York, 1920–21), pp. v–vi.

[141] James Brown Scott, "The Central American Peace Conference of 1907," *American Journal of International Law*, II (1908), 127–33.

[142] William I. Buchanan, report of *The Central American Peace Conference, Held at Washington, D.C., 1907* (Washington, D.C., 1908), pp. 11–12; "General Treaty of Peace and Amity, Concluded at the Central American Peace Conference, December 20, 1907," given in Hicks, *op. cit.*, pp. 393–99; Scott, "The Central American Peace Conference of 1907," *op. cit.*, p. 133.

tendance of five justices was necessary to make a legal quorum. The salaries of the justices and other expenses of the Court were paid by the states.[143] Article XIII declared that the Central American Court of Justice represented the national conscience of Central America, wherefore the justices who composed the tribunal were not to consider themselves barred from the discharge of their duties because of the interest which the republics, to which they owed their appointment, may have in any case or question. In deciding points of fact the Court was governed by its free judgment and, with respect to points of law, by the principles of international law. The Court was competent to determine its jurisdiction. All controversies between the five states were to be submitted to it,[144] and the Court could take cognizance of questions which individuals of one country might raise against any of the other governments. Article XXV declared: "The interested parties solemnly bind themselves to submit to said judgments, and all agree to lend all moral support that may be necessary in order that they may be properly fulfilled, thereby constituting a real and positive guaranty of respect for this Convention and for the Central American Court of Justice."[145]

The unique features of the Court have been described by one writer on international law as being "its unlimited jurisdiction, its power to give orders to the parties before it along the lines of the equity decrees of our local courts, and the fact that individuals were allowed to appear directly before the Court even if their governments did not espouse their

[143] Manley O. Hudson, "The Central American Court of Justice," *American Journal of International Law*, XXVI, No. 4 (October, 1932), 762–64.

[144] Luis Anderson, "The Peace Conference of Central America," *American Journal of International Law*, II, No. 1 (January, 1908), 144.

[145] "Convention for the Establishment of a Central American Court of Justice, Concluded December 20, 1907," given in Hicks, *op. cit.*, pp. 399–405.

claims."[146] In the ten years of the Court's existence nine cases were decided. At the end of the ten-year period the convention was not re-enacted, and the Court went out of existence, March 17, 1918. Hudson thinks that in a period of greater relative stability it is altogether possible that the Court may have continued its functions and had a useful future.[147]

Nicaragua was unwilling to renew the treaty because two decisions of the Court in 1911 and 1917 were adverse to her. Nicaragua had made a treaty with the United States in 1914 by which the United States, in payment of $3,000,000, acquired exclusive right to construct a canàl through Nicaragua, a lease of Great and Little Corn Islands, and the right to construct a naval base in the Gulf of Fonseca. The complaint was made that this treaty was in violation of former treaties, and the Court declared Nicaragua to be under the obligation to re-establish and maintain the legal status that existed prior to the treaty of 1914 with the United States. Nicaragua did not annul the treaty; and the United States, which had been instrumental in the creation of the Court, remained silent.[148] Thus the Central American league of nations experiment came to an end.

Nevertheless, in its short life, it demonstrated clearly how useful the existence of a judiciary power between sovereign and independent states really is. It was the first actual historical example of such a judiciary power, and it will always have the place of honor in the history of the development and life of international justice. The New World may well be proud that the first permanent international court ever known was a Latin-American institution.[149]

[146] Jessup, op. cit., p. 188.

[147] "The Central American Court of Justice," op. cit., XXVI, 786.

[148] Florence Brewer Boeckel, Between War and Peace: A Handbook for Peace Workers (New York, 1928), p. 220.

[149] De Bustamante, op. cit., p. 78.

CHAPTER IV
PROGRAMS OF THE GREAT WAR PERIOD
(1914–18)

I T WAS World War I that aroused men, as never before, to the tragedy of war and the overwhelming necessity of permanent peace. Face to face with the horrors of the battlefield, men turned with great ardor to the hope that this war would end war and began to contemplate schemes which would fulfil that hope at the close of the struggle. Many agreed with Lord Bryce: "If we do not try to end war, war will end us. . . . ."[1] Realizing the strength that comes from concerted action, men banded together in peace societies and groups which were highly productive of schemes for the establishment of a new international order to secure lasting peace. These plans challenged much attention and were fruitful of further consideration and study. By the termination of the war considerable thought had been evoked, many detailed projects had been presented, and a working basis existed for the formulation of a league of nations. Only some of the best known of these programs are considered here.

Early in 1915 a group presided over by Viscount Bryce drafted a scheme by which wars might be prevented in the future. The project[2] was first circulated privately to a small number of persons who were believed to be in general accord with the object in view. The authors expressed themselves

[1] Viscount James Bryce, Introduction to Viscount Grey et al., The League of Nations (London, 1918, 1919), p. 18.

[2] Viscount James Bryce, Proposals for the Avoidance of War (Private and Confidential, Not for Publication), with a prefatory note by Viscount Bryce (as revised up to February 24, 1915) (n.p., n.d.).

as being grateful for any criticisms or suggestions from those to whom the plan was confidentially submitted.[3] The work had considerable influence upon the formation of European and American opinion.[4]

According to Lord Bryce and his group in England, the causes for war could only be dissipated gradually by the dissemination of intelligence, knowledge, and good will. In the meantime they believed the risk of war could be greatly diminished by the arrangement which they suggested.[5] States were to enter into an arrangement to preserve peace, at the same time retaining their sovereignty. All the great powers were to be included; and other lesser states, such as Holland, Belgium, the Scandinavian countries, Switzerland, and the chief South American countries, were also to be included. Later on, after the plan got on a working basis, all the other nations might be admitted.[6]

In formulating his plan Bryce took as his starting-point the series of treaties generally known as the "Bryan treaties," concluded between the United States and a number of other powers. The essence of the treaties was that disputes of every nature whatsoever which diplomacy had failed to adjust and where recourse was not had to arbitration were to be referred to a permanent commission for investigation and report,[7] during which time no hostile action was to be taken by the contracting parties.[8] Bryce's program also contem-

[3] *Ibid.*, prefatory note, p. 6.

[4] Introduction, *Contributions by Various Writers on the Project of a League of Nations* (London, n.d.), p. 3.

[5] Viscount James Bryce *et al.*, Introduction to *Proposals for the Prevention of Future Wars* (London, 1918), p. 12.

[6] *Ibid.*, p. 14.   [7] *Ibid.*, pp. 14–16.

[8] The permanent commissions as provided in the Bryan treaties were to be composed of five members: one from each nation, one from a foreign nation chosen by each of the contracting states, and one chosen by the two countries

plated economic pressure[9]—an embargo on the shipping of
the recalcitrant state, a prohibition of loans or exports to or
imports from it, or a severance of railway, postal, telegraphic, and telephonic communication.[10] This plan implied such
a measure of popular control over international affairs as
was involved in the publication of the inquiry and discussion
in representative assemblies and in the press.[11] In studyng
the plan[12] it will be noticed that no executive power was conferred on the council of conciliation and that Bryce distin-

---

together. The commissions were to render their services without waiting to
be called upon by one of the states. A period of one year was to be allowed
before hostilities could commence. It was expected that the lapse of this period of time would have a cooling influence upon the excited countries and
that the report made by the commission would have a clarifying effect. The
treaties possessed no finality of decision; their value lay in their automatic
character, the inclusion of nonjusticiable disputes, and the ease with which
the commission could be employed as a supplement to good offices, mediation, and diplomacy. "It [the commission] was unique among arbitral groups
until the formation of the League Permanent Court in that it was not selected
for the occasion, but a body 'created in advance of the dispute or existing at its
outbreak' " (Jessie Wallace Hughan, *A Study of International Government* [New
York, 1923], pp. 84–85). See also *Treaties for the Advancement of Peace between
the United States and Other Powers Negotiated by the Honourable William J. Bryan,
Secretary of State of the United States*, with an Introduction by James Brown
Scott (New York, 1920).

[9] Bryce explained his point of view on economic compulsion as follows:
"Such a method might often be speedier than war and quite as effective. But
its efficacy would depend upon its being reserved as a weapon to check some
aggressive action against a member of the League. An economic boycott applied in normal times by one nation or group of nations, to another, would be
a means of provoking, rather than preventing, war" (Introduction to Grey
et al., op. cit., p. 14).

[10] Bryce, Introduction to Bryce *et al., Proposals for the Prevention of Future
Wars*, p. 17.

[11] *Ibid.*, p. 23.

[12] The project is also given in Leonard S. Woolf, *The Framework of a Lasting
Peace* (London, 1917), pp. 85–90.

guished two classes of disputes, namely, justiciable and non-justiciable, and two processes of settlement.

In the treatment of justiciable disputes[13] the Bryce group planned to refer to an arbitral tribunal all cases including those affecting honor and vital interests which were of a justiciable nature and which the powers had failed to settle by diplomatic means.[14] The arbitral parties were to agree to accept the award of the tribunal.[15] Justiciable disputes were defined as embracing "disputes as to the interpretation of a treaty, as to any question of international law, as to the existence of any fact which, if established, would constitute a breach of any international obligation, or as to the nature and extent of the reparation to be made for any such breach."[16] The court was to decide whether a dispute was justiciable.[17] A permanent council of conciliation[18] was to be established with a view to the prevention and settlement of disputes which were not of a justiciable character.[19] The members of the council were to be appointed by the signatory powers for a fixed term of years.[20] In case a nonmember was desirous of submitting its case to the council, provision was to be made for its temporary representation.[21] The powers were to submit their nonjusticiable cases to the council.[22] The council was to publish a report of its recommendations for the settlement of any dispute referred to it.[23] The

[13] Bryce, *Proposals for the Avoidance of War*, pp. 15–16; Bryce et al., *Proposals for the Prevention of Future Wars*, pp. 31–32; Viscount James Bryce, *Essays and Addresses in War Time* (New York, 1918), p. 206.

[14] Art. II.   [16] Art. IV.

[15] Art. III.   [17] Art. V.

[18] Bryce, *Proposals for the Avoidance of War*, pp. 16–18; Bryce et al., *Proposals for the Prevention of Future Wars*, pp. 32–34; Bryce, *Essays and Addresses in War Time*, pp. 206–7.

[19] Art. VI.   [21] Art. VIII.

[20] Art. VII.   [22] Art. IX.   [23] Art. XI.

council was empowered to make suggestions for the limitation of armaments.[24]

The program provided for a moratorium on hostilities.[25] Every power adhering to the arrangement was to agree not to declare war, begin hostilities, or make hostile preparations against any other signatory power (a) before the dispute was submitted to an arbitral tribunal or to the council, (b) within a period of twelve months after such submission, or (c), if the award had been published within that time, not to go to war or take hostile steps until six months had elapsed after the publication of the award.[26] The scheme placed a limitation on the effect of the alliance.[27] It was agreed that no signatory power commencing hostilities against another, without first complying with the foregoing provisions, was entitled to military or other support of any other member-state.[28] The plan provided for enforcement[29] by pledging all signatories to take action against any state, whether or not a signatory power, that declared war, began hostilities, or made hostile preparations against a signatory power without first submitting its case to an arbitral tribunal or to the council or complying with the moratorium requirement. In such case the states were to take concerted action, economic and forcible, which they felt appropriate against the offending country.[30]

[24] Art. XII.

[25] Bryce, *Proposals for the Avoidance of War*, p. 18; Bryce *et al.*, *Proposals for the Prevention of Future Wars*, p. 34; Bryce, *Essays and Addresses in War Time*, p. 207.

[26] Art. XVII.

[27] Bryce, *Proposals for the Avoidance of War*, p. 18; Bryce *et al.*, *Proposals for the Prevention of Future Wars*, p. 35; Bryce, *Essays and Addresses in War Time*, p. 208.

[28] Art. XVIII.

[29] Bryce, *Proposals for the Avoidance of War*, pp. 18–19; Bryce *et al.*, *Proposals for the Prevention of Future Wars*, pp. 35–36; Bryce, *Essays and Addresses in War Time*, p. 208.

[30] Art. XIX.

In Bryce's own eyes the outstanding merits of the program were, first, that the union was not confined to Europe; second, that it bound the signatory powers to submit their disputes to peaceable settlement before having recourse to arms; third, that it created an impartial and permanent council before which were to be discussed the most difficult and contentious questions.[31]

A program which was similar in a number of respects to the Bryce plan was that of the British League of Nations Society, an organization which was constituted on March 10, 1915.[32] The aim of this league[33] was evident from the subtitle of the Society: "Founded to advocate an Agreement among civilized States, which will serve as a basis of permanent peace among them, by providing for the Peaceful Settlement of Disputes, for Mutual Defence, and the Observance of Treaties and International Law." This organization presented a program of six "Objects."[34] A treaty was

[31] Bryce, prefatory note to *Proposals for the Avoidance of War*, pp. 12–13.

[32] Introduction to *Contributions by Various Writers on the Project of a League of Nations*, p. 4.

[33] *The League of Nations Society* (London, 1917), p. 5.

[34] The program is given in a large number of the "Publications of the League of Nations Society," among which the following may be considered as representative: *The League of Nations Society* (No. 2 [London, 1917]); Aneurin Williams, *A League of Nations: How To Begin It* (No. 8 [London, 1917]); *idem, The Minimum of Machinery* (No. 18 [London, 1917]); Lord Shaw of Dunfermline, *Speech: The League of Nations in the House of Lords, June 26th, 1918* (No. 39 [London, 1918]); *League of Nations: Scheme of Organisation Prepared by a Sub Committee of the League of Nations Society*, with a Foreword by W. H. Dickinson (No. 42 [London, 1918]); *The League of Nations: "The Final Triumph of Justice and Fair Dealing," Speech by President Wilson, New York, Sept. 27, 1918* (No. 43 [London, 1918]). The Society actively engaged in spreading information concerning a league of nations. In addition to the foregoing, the following are among representative issues: Raymond Unwin, *Functions of a League of Nations* (No. 19 [London, 1917]); *General Smuts and a League of Nations: Includes Also Speeches by Lord Bryce, the Archbishop of Canterbury, Lord Buckmaster, Lord Hugh Cecil, and*

to be made, as soon as possible, whereby as many states as were willing were to form a league for the peaceful settlement of disputes arising among them.[35] It will be noticed that the program did not say "all nations." The Society explained that it might not be possible for the smaller states or some of them to take part in the founding of the league of peace. The fact remained, too, that some of the great powers might refuse to join; but, according to the British League of Nations Society's provision, it would still be possible for the others to go forward.[36] The program distinguished between two types of disputes: justiciable and nonjusticiable. The first, arising out of questions of international law or the interpretation of treaties, was to be referred to the Hague Court of Arbitration or some other tribunal. The decisions were to be considered as final. The second type of disputes, the nonjusticiable, were to be referred to a council of inquiry, which was to be representative of the states which formed the league.[37] The program did not settle the question whether the council was to be composed of one representative from each of the member-states or a varying number depending on the respective importance of the different countries.[38] The Society held that, where nations were un-

Others, *Report of Meeting Held at the Central Hall, Westminster, May 14, 1917* (No. 11 [London, 1917]); *A Sense of a Community of Nations: An Address by Sir Francis Younghusband* (No. 13 [London, 1917]); H. N. Spalding, *What a League of Nations Means* (No. 22 [London, 1918]); *Tentative Draft Convention by an American Committee* (No. 30 [London, 1918]). For a list of the pamphlets of the League of Nations Society: *Handbook for Speakers on a League of Nations*, Appen. II, pp. 66–67. The objects and platform of the Society are also given in the following: Woolf, *op. cit.*, pp. 65–66; Edith M. Phelps (comp.), *A League of Nations* (New York, 1919), pp. 48–49.

[35] Object I.
[36] *The League of Nations Society*, p. 7.
[37] Object II.
[38] *The League of Nations Society*, p. 12.

willing to give way, the best hope of a peaceful settlement lay in conciliation. Referring the dispute to a council of conciliation for investigation and report provided a period for the cooling of passions.[39]

The states were to unite in any action necessary to insure that every member abide by the treaty. They were to use jointly their economic and military forces against any member that went to war or committed acts of hostility before submitting the question to a court or the council of conciliation.[40] The league-states were to make provision for mutual defense—diplomatic, economic, and military—in the face of attack by a nonmember which refused to submit the case to a tribunal or to the council.[41] Conferences between members of the league were to be held from time to time to consider matters of an international character and to formulate and codify rules of international law. Unless a member dissented, the rules of international law as adopted were to govern in the decisions of the judicial tribunal.[42] The Society felt that it was here dealing with two of the greatest difficulties in international relations, that is, the uncertainties of international law on many important matters and the need to provide for modification of the status quo among nations as world conditions change.[43] The program stated that any civilized state desiring to join the league was to be admitted to membership.[44]

It will be noticed that this plan was similar to Lord Bryce's in accepting the same division of disputes. In both programs justiciable disputes were to be referred to an arbitral tribunal and nonjusticiable disputes to a council of conciliation. Both programs contemplated forcible action

[39] *Ibid.*, p. 10.
[40] Object III.
[41] Object IV.
[42] Object V.
[43] *The League of Nations Society*, p. 22.
[44] Object VI.

by member-states, who were to use economic or military pressure against one of their number who might go to war before submitting the controversy in question to arbitration or conciliation. The parties were bound by the treaty to consider the decision of the arbitral court as final and to carry out the award. If the case involved a nonjusticiable issue, there was no provision made to compel an unwilling government to accept the report of the council. A country was free to go to war as a last resort. In both programs force was to be used only to secure the moratorium while the case was being considered. In both plans the parties were pledged to take action against a state outside the league which declared war or made hostile preparations without first submitting the dispute to pacific settlement. Both projects, therefore, did not seek a world-wide league, as they provided for mutual defense by members against nonmembers.[45]

One of the most influential associations of the time was the American League To Enforce Peace. It was formed[46] upon the call of one hundred and twenty influential citizens[47] of

[45] Baron Walter G. F. Phillimore, *Schemes for Maintaining General Peace* (London, 1920), p. 31.

[46] A series of preliminary conferences were held in January, 1915, by a group of thirty professors, statesmen, and students of public affairs. After three months the group substantially united on a program and decided to call a national conference to bring their proposals prominently before the American people (John H. Latané [ed.], *Development of the League of Nations Idea: Documents and Correspondence of Theodore Marburg* [New York, 1932], II, 703–17, 790; William H. Short, "The History of the Conference," in *Independence Hall Conference Held in the City of Philadelphia, Bunker Hill Day [June 17th], 1915, Together with the Speeches Made at a Public Banquet in the Bellevue-Stratford Hotel on the Preceding Evening* [New York, 1915], p. 6).

[47] For the names of the one hundred and twenty prominent citizens see *Independence Hall Conference*, pp. xi, xii.

the United States. About three hundred men[48] assembled in Independence Hall, Philadelphia, June 17, 1915,[49] to organize an association whose object was to adopt a program of action to follow the war which would look toward the prevention of future wars.[50] The League To Enforce Peace received the indorsement of many eminent statesmen.[51] The idea embodied in its proposal, which Lord Bryce said was "about the same"[52] as that submitted by his group, was warmly approved by President Wilson and by Charles E. Hughes. Former President William Howard Taft accepted the presidency of the organization. The League published a collection of speeches made at the Philadelphia conference.[53]

[48] *Ibid.*, p. 6; Charles Frederick Carter, "A Remarkable Gathering," in *Enforced Peace: Proceedings of the First Annual National Assemblage of the League To Enforce Peace, Washington, May 26–27, 1916* (New York, 1916), p. 6.

[49] An interesting report of the proceedings was made by Mr. Ashbee, who was present at the Conference. He wrote: "I recall few more significant and dramatic moments than at the close of the afternoon of June 17, 1915, in the intense heat of the Philadelphia summer. The delegates had dropped off one by one from sheer heat exhaustion, and the gathering was reduced to less than half its number when the peace-at-any-price party, who hold Peace to be an end in itself, backed by the pro-Germans of Milwaukee, brought in their amendment to cut out the word 'enforce.' Here was Christian pacifism caught in the German militarist net. It was equivalent to wrecking the whole thing. President Lowell, of Harvard, sprang up and cried, 'Either we are here to *enforce* Peace, or we are here for nothing at all.' The chairman put the amendment, and, because extremists, especially when they are pacifists, have louder voices, the Ayes had it. For a moment everything seemed lost: then the party of reason called for a count, and by only eleven votes the amendment was reversed and the American League to Enforce Peace came into being" (C. R. Ashbee, *The American League To Enforce Peace: An English Interpretation*, with an Introduction by G. Lowes Dickinson [London, 1917], pp. 21–22).

[50] William Howard Taft, "Address," in *Independence Hall Conference*, p. 13.

[51] Theodore Marburg, "The League To Enforce Peace: A Reply to Critics," in *Enforced Peace*, p. 142.

[52] Bryce, prefatory note to *Proposals for the Prevention of Future Wars*, p. 8.

[53] *Independence Hall Conference.*

The first annual assemblage met in Washington, May 26 and 27, 1916, to give effect to the proposals adopted at the Philadelphia meeting. President Wilson addressed the group. "So sincerely do we believe in these things," he said, "that I am sure that I speak the mind and wish of the people of America when I say that the United States is willing to become a partner in any feasible association of nations formed in order to realize these objects and make them secure against violation."[54]

The objectives of the League To Enforce Peace were three:[55] first, ultimate; second, political; and, third, moral or educational. The first was to assemble a conference of the nations to work out and agree upon the terms of a treaty establishing a league of nations to enforce peace. The political or legislative objective consisted of four parts: first, adoption of the League's platform by all political parties; second, adoption by the legislatures of the several states of resolutions favoring the establishment of a league and calling upon the national government to take the necessary steps; third, obtaining from Congress a national charter for the League to lend it prestige; and, fourth, adoption by Congress of a resolution of the same character as sought from the state legislatures. The moral or educational objective was "to implant the principles of the League in the minds and consciences of the American people as deeply as the Monroe Doctrine."

At the time that the League's platform was promulgated in the Hall of Independence at Philadelphia, "its reasonable nature" was set forth in a preamble,[56] which one enthusias-

[54] Woodrow Wilson, "The Thought and Purpose of the People," in *Enforced Peace*, pp. 162–63.

[55] William H. Short, *Program and Policies of the League To Enforce Peace: A Handbook for Officers, Speakers and Editors* (New York, 1916), pp. 5–9.

[56] *Independence Hall Conference*, p. 3.

tic supporter described as being written in language worthy of Jefferson and Lincoln.[57]

WARRANT FROM HISTORY

Throughout five thousand years of recorded history peace, here and there established, has been kept, and its area has been widened, in one way only. Individuals have combined their efforts to suppress violence in the local community. Communities have co-operated to maintain the authoritative state and to preserve peace within its borders. States have formed leagues or confederations, or have otherwise co-operated, to establish peace among themselves. Always peace has been made and kept, when made and kept at all, by the superior power of superior numbers acting in unity for the common good.

Mindful of this teaching of experience, we believe and solemnly urge that the time has come to devise and to create a working union of sovereign nations to establish peace among themselves and to guarantee it by all known and available sanctions at their command, to the end that civilization may be conserved, and the progress of mankind in comfort, enlightenment and happiness may continue.

This platform was briefly summarized in the publications of the League: "To secure the maintenance of peace after the close of the present war by the use of economic and military force."[58] The association wanted the United States to join a league of nations binding the signatories to a program of four points. The platform[59] of the League To Enforce Peace requested that all justiciable disputes of the signatory powers, not settled by negotiation, were to be submitted,

[57] Ashbee, *op. cit.*, p. 29.

[58] Short, *Program and Policies of the League To Enforce Peace*, p. 4.

[59] *Independence Hall Conference*, p. 4; Short, *Program and Policies of the League To Enforce Peace*, p. vii; Robert Goldsmith, Preface to *A League To Enforce Peace*, with an Introduction by A. Lawrence Lowell (New York, 1917), pp. xx–xxi; *Enforced Peace*, pp. 7–8, 189–90; Theodore Marburg and Horace E. Flack (eds.), *Taft Papers on League of Nations* (New York, 1920), pp. 1–2; Woolf, *op. cit.*, pp. 61–62; Bryce, *Essays and Addresses in War Time*, p. 205; Phelps (comp.), *op. cit.*, p. 42; Latané (ed.), *op. cit.*, pp. 790–91; Ashbee, *op. cit.*, pp. 33–34.

"subject to the limitations of treaties," to a judicial tribunal
for hearing and judgment.[60] All other questions were to be
referred to a council of conciliation for hearing, consideration, and recommendation.[61] The signatory powers were to
use their economic and military forces against any member
that went to war or committed acts of hostility against any
other signatory before the question was submitted to pacific
settlement as provided. The following interpretation of this
provision was authorized by the Executive Committee of the
League To Enforce Peace:

> The signatory powers shall jointly use forthwith, their economic forces
> against any of their number that refuses to submit any question which
> arises to an international judicial tribunal or council of conciliation before
> issuing an ultimatum or threatening war. They shall follow this by the
> joint use of their military forces against that nation if it actually proceeds
> to make war or invade another's territory.[62]

The platform required that conferences were to be held
from time to time to formulate and codify rules of international law which, unless a signatory dissented, were to
govern in the decisions of the judicial tribunal.[63]

The program, it will be noted, began with a proposal in
essence the same as that contained in the Bryan treaties[64]
and which provided that all disputes be submitted for a public hearing before issuing an ultimatum or threatening war.
Provision was made for the holding of international conferences for the purpose of clarifying international law which
was to govern in the decisions of the court. The platform
called for a judicial court and a council of conciliation. To
the judicial court were to go all disputes which could be de-

[60] Art. I.   [62] Art. III.

[61] Art. II.   [63] Art. IV.

[64] The secretary of the League To Enforce Peace said: "The League's
program includes all the good features of the Bryan treaties" (Short, *Program
and Policies of the League To Enforce Peace*, p. 32).

cided in accordance with the rules of law and equity—that is, questions of boundaries, meaning of treaties, and all other justiciable questions. To the council of conciliation were to go the nonjusticiable questions—that is, matters of a political nature involving national policy, "national honor," and "vital interests." No provision was made for the enforcement of the decisions of either the judicial court or the council of conciliation. The council of conciliation was not to be confined to the principles of international law and the precedents of past decisions; it was to be diplomatic and arbitral in its nature and could made any short cut to justice that it might see fit.[65] Only on one occasion was the league to resort to force, and that was if a member of the league who had pledged itself to submit all questions to a hearing before resorting to arms broke its promise and attacked a neighbor.[66] "The League would then go to the defense of the innocent nation and as an international sheriff or posse comitatus of the nations see to it that the quarrel was carried before a proper tribunal."[67]

It will be seen that the League To Enforce Peace did not assert that war can be abolished. The scheme did not claim to make war impossible; but it did offer a means by which, the League held, most wars could be avoided.[68] The league of nations would insist that member-states would first attempt to settle the dispute peacefully. The president of the organization, the Hon. William Howard Taft, speaking of the proposed peace league, said that its "primary and

[65] *Ibid.*, pp. 25–26.   [66] Taft, *op. cit.*, p. 15.

[67] Short, *Program and Policies of the League To Enforce Peace*, p. 28.

[68] William Howard Taft, *Why a League of Nations Is Necessary* (New York, n.d.), p. 16. See also Theodore Marburg, *League of Nations: A Chapter in the History of the Movement* (New York, 1917); *idem, League of Nations: Its Principles Examined* (New York, 1918); William Howard Taft and William Jennings Bryan, *World Peace: A Written Debate* (New York, 1917).

fundamental principle shall be that no war can take place between any two members of the League until they have resorted to the machinery that the League proposes to furnish to settle the controversy likely to lead to war."[69]

The American League To Enforce Peace and the British League of Nations Society were closely allied in their aim and were similar in their program. The two organizations kept in close touch with each other.[70] Mr. Marburg of the American League (March 17, 1916) explained that the objects of the English and American societies were almost the same and differed in no essentials. He stated that the Americans did not intend to form a branch in the United Kingdom, as they regarded the British Society as sufficient to cover the ground.[71] It will be noticed that the American League made the same division of disputes into justiciable and nonjusticiable as did the Bryce group and the British League of Nations Society. The proposals of the League To Enforce Peace were not as drastic as those of the British Society or the Bryce plan, in that the Americans omitted the provision for considering the decisions of the tribunal as final and as necessarily being carried into effect. Former President Taft explained the organization's stand as follows:

We do not propose in our plan, to enforce compliance either with the Court's judgment or the Conciliation Commission's recommendation. We feel that we ought not to attempt too much. We believe that the

[69] Taft, "Address," in *Independence Hall Conference*, pp. 14–15.

[70] The British Society felt that the American organization was attracting greater public attention than it was able to obtain for itself, but the British Society pointed out that the conditions that prevailed in Europe "rendered it advisable that the British Society should proceed with the work more quietly and with much deliberation . . . ." (W. H. Dickinson, *A League of Nations and Its Critics* [London, 1917], p. 3).

[71] *Proceedings of the First Annual Meeting Held at the Caxton Hall, July 20th, 1917* (London, 1917), pp. 9–10.

forced submission, the truce taken to investigate and the judicial decision, or the conciliatory compromise recommended will form a material inducement to peace. It will cool the heat of passion and will give the men of peace in each nation time to still the jingoes.[72]

Samuel Gompers thought the League To Enforce Peace was wise in recommending a league of nations that would content itself with enforcing submission of disputes to judicial decision or conciliation. He declared: "Until democracy is more nearly universal, until democracy becomes a social and industrial fact as well as a political catchword, a League with power to enforce decisions would almost certainly become the repressive tool of the reactionary and privileged forces of the world."[73] On this point in the League's plan Lord Shaw made the following observation:

But upon the question of force the Taft proposal is that all the nations so binding each other shall compel the particular power involved to listen for a sufficient time to the statement and consideration of the case. If it will not do so it is to be treated as a mutinous rebel, and to incur the joint and armed coercion of all the other powers. Observe, as I say, how guarded that is. As I read the Taft proposal it is not exactly a League to enforce peace. It is called that, but it is not quite that; it is a League to enforce consideration.[74]

The American League To Enforce Peace, unlike the British League of Nations Society and the Bryce program, wrote no clause into the platform which contemplated making the association into an alliance against any nonmember which might attack a league-state. Lord Bryce saw in this the principal difference between his draft and that of the American League.[75] "This difference," he said, "seems to be

[72] Taft, "Address," in *Independence Hall Conference*, p. 17.

[73] Samuel Gompers, "American Labor and a Constructive Settlement of the War," in *Enforced Peace*, pp. 113–14.

[74] *Lord Shaw of Dunfermline: An Address at a General Meeting of the Society, 15th December, 1916* (London, 1916), p. 6.

[75] Latané (ed.), *op. cit.*, p. 818.

due to the geographical situation and political traditions of the United States."[76] It appears that the American association aimed at merely a league, not an indissoluble union, and that members were to have the right to withdraw at will.[77] The platform did not insist upon disarmament, which the framers evidently considered as being impracticable and impossible of achievement at the time. Nationalists were assured that "the creation of a League of Nations *does not* mean the loving of any other country as much as our own; nor complete disarmament of nations; nor making ineffective national defense; nor giving up national rights; nor abandoning the Monroe Doctrine; nor free trade; nor letting Germany off easy."[78]

The League To Enforce Peace was careful to emphasize that it was not a "stop-the-war" movement. It stressed that the Germans must be conquered if a just and lasting peace was to be secured, that the cry of the United States and the Allies must be "Victory with Power."[79] In *Suggestions for League Speakers* of the League To Enforce Peace the following appeared:

Merely to whip the Kaiser will be poor compensation for the losses of this war. Germany wants peace but her requests should not be granted. We should not have peace until Germany has been taught the necessity of a right attitude towards other nations. That will require punishment, as it often does in the case of a wilful child. It may even require the destruction of Germany as a nation, but to that extreme we must, if necessary, be ready to go.[80]

[76] Bryce *et al.*, *Proposals for the Prevention of Future Wars*, p. 29.

[77] John Spencer Bassett, *The Lost Fruits of Waterloo* (New York, 1918), p. 40.

[78] W. R. Boyd, Jr., Foreword to *League To Enforce Peace* (New York, n.d.), p. 2.

[79] Marburg and Flack (eds.), *op. cit.*, p. 132.

[80] *Suggestions for League Speakers, Taken from the Organization Speech Delivered by Justice S. Harrison White, Colorado Supreme Court, at the Win-the-War-for-Permanent-Peace Convention, Colorado Branch, League To Enforce Peace, Denver, September 20, 1918* (New York, 1918).

This stand won newspaper comments which declared that the League To Enforce Peace was a laudable organization in contrast to the pacifist organizations, which were pro-German. A New England paper, in an item under the title "Peace Societies," stated:

There are several peace societies, but only one peace society. The organization headed by Mr. Taft, which plans to enforce a world peace, realizes that only the vigorous prosecution of the war to a decisive end can bring about lasting peace. In all parts of the country there are peace societies which aim to bring about peace. The authorities have many of these societies under surveillance and some of the organizers are likely to get their peace in jail.

If you probe any of these societies you will find something pro-German back of it. If it be Socialist, or I.W.W., or anything else of the sort, there is German money, or German influence, or German cunning back of the movement.[81]

The League To Enforce Peace was able to claim a favorable press. Of one hundred and fifty-two editorials over a six-week period, only three expressed views unfavorable to the principles of the League.[82] By May, 1918, the League To Enforce Peace was organized in forty-five states with more than four thousand state and county officers and committeemen.[83]

After the signing of the armistice with Germany, the League expanded its plan into what was called a "Victory Program," adopted November 23, 1918. The League To Enforce Peace stated that the original program was the nar-

[81] *Meriden* (Connecticut) *Journal*, cited in the *League Bulletin* (issued weekly by the League To Enforce Peace, New York), No. 48 (August 17, 1917), p. 44.

[82] *League Bulletin*, No. 52 (September 14, 1917), p. 60.

[83] *Report of the Executive Committee, League To Enforce Peace, to the National Committee and League Members at the Biennial Meeting in Connection with the "Win the War for Permanent Peace" Convention, Philadelphia, May 15–17, 1918* (n.p., n.d.), p. 5.

rower one adopted by the statesmen of Europe and America since it was formulated at Philadelphia. The new program, the League said, incorporated the co-operative lessons of the war and corresponded with the needs of international existence. The League claimed that it was generally accepted by other organizations as a minimum on which all could agree.[84] The Victory Program went further than the original proposals in three respects: first, provision for enforcing the decisions of the court in justiciable disputes; second, provision for consultation in case of failure to accept and give effect to the recommendations of the council of conciliation; third, the implication of action against nonmembers. "None of the other features of the new program are inconsistent with the old program. On the contrary, they are all possible, even probable, developments under the old program."[85] The Victory Program serves as a splendid example of the evolution of a scheme from a general plan to a more detailed one. In many respects the plan bears resemblance to the Covenant of the League of Nations. The new platform, it was felt, put the organization "abreast of the progress of liberal thought" during the preceding three and one-half years.[86] It expressed confidence in a new order that came with victory.[87]

In announcing the Victory Program the League stated:[88]

[84] *The Basis of Permanent Peace: Outline Study of a League of Nations; The Background, Purpose and Problems of the Movement* (New York, n.d.), p. 9.

[85] Latané (ed.), *op. cit.*, p. 799 n.

[86] *League Bulletin*, No. 115 (November 30, 1918), p. 313.

[87] Just a few days before the adoption of the Victory Program, former President Taft exclaimed: "I verily believe that we are in the sight of the Promised Land. I hope we may not be denied its enjoyment" (William Howard Taft, *The Obligations of Victory: An Address Delivered at the Convention of the League To Enforce Peace, at Madison, Wisconsin, under the Auspices of the University of Wisconsin, November 9, 1918* [New York, n.d.], p. 8).

[88] *League Bulletin*, No. 115 (November 30, 1918), pp. 313–14; *The Basis of Permanent Peace: Outline Study*, pp. 9–10.

The war now happily brought to a close has been above all a war to end war, but in order to ensure the fruits of victory and to prevent the recurrence of such a catastrophe there should be formed a League of Free Nations, as universal as possible, based upon treaty and pledged that the security of each state shall rest upon the strength of the whole. The initiating nucleus of the membership of the League should be the nations associated as belligerents in winning the war.

The League should aim at promoting the liberty, progress, and fair economic opportunity of all nations, and the orderly development of the world.

It should insure peace by eliminating causes of dissension, by deciding controversies by peaceable means, and by uniting the potential force of all the members as a standing menace against any nation that seeks to upset the peace of the world.

The advantages of membership in the League, both economically and from the point of view of security, should be so clear that all nations will desire to be members of it.

The Victory Program[89] consisted of five articles. It provided that for the decision of justiciable disputes an impartial tribunal was to be established. Jurisdiction was not to depend upon the assent of the parties to the controversy. Its decisions were to be enforceable.[90] For nonjusticiable questions a council of conciliation was to be set up as a mediator. It was to hear, consider, and recommend. If the parties concerned failed to acquiesce, the league was to determine what action, if any, was to be taken.[91] An administrative organization was to be formed to look after common interests, to protect and care for backward regions and internationalized places and such matters as were jointly administered before and during the war. This was to be attained by methods and through machinery that would prevent, on the one hand, any crystallization of the status quo and that

[89] *League Bulletin*, No. 115 (November 30, 1918), p. 314; *The Basis of Permanent Peace: Outline Study*, pp. 10–12; Latané (ed.), *op. cit.*, pp. 798–99; Marburg and Flack (eds.), *op. cit.*, pp. 2–4; Phelps (comp.), *op. cit.*, pp. 43–44.

[90] Art. I.   [91] Art. II.

would provide, on the other hand, a way by which necessary change could be obtained without recourse to arms.[92]
A representative congress was to formulate and codify international law, to inspect the work of administrative bodies,
and to consider any matter which might affect the peace of
the world or the progress of mankind. The meetings were to
be open to the public.[93] There was to be an executive body
to act in case peace was endangered. Representation of the
nations was to be in proportion to the responsibilities and
duties assumed. The rules of international law were not to
be defeated for lack of unanimity. Any aggression was to be
met by the member-states with "such an overwhelming economic and military force that it will not be attempted." No
member was to make an offensive or defensive alliance. All
treaties were to be made public. "Such a League must be
formed at the time of the definitive peace, or the opportunity may be lost forever."[94]

Another American peace society was the American
League of Free Nations Association, which had for its object
the promotion of "a more general realization and support
by the public of the conditions indispensable to the success,
at the Peace Conference and thereafter, of American aims
and policy as outlined by President Wilson." The Association hoped to obtain, through a league of nations for all
peoples, security, that is, the due protection of national existence, and equality of economic opportunity. The fundamental principle underlying the proposed league of nations
was that the security and rights of each member were to rest
upon the strength of the whole league, "pledged to uphold
by their combined power international arrangements ensur-
ing fair treatment for all." The American League of Free

[92] Art. III.
[93] Art. IV.   [94] Art. V.

Nations Association emphasized the need for effective popular representation and insisted upon representation of the peoples, including minority elements, in a body with legislative powers over international relations.[95]

A very detailed program, in comparison to the foregoing plans, was the offering of the celebrated Fabian Society of England.[96] The program[97] presented a detailed constitution for the league and a list of questions which were to be considered justiciable. It suggested twelve nonmilitary sanctions to enforce the decrees of the international high court to which justiciable questions were to be taken. The decrees of the international council to which nonjusticiable questions were to be submitted were to be enforceable, and a nation would not be prevented from going to war as a final recourse. In addition to the international council and the international high court, there was to be an international secretariat.

The constituent states were to be drawn from the belligerents in the war and from such other states as were represented at either of the peace conferences at The Hague and such states as might be admitted by the council.[98] The con-

[95] For the platform see the following: *League of Free Nations Association: Statement of Principles* (New York, 1918); Phelps (comp.), *op. cit.*, pp. 45–46.

[96] For an account of the Fabian Society see Edward R. Pease, *The History of the Fabian Society* (New York, 1926).

[97] The Fabian program was published as Part III, "Articles Suggested for Adoption by an International Conference at the Termination of the Present War, by the International Agreement Committee of the Fabian Research Department," in Leonard S. Woolf, *International Government: Two Reports, Prepared for the Fabian Research Department, Together with a Project by a Fabian Committee for a Supernational Authority That Will Prevent War* (New York, 1916), pp. 376–410, and in *idem, The Framework of a Lasting Peace*, pp. 95–123. See also R. S. Bourne (ed.), *Towards an Enduring Peace: A Symposium of Peace Proposals and Programs, 1914–1916*, with an Introduction by Franklin H. Giddings (New York, 1916), pp. 278–96; Latané (ed.), *op. cit.*, pp. 777–79.

[98] Art. II.

stituent states disclaimed all desire or intention of aggression on any other state and agreed never to pursue any claim or complaint beyond the stage of courteous representation without first submitting the issue to the court or to the council.[99] They bound themselves not to declare war or make hostile preparations against a constituent state until the matter in dispute had been submitted to the court or to the council and until the expiration of one year from the date of such submission.

On the other hand, no Constituent State shall, after submission of the matter at issue to the International Council and after the expiration of the specified time, be precluded from taking any action, even to the point of going to war, in defense of its own honor or interests, as regards any issues which are not justiciable within the definition laid down by these Articles, and which affect either its independent sovereignty or its territorial integrity, or require any change in its internal laws, and with regard to which no settlement acceptable to itself has been arrived at.[100]

The council was to be composed of five representatives from each of the eight great powers—Austria-Hungary, the British Empire, France, Germany, Italy, Japan, Russia, and the United States—and two representatives from each of the minor constituent states.[101] Elaborate provisions were made for different sittings of the council: council of the eight great powers, council for America, council for Europe. Each was to be restricted to the representatives of the states indicated. A statement was then made as to what business was to be referred to each.[102] When the council was to sit as the council of the eight great powers or as the council of the states other than the eight great powers, each of the states represented was to have only one vote. When the council was to sit as a whole or as the council for Europe or as the council for America, the scale of voting was such as to permit the

[99] Art. III.
[100] Art. IV.
[101] Art. V.
[102] Art. VI.

great powers to outvote the small states.[103] It was to be within the competence of the council to codify and declare international law and also to amend the same, whether or not this was codified.[104] To the council was to go nonjusticiable issues, and the powers were pledged to submit such questions. The decision of the council was to be binding on all member-states if passed unanimously by the members of the council present and voting or if passed by a three-fourths majority in cases where the proposed enactment did not affect the sovereignty, territorial integrity, or require any change in the internal laws of any state.[105] There was also to be established a permanent international secretariat.[106]

Fifteen judges were to compose the international high court. Eight were to be appointed by the great powers, and seven by the others.[107] The court was to deal only with justiciable questions.[108] The program carefully listed the justiciable issues with which the court was competent to deal. If a question arose as to whether or not an issue was justiciable, this was to be determined by the court.[109] There was to be immediate publication of all treaties. These were to be deposited in the registry of the court and were to be published in the official gazette.[110] In the event of noncompliance with the decrees of the court the Fabian scheme made definite recommendations on the matter of sanctions. It prescribed an embargo on ships belonging to the recalcitrant state. It placed a prohibition on loans, dealing on the stock exchange, all communication, imports, exports, passenger traffic, entrance into any port of ships belonging to the recalcitrant state, and payment of debts. The program indorsed a decree of complete nonintercourse and a levying of a special export duty on all goods belonging to the offending state. The association was to furnish a contingent of warships to maintain a blockade.[111]

Leonard S. Woolf prepared two reports for the Fabian Society in which he presented his own plan. The work bears the title *International Government* (1916) and should be studied in connection with the Fabian program. Woolf's plan called for international conferences to examine facts, express an opinion, issue a report, and act as a council of conciliation or mediation between two or more disputing states. The conditions under which the conferences were to be called were to be definitely stipulated. He proposed that the decisions of the conferences were to be binding upon the states represented. The conferences were to be full international legislative bodies. He proposed a permanent tribunal, the decisions of which were to be accepted by the parties. Woolf did not believe in the theory of the equality of independent states.

> The practical result of insisting upon this mystic equality of things radically unequal, of trying to make thousands balance millions in the international scales . . . . made a fair representation of international interests impossible, and therefore a reasonable settlement of any question in which those interests were really involved became equally impossible.[112]

His second report, or Part II, was an elaborate analysis of the association and interpenetration of nations in various unions, such as postal, telegraphic, and sanitary.[113]

It will be observed that the Fabian program agreed with the Bryce group, the League of Nations Society, and the

[111] Art. XVII.

[112] Woolf, *International Government*, p. 119. See also *idem, A Durable Settlement after the War by Means of a League of Nations* (London, 1917).

[113] For a brief survey of international agreements as "forerunners of the League" see M. Erzberger, *The League of Nations: The Way to the World's Peace*, translated by Bernard Miall (New York, 1919), pp. 120–36.

American League To Enforce Peace in proposing the establishment of a court to decide justiciable disputes and a council to deal with nonjusticiable disputes. The Fabian Society was most definite in its recommendations, and its program was clear-cut and left little to the imagination. It pointed out explicitly how the court and council both were to be composed. Its proposals in regard to making the decisions of the court enforceable took the definite form of twelve nonmilitary sanctions. It stated very clearly that a state, after submitting the issue to the council and waiting the specified time, could go to war as a final resort. The project therefore did not plan to abolish armed conflict. Like the Victory Program, it sought the publication of all treaties in an endeavor to do away with what was considered as the evils of secret diplomacy. The Fabian scheme differed from the others in recommending a secretariat and in giving to the council the function of codifying and declaring international law.

An organization that attracted considerable attention in England was the Union of Democratic Control. It was started in the first days of the war by a "small group of men who determined to take hope as their inspiration in the darkest hour."[114] They believed that the exclusive management of international relations in each country unfortunately rested in the hands of a small number of men and that it was the governments which had led the world to war. The people would take a broader view and, if given the opportunity, would direct a country's policies in pacific channels.[115] But, before the people can form a judgment, they

[114] Charles Trevelyan, *The Union of Democratic Control (an Organisation Created To Secure the Control over Their Foreign Policy by the British People, and for the Promotion of International Understanding), Founded in November, 1914: Its History and Its Policy* (London, 1919; Hertford, 1921), p. 1.

[115] Arthur Ponsonby, *Parliament and Foreign Policy* (London, n.d.), p. 2.

must be properly informed, and this was the duty which the Union of Democratic Control took upon itself. The first step toward the organization of the society was taken by Mr. Charles Trevelyan in a letter to Mr. E. D. Morel of August 5, 1914, telling him of the projected society and expressing a wish that he would act as secretary.[116] Mr. Morel replied immediately to Mr. Trevelyan, stating that he would be honored to accept.[117] In the second week of August a letter,[118] dated from Mr. Trevelyan's house, was sent to those who, it was presumed, would be favorably disposed. The letter was signed by J. Ramsay MacDonald, Charles Trevelyan, Norman Angell, and E. D. Morel. The letter began:

There are very many thousands of people in the country who are profoundly dissatisfied with the general course of policy which preceded the war. They are feeling that a dividing-point has come in national history, that the old traditions of secret and class diplomacy, the old control of foreign policy by a narrow clique, and the power of armament organizations have got henceforth to be combatted by a great and conscious and directed effort of the democracy.[119]

This private letter came into possession of the *Morning Post*, which then claimed to have unearthed a conspiracy against the government and insinuated that the authors were acting at the request of the German government. Other papers took up the cry. It was thought advisable by the leaders of the projected association to open immediately the entire matter to the public; and, accordingly, in the first week in September a second letter was written, and this was given to the press. The letter announced the formation of the Union of Democratic Control and was signed by the

[116] H. M. Swanwick, *Builders of Peace, Being the Ten Years' History of the Union of Democratic Control* (London, 1924), p. 30.

[117] *Ibid.*, p. 31.

[118] For text of the letter see Swanwick, *ibid.*, pp. 31–32.

[119] *Ibid.*, p. 31; Trevelyan, *op. cit.*, 1919 ed., p. 2; 1921 ed., pp. 1–2.

original four with the additional signature of Arthur Ponsonby.[120] The letter was followed by a printed statement,
which said in part:

It will be remembered how short was the period between the crisis
arising out of the presentation of the Austrian Note to Servia and Britain's
declaration of war against Germany. It will be remembered, too, that the
Foreign Secretary's announcement in the House of Commons on August
3rd, to the effect that the country had been definitely committed to support France against Germany, was made in the midst of great public
excitement occasioned by the sudden order for mobilisation of the entire
Russian Army and the ensuing German Ultimatum to Russia. Event succeeded event with bewildering rapidity. Neither in this nor in any of the
belligerent countries had public opinion time to become articulate, or to
concentrate upon any course of action in order to check or control in any
way the acts of rulers and diplomatists executing a policy conceived in
secret and finally imposed upon the peoples as an accomplished fact.

If a similar situation is not to mark the close of hostilities, if, that is, we
are to avoid being suddenly confronted with a Peace framed in secret by
the diplomatists who made the war inevitable, a Peace in no way, it may
be, reflecting the wishes of the people, then steps must be taken to see that
public opinion is in a position quickly and vividly to assert itself when the
time comes.[121]

The Union of Democratic Control was an organization
whose particular object was, as the name tells us, the
democratic control of foreign policy. While various members of the Union in the publication of their pamphlets differed as to the range of subject matter, all agreed upon this
fundamental. The Union held that, while during the previous fifty years there had been a rapid expansion of democratic institutions and a great increase in the control by the
people over domestic legislation and administration, in the
matter of directing foreign policy the world was still in the
same stage it had been for centuries past.[122] If we are to be

[120] Swanwick, op. cit., pp. 32–33.

[121] Cited in Trevelyan, op. cit., 1919 ed., p. 3; 1921 ed., p. 3.

[122] Ponsonby, op. cit., p. 1.

guided by public opinion, the Union emphasized, public opinion must have the opportunity of judging policies to which it gives its consent. That means that public opinion must be enlightened, that it cannot be kept in ignorance of the engagements to which its government is pledged, for "the whole basis of constitutional and democratic government is public discussion."[123] The Union, therefore, stood for a new system in place of the old secret diplomacy.[124] All treaties were to be sanctioned by Parliament and were to be revised periodically. All secret treaties and secret clauses in treaties were to be forever abolished. Greater opportunity was to be given in the House of Commons for the discussion of foreign policy. A parliamentary foreign-affairs committee was to be established. The foreign office and the diplomatic service were to be united, and positions in the diplomatic service were to be open to all.[125]

The "cardinal points" in the policy[126] of the Union of Democratic Control provided that no transfer of territory was to be made by one nation to another without the consent of the population of that territory by plebiscite or otherwise.[127] Great Britain was to enter upon no treaty, arrange-

[123] Herbert H. Asquith *et al.*, *The National Policy* (London, n.d.), p. 13.

[124] *Secret Diplomacy as a Menace to the Security of the State: The National and Imperial Problem (from a Speech by Mr. E. D. Morel at the Christian Institute, Glasgow, November 23, 1915)* (London, n.d.).

[125] Arthur Ponsonby, *The Control of Foreign Policy* (London, 1918), pp. 9–13.

[126] Swanwick, *op. cit.*, pp. 39–40; Trevelyan, *op. cit.*, 1919 ed., pp. 4–5; 1921 ed., p. 4; *The Union of Democratic Control: Rules and Constitution, 1917–1918* (London, n.d.), pp. 3–4; *The Morrow of the War* (London, n.d.), pp. 1–12; Phillimore, *op. cit.*, pp. 43–44; Bourne (ed.), *op. cit.*, p. 277. For an explanation of the program, its chief ends, and its policy see E. D. Morel, *The Union of Democratic Control* (London, n.d.); *The Union of Democratic Control, Its Motives, Objects and Policy* (London, 1916). See also the handbook for lecturers: B. N. Langdon-Davies, *The A.B.C. of U.D.C.* (London, n.d.).

[127] Art. I.

ment, or undertaking without the consent of Parliament. Adequate machinery was to be created to insure democratic control of foreign policy.[128] Great Britain's foreign policy was not to be aimed at the creation of alliances to maintain the balance of power but rather at concerted action between the nations and the institution of an international council with deliberations to be public. Adequate machinery was to be established for securing international agreement.[129] Great Britain was to propose, as part of the peace settlement, a drastic reduction in armaments of all the belligerent powers and was to attempt to secure the general nationalization of the manufacture of armaments and the control of their exportation from one country to another.[130] Following the war, economic conflict was to cease, and British policy was to foster free commercial intercourse between all nations and the extension of the doctrine of the open door.[131]

The Union was bitterly assailed[132] and charged with being pro-German. In particular was there criticism of the thesis of the Union that the Central Powers were by no means solely responsible for the conflict and that British policy was a contributing factor.[133] The Union vehemently denied the charges freely circulated in the press that it was pro-German and that it was hindering recruiting. It asserted time and again that it was not a "stop-the-war" movement.[134] Op-

[128] Art. II.   [130] Art. IV.

[129] Art. III.   [131] Art. V.

[132] A scorching indictment of the Union of Democratic Control was made by G. G. Coulton in his *The Main Illusions of Pacifism: A Criticism of Mr. Norman Angell and of the Union of Democratic Control* (Cambridge, England, 1916).

[133] Lindsay Rogers, "Popular Control of Foreign Policy: A Review of Current Literature," in *Recueil de rapports sur les différents points du Programme-Minimum* (La Haye, 1918), IV, 455.

[134] *The Union of Democratic Control: What It Is and What It Is Not* (London, 1915), p. 2.

position at times took more violent turns, and meetings of
the Union were sometimes forcibly broken up.[135] Mr. Morel
himself was imprisoned.[136]

After the war the Union proffered a revised program.[137]
In addition to demanding again that no treaty, arrangement, or undertaking was to be concluded without the
sanction of Parliament,[138] the Union called for the abolition
of industrial and military conscription. It sought a drastic
reduction in armaments as a preliminary to eventual abolition. It also stood for the nationalization of armaments and
control by the League of Nations of the export of armaments
from one country to another.[139] It asked for free commercial
intercourse between all nations and the extension of the
open-door policy.[140] The program indorsed the doctrine of
the self-determination of peoples.[141] The constitution of the
League of Nations was to be made more flexible, inclusive,
and democratic. The Union of Democratic Control wanted
the League to insure admission into its membership of all
nations, to prohibit partial military alliances, and to insure
the rights and interests of all peoples placed under the man-
dates system.[142] The last article stated: "Provision shall be
made for the revision of the Peace Treaties of 1919, so as to

[135] *The Attack upon Freedom of Speech: The Broken-up Meeting at the Memorial
Hall, 29th November, 1915, an Elaborate Conspiracy and Its Origin: Full Text of the
Speeches Which Were To Be Delivered* (London, n.d.); *The Attack upon Freedom of
Speech: Astounding Official Defense; House of Commons Sequel to the Broken-up
Meeting at the Memorial Hall, November 29th, 1915* (London, n.d.).

[136] *Rex v. E. D. Morel, Being a Verbatium* [*sic*] *Report of the Court Proceedings at
Bow Street on Sept. 1 and 4, 1917, before Mr. E. W. Garrett* (London, n.d.);
Vindication of Mr. Morel in the House of Commons (London, n.d.).

[137] Trevelyan, *op. cit.*, 1919 ed., pp. 9–11; 1921 ed., pp. 9–10; Swanwick,
op. cit., pp. 125–26.

[138] Revised program, Art. I.

[139] Revised program, Art. II.   [141] Revised program, Art. IV.

[140] Revised program, Art. III.   [142] Revised program, Art. V.

remove those obvious and manifold injustices therein, which contain the seeds of further and future wars."[143] The stand of the Union of Democratic Control against the peace settlement[144] as represented by the peace treaties, the League of Nations, and reparations made it unique among the peace societies called into being during World War I. Concerning the points in the first program of the Union of Democratic Control, Trevelyan claimed: "They represent the terms of the settlement which ought to have been arrived at to conclude the war. *It is the failure to adopt them which has condemned the world to a new era of unrest and armaments.*"[145]

A rather unique plan was that of the Community of Nations.[146] The essential basis of the proposed new world order was "consent and not the coercion of armed force." While the scheme called for a court to settle justiciable disputes and a council to handle nonjusticiable disputes as so many of the other societies provided, this plan requested that a congress of national representatives be established to promote the common interests of nations. A feature of the plan was the recommendation that foreign secretaries were to meet one another at regular intervals and at critical times for a direct

[143] Revised program, Art. VI.

[144] Arthur Ponsonby, *The Covenant of the League of Nations: An Analysis with Full Text* (Letchworth, England, 1920); E. D. Morel, *The Fruits of Victory: Have Our Statesmen Won the Peace Our Soldiers Fought For?* (London, 1919); *Three Notable Protests against the Peace Treaty: A Christian Protest by Canon Peter Green; an Historical Protest by Dr. Charles Sarolea; a University Protest by the Bishop of Oxford (and Others)* (London, 1919); *The Betrayal of the Peoples, Issued by the Executive Committee of the Union of Democratic Control (with Map Illustrating the Territorial Changes Involved in the Peace Treaty)* (London, n.d.); J. A. Hobson, *The New Holy Alliance: U.D.C. Memoranda on a Democratic Peace* (London, 1919); Charles Roden Buxton, *Memorandum on Territorial Claims and Self-determination* (London, 1919); F. W. Pethick Lawrence, *Making Germany Pay: U.D.C. Memoranda on a Democratic Peace* (London, 1919).

[145] Trevelyan, *op. cit.*, 1919 ed., p. 5; 1921 ed., p. 5.

[146] Woolf, *The Framework of a Lasting Peace*, pp. 124–25.

interchange of ideas instead of acting always through ambassadors.

The British League of Free Nations Association made several interesting proposals.[147] The program[148] followed the
popular course of dividing disputes into those to be submitted to a court whose decisions were to be enforceable and
those submitted to a council which was to act as a mediator.[149] The members were to promise to submit all questions
to peaceful settlement[150] and to suppress jointly any attempt
to disturb the peace of the world by acts of war.[151] All countries were to be admitted to the proposed league of nations[152]
except Germany, which, however, would be welcomed
when it relinquished "clearly and convincingly the dreams
of imperial conquest and world dominion" and when it was
"no longer war-proud and war-greedy." In the supreme
court, states might sue and be sued. The permanent council
was to provide for the codification and extension of international law and was to consider questions affecting transit,
tariffs, access to raw materials, migration, and health. The
council also was to supervise, limit, and control the military
and naval forces and the armament industries of all member-states. The association was definitely opposed to any
attempt to perpetuate boundaries and existing political conditions.

In 1918 the British League of Free Nations Association
and the League of Nations Society combined to form the
League of Nations Union. The program which was ad-

[147] *War after War: The Inaugural Meeting of the League of Free Nations Association Held in the Town Hall, at Northampton on September 13, 1918; Speech by Viscount
Bryce* (London, 1918).

[148] Latané (ed.), *op. cit.*, pp. 818–19.

[149] Arts. III, IV.   [151] Art. II.

[150] Art. I.   [152] Art. V.

vanced, while it resembled the plan of the League of Nations Society in many respects, was almost identical with that of the League of Free Nations Association. The Union was constituted to promote the formation of a world league of free peoples for the securing of international justice, mutual defense, and permanent peace. The presidency was accepted by Viscount Grey. The Union actively engaged in spreading information concerning a league of free peoples desirous of ending war forever.[153] The program[154] demanded that all disputes of member-states were to be submitted to peaceful settlement.[155] The signatories were to use all the means at their disposal to suppress jointly any attempt made by any state to disturb world peace by acts of war.[156] A supreme court was to be founded, and the members were to respect and enforce its decisions.[157] A permanent council was to be established to provide for the development of international law and for the settlement of disputes not suitable for submission to the court. The council was also to supervise and control armaments. It was to take action in

[153] The Union issued a large number of pamphlets, among which the following (in the "Publications of the League of Nations Union") may be cited as representative: Sir Henry Jones, *Form the League of Peace Now: An Appeal to My Fellow-Citizens* (Ser. 2, No. 5 [London, 1918]); John Clifford, *The League of Free Nations: Facing the Facts* (Ser. 2, No. 18 [London, 1918]); David Davies, *Some Problems of International Reconstruction and a League of Nations* (Ser. 2, No. 23 [London, 1918]); *The League of Nations Union* (Ser. 2, No. 10 [London, 1918]); G. A. McCurdy, *The League of Free Nations* (Ser. 2, No. 3 [London, 1918]); Arthur James Grant, *The Holy Alliance and the League of Nations*, with a Foreword by Lord Robert Cecil (No. 112 [London, 1923]); *The Problems of a League of Nations* (Ser. 1, No. 1 [London, 1918]); Harry R. Reichel, *Why a League of Free Nations?* (Ser. 2, No. 21 [London, 1918]); *A Scheme for the World League: Speech Delivered by the Late Lord Parker in the House of Lords on March 19, 1918* (Ser. 2, No. 16 [London, 1918]).

[154] *The Constitution of the League* (London, 1918). The program is also given in a large number of publications of the Union.

[155] Art. I. [156] Art. II. [157] Art. III.

matters of common concern.[158] The league was to admit all
peoples "able and willing to give effective guarantees of
their loyal intention to observe its covenants." The league
was to act as the trustee and guardian of uncivilized races
and undeveloped territories and maintain international
order.[159]

Early in the war the Nederlandsche Anti-Oorlog Raad
("Dutch Anti-war Council") was formed at The Hague.
This society convoked an international meeting, April 7–10,
1915, which was composed of about thirty international
jurists, statesmen, and publicists representing Austria, Germany, Great Britain, Holland, Belgium, Norway, Sweden,
Denmark, Switzerland, and the United States.[160] The result was the creation of the Central Organization for a Durable Peace. Its executive committee[161] was representative of
neutrals and belligerents of both sides. The meeting made
an appeal to world opinion by offering the "Minimum Program" as a basis for discussion of the means to secure permanent peace. Since the war made it difficult to hold international meetings, the method was adopted of collecting information and making reports on various topics concerned.[162] The *Recueil de rapports*,[163] published by the Central
Organization, began in 1916 and reached four volumes.

[158] Art. IV.   [159] Art. V.

[160] *Central Organisation for a Durable Peace: Manifesto* (The Hague, 1915),
p. 4; Fannie Fern Andrews, "The Central Organization for a Durable Peace,"
Journal of the National Institute of Social Sciences, III (January, 1917), 119–20.

[161] The list of members of the executive committee is given in C. L. Lange,
Exposé des travaux de l'organisation (The Hague, 1917), p. 29; *Une paix durable,
commentaire officiel du Programme-Minimum* (La Haye, n.d.), pp. ix–xv.

[162] G. Lowes Dickinson, Introduction to *Problems of the International Settlement* (London, 1918), p. vi.

[163] *Recueil de rapports sur les différents points du Programme-Minimum* (The
Hague), Vols. I, II (1916); III (1917); IV (1918).

Various subjects were treated, such as plebiscites, the problem of nationalities, an international court of justice and a council of conciliation, sanctions, freedom of the sea, limitation of armaments, and parliamentary control of foreign policy. These research studies were widely used for the discussion of the problems of a durable peace.[164] Lange[165] feels that the *Recueil* made a very important contribution in this respect.

The Minimum Program[166] provided that no transfer of territory was to be made without consulting the wishes of the population. The states were to guarantee to their minorities liberty of law, religion, and free use of their native languages.[167] The states were to agree to introduce liberty of commerce or equal treatment to all nations in their colonies, protectorates, and spheres of influence.[168] The work of the Hague conferences was to be expanded and given a permanent organization with meetings at regular intervals.[169] The states were to promise to submit all disputes to peaceful settlement. In addition to the existing Hague Court, there was to be created a permanent court of international justice and a permanent international council of investigation and

[164] Andrews, *op. cit.*, p. 124.   [165] *Op. cit.*, p. 16.

[166] Before the Preface to Vols. I–IV of *Recueil de rapports; Central Organisation for a Durable Peace: Manifesto* (The Hague, 1915), p. 3; *Une paix durable, commentaire officiel du Programme-Minimum*, p. iv; Lange, *op. cit.*, pp. 5–6; Woolf, *The Framework of a Lasting Peace*, pp. 63–64; Latané (ed.), *op. cit.*, pp. 821–22; Phillimore, *op. cit.*, pp. 44–45.

[167] Art. I.   [168] Art. II.

[169] G. Lowes Dickinson points out that the Minimum Program called for the developing of the Hague institutions, whereas the English League of Nations Society and the American League To Enforce Peace tacitly ignored The Hague. On this point there may be, he says, an important cleavage between Continental and Anglo-Saxon advocates of a league (Introduction to *Problems of the International Settlement*, pp. xiv–xv).

conciliation. The states were to take concerted economic, diplomatic, or military action in case any state resorted to war without submitting the issue to judicial decision or to settlement by the council.[170] The powers were to reduce their armaments. The right of capture was to be abolished, and the freedom of the seas assured.[171] Foreign policy was to be controlled by the parliament in each country. Secret treaties were to be void.[172]

The most important document of the Central Organization was the "Draft Treaty" prepared by the Dutch commission. This was the detailed plan. The Draft Treaty[173] provided that there was to be established at The Hague an international court of arbitration and an international council of conciliation.[174] The contracting states were to promise to submit their disputes to the court or to the council.[175] The court was to be composed of judges and deputy judges appointed by the states. Each power was to appoint two or at the most four judges, and the same number of deputies, to serve for a period of twelve years.[176] The court was to handle all disputes of a justiciable nature. The following were defined as justiciable: "All disputes concerning the interpretation of treaties and the application of rules and principles of international law, including the fixing of the amount of the indemnities for the violation of treaties or of the rules and principles of international law." The court was also to have cognizance over disputes which were subject to arbitration according to treaty.[177] The award was not to be binding except on the parties concerned. In case the disputes involved the interpretation of a treaty and thus

[170] Art. III.   [171] Art. IV.   [172] Art. V.

[173] B. C. J. Loder (presented by), *Institutions judiciaires et de conciliation: rapport* (The Hague, 1917), pp. 20–43; Woolf, *The Framework of a Lasting Peace*, pp. 126–54; Bourne (ed.), *op. cit.*, p. 247.

[174] Art. I.   [175] Art. II.   [176] Art. IV.   [177] Art. XVI.

concerned other parties, the third parties might intervene, but the decision was then equally binding on them.[178] To facilitate the solution of disputes involving neither honor nor vital interests, an international commission of inquiry was to be established. The commission was to elucidate the facts by making an impartial investigation.[179] Each of the contracting states was to appoint at least two and not more than four members and deputy-members, who were to serve for six years.[180] The council was to take cognizance of disputes upon the request of all the parties or on request of one of the parties if the court declared the case outside its jurisdiction. The council likewise was to take cognizance if, according to the opinion of the parties, the case was not subject to arbitration or if it did not admit of doubt that the case was outside the jurisdiction of the court.[181] Members were to have only one vote.[182] Decisions were to be made by majority vote, but the majority must include at least one vote of a member of each party.[183] Decisions arrived at in this manner were to be binding.[184] In addition, an international bureau was to be established at The Hague to serve as a registry for the court and the council. It was to have charge of the archives. The contracting powers were to communicate to the bureau, as soon as possible, a certified copy of every agreement of arbitration, all laws, regulations, and documents relating to the ultimate carrying-out of the decisions of the court.[185]

[178] Art. LI.

[179] Art. LVIII.   [182] Art. CIV.

[180] Art. LXXXVI.   [183] Art. CV.

[181] Art. XCVIII.   [184] Art. CVI.

[185] Art. CXI. The Draft Treaty of the Dutch commission is most elaborate and in the opinion of Lord Phillimore "comes to very little." He thinks its principal value is perhaps in "showing that writers not of Anglo-American origin are more averse than others from interfering with the independence and sovereignty of various States" (*op. cit.*, p. 48).

One of the most influential organizations in France was the Association de la Paix par le Droit. Its platform was similar to that of the Central Organization for a Durable Peace. The Association denounced "as a perpetual menace to international society the fact that certain dynasties or castes have an absolute right to declare war; it sees in the general evolution of modern societies towards democracy the most efficacious condition of a lasting peace. . . . ."[186] The work of the Hague conferences was to be completed "especially by the establishment of an obligatory arbitral jurisdiction, the decisions of which would be carried out by means of effective sanctions, such as economic blockades or the employment of an international police force."[187] Membership was to be open to every power which would accept the convention in its entirety. The Association urged the allies to negotiate among themselves as liberal commercial treaties as possible. It advocated unification of metric and monetary systems, labor laws, transport rates, and the reduction of postal and customs tariffs. The Association recommended the principle of "the open door" in colonies not yet formed into autonomous states. As regards neutrals, it urged the allies to grant them, as far as possible, the "most-favored-nation" clause.[188]

In particular the Association expressed the wish that, without delay, the allies would conclude a general convention[189] among themselves binding them to submit all disputes not settled diplomatically to a permanent commission of inquiry and conciliation.[190] All differences incapable of solution by the commission were to be submitted to the Hague Court.[191] The member-states were to unite against any signatory which declared war or committed hostile acts

---

[186] *Problems of the International Settlement*, p. 202.
[187] *Ibid.*
[188] *Ibid.*, p. 204.
[189] *Ibid.*, pp. 203–4.
[190] Art. I.
[191] Art. II.

against any other signatory.[192] Conferences were to be held periodically to formulate and perfect the code of international law which was to be binding upon all states not having repudiated the convention within certain time limits.[193] A Society called "Ligue pour une Société des Nations" was formed in France in January, 1917. One of the founders was M. Paul Otlet, who was closely associated in the publication of the "World Charter" issued by the Union des Association Internationales at The Hague in October, 1914.[194] The organization engaged largely in the educational work of popularizing the idea of a league of nations.[195]

Credit should be given to the Socialist party in the different countries for its influence upon the peace movement and its voicing of the need for an international organization.[196] For example, M. Albert Thomas stated in the interview with John Bell (January 7, 1918): "We [the French Socialist party] are firmly persuaded that a durable peace can only be secured by an international organization, a Society of Nations based on the right of peoples to dispose of themselves."[197] The league-of-nations idea was further indorsed by many conferences of labor and Socialist organizations.[198]

[192] Art. III.   [193] Art. IV.

[194] *Proceedings of the First Annual Meeting Held at the Caxton Hall, July 20th, 1917*, p. 10.

[195] *Appel-Programme, Status: Composition du conseil et du bureau* (Paris, 1918); Phelps (comp.), *op. cit.*, p. 54.

[196] For the program of the Socialist party of America and other countries see Bourne (ed.), *op. cit.*, pp. 271–73.

[197] *Pronouncements on a League of Nations* (London, 1918), p. 3.

[198] E.g., Inter-allied Socialist and Labor Conference in London, February 4, 1915; Inter-allied Socialist and Labor Conference in London, August, 1917; Inter-allied Trade Union Conference, September 10–11, 1917; Inter-allied Socialist and Labor Conference in London, February, 1918; Union of Belgian Socialists Resident in France, May, 1918; French Socialist-Radical Congress, October 27, 1917; General Confederation of Labor (French), December 26, 1917; National Council of the French Socialist Party, February

Societies indorsing a league of nations were also established in Italy, Switzerland, Denmark, Norway, Sweden, and other countries.[199] The plans issuing from the United States, Great Britain, and France, to which particular attention has been given here, were undoubtedly of greatest influence, as it was these nations which took a dominant part in the drawing-up of the Peace Treaty, which included the establishment of the League of Nations. Many individuals likewise presented their plans for permanent peace.[200] The World War period of 1914–18, in fact, was productive of a multitude of schemes and indorsements.[201] Some of the books of this period proposing a peace league were worthy contributions.[202]

18, 1918; Socialist Parliamentary Group (Italian), January 27, 1917; National Executive of German Social Democratic Party, July 1, 1915; German Social Democratic Labor Association, January, 1917; National Conference of Social Democrats in Austria, June, 1918; Workmen's Council of Vienna, June, 1918. See *World-Wide Support for a League of Nations* (London, 1918), p. 4; Bourne (ed.), *op. cit., passim.* For interallied labor and Socialist conferences of 1918 and Dutch-Scandinavian Socialists see Latané (ed.), *op. cit.,* pp. 781–84.

[199] C. L. Lange, "Préparation de La Société des Nations pendant la Guerre," in P. Munch (director), *Les Origines et l'œuvre de la Société des nations* (Copenhagen, 1923), I, 8–61; Bourne (ed.), *op. cit., passim.*

[200] For a list of further references on plans for peace for this period, including an extensive listing from medieval times to 1936, see Mary Alice Matthews (comp.), *Peace Projects: Select List of References on Plans for the Preservation of Peace from Medieval Times to the Present Day* (Washington, D.C., 1936).

[201] Reprints of some contemporary articles concerning the formation of a league of nations: Phelps (comp.), *op. cit.,* pp. 79–319; Bourne (ed.), *op. cit.,* pp. 243–326.

[202] As typical works the following few may be mentioned: Alfred Owen Crozier, *Nation of Nations: The Way to Permanent Peace* (Cincinnati, 1915); H. E. Hyde, *The International Solution* (London, 1918); J. A. Hobson, *Towards International Government* (New York, 1915); Raleigh C. Minor, *A Republic of Nations: A Study of the Organization of a Federal League of Nations* (New York, 1918); Horace Meyer Kallen, *The League of Nations—Today and Tomorrow: A Discussion of International Organization Present and To Come* (Boston, 1919); Henry N. Brailsford, *A League of Nations* (New York, 1917); George Paish, *A Permanent League of Nations* (London, 1918); Lassa Oppenheim, *The League of*

The hope that World War I would be the last war, that the struggle would be followed by an agreement to establish an international order for peace,[203] was the hope expressed not only by political philosophers but by the most prominent statesmen. The idea of a league of nations entered the realm of "real politics." President Wilson was the most important single exponent of the idea of a league of nations. His speeches[204] on the necessity of forming a general association of nations under specific covenants had a profound impression on world opinion. In the meantime, the Allies included some such plan among the objects for which they were contending.[205] The European governments gave almost universal assent to the idea of a league of nations, and in January, 1917, they expressed to President Wilson their wholehearted agreement with the proposal to cre-

Nations and Its Problems: Three Lectures (London, 1919); G. Lowes Dickinson, *The Choice before Us* (New York, 1917); Ernest C. Fayle, *The Fourteenth Point: A Study of the League of Nations* (New York, 1919); Erzberger, *op. cit.;* Frank Noel Keen, *The World in Alliance: A Plan for Preventing Future Wars* (London, 1915); idem, *Hammering Out the Details* (London, 1917); Henri La Fontaine, *The Great Solution: Magnissima charta* (Boston, 1916); James Walker and M. D. Petre, *State Morality and a League of Nations* (London, 1919); H. G. Wells *et al.*, *The Idea of a League of Nations* (Boston, 1919); Oscar Crosby, *International War: Its Causes and Its Cure* (London, 1919); Viscount Grey *et al., op. cit.;* Theodore Marburg (description and comment by), *Draft Convention for League of Nations by Group of American Jurists and Publicists* (New York, 1918); Gilbert Murray, *The League of Nations and the Democratic Idea* (New York, 1918); Sir Frederick Pollock, *The League of Nations and the Coming Rule of Law* (London, 1918).

[203] Concerning the demand for a league of nations during the war period see, further, Erzberger, *op. cit.*, pp. 1–57.

[204] *Pronouncements of Leading Statesmen* (London, 1917); *The League of Nations: "The Final Triumph of Justice and Fair Dealing," Speech by President Wilson, New York, Sept. 27, 1918* (London, 1918), pp. 4–7; for excerpts from the addresses and state papers of Woodrow Wilson see "A League of Nations as Advocated by Woodrow Wilson," in Phelps (comp.), *op. cit.*, pp. 5–14.

[205] *Nations Unite! Speeches on a League of Nations* (London, 1918); *Viscount Grey on a League of Nations, at a Meeting Held at Central Hall, Westminster, October 10, 1918* (London, 1918); *Pronouncements of Leading Statesmen;* "Governments Pledge Support to a League of Nations," in Phelps (comp.), *op. cit.*, pp. 59–63.

ate a league of nations.[206] In August, 1917, the pope addressed a note to the heads of the belligerent peoples in which he pleaded that moral right be substituted for the material force of arms.[207] The governments declined to act upon the proposals of the pope.[208] The league-of-nations proposal found support among statesmen the world over. The fundamental principle of a league of nations was thus generally accepted.[209]

President Wilson, in his final note of November 5, 1918, stated that the Allied governments agreed to make peace with the government of Germany on the terms laid down in his address to Congress of January 8, 1918, and the principles enunciated in his subsequent addresses. The address of January 8 included the famous Fourteen Points, of which the Fourteenth Point was that "a general association of nations must be formed under specific covenants for the purpose of affording mutual guarantees of political independence and territorial integrity to great and small States alike."

It was the duty, therefore, of the Paris Peace Conference, when it met, to give serious attention to the preparation of a scheme for a league of nations. The question was immediately raised at the peace conference whether the Covenant of the League of Nations should be included in the peace treaty or placed in a separate document. There was a disposition among many to postpone the final settlement of the Covenant until the immediate problems which they considered more pressing were settled. President Wilson felt

[206] Bryce, Introduction to *Proposals for the Prevention of Future Wars*, p. 11.

[207] *Appeals for Peace of Pope Benedict XV (August 1, 1917) and Pope Pius XI (December 24, 1930)* (Baltimore, 1931), pp. 4–5.

[208] In his encyclical, "International Reconciliation," Pentecost Sunday, 1920, Pope Benedict XV laid stress on forming an association of nations (*International Ethics* [New York, 1928], pp. 36–37).

[209] See "Men and Organizations Endorse a League of Nations," in Phelps (comp.), *op. cit.*, pp. 63–74.

that the preliminary treaty would be the final treaty and that not to include the League of Nations Covenant in it would not only weaken it but might indefinitely postpone the creation of the League. It was due to his insistence, with the support of a few others, that the Covenant was not tabled but became an integral part of the treaty. It became not only a part of the Treaty of Versailles but a part of the subsequent treaties with Austria, Hungary, Bulgaria, and Turkey. A special commission, with President Wilson as chairman, was appointed for the purpose of drafting the Covenant of the League of Nations. The commission considered several drafts.[210] After ten days of concentrated work the commission's report was presented by President Wilson to a plenary sitting of the peace conference on February 14, 1919. The Covenant was then published, submitted to close re-examination, and a number of amendments were adopted. The Covenant in its final form was then submitted at a plenary session and unanimously adopted on April 28, 1919.

[210] Consult: J. C. Smuts, *The League of Nations: A Practical Suggestion* (London, 1918); Florence Wilson, *The Origins of the League Covenant: Documentary History of Its Drafting* (London, 1928); David Hunter Miller, *The Drafting of the Covenant*, with an Introduction by Nicholas Murray Butler (2 vols.; New York, 1928); *League of Nations: Comparison of the Plan for the League of Nations Showing the Original Draft as Presented to the Commission Constituted by the Preliminary Peace Conference in Session at Versailles, France, Together with the Covenant as Finally Reported and Adopted at the Plenary Session of the Peace Conference, Also the Presentation Speeches of the President of the United States Relating Thereto* (Washington, D. C., 1919); C. A. Kluyver (comp.), *Documents on the League of Nations* (Leiden, 1920); "A Draft of the Composite Covenant Made by the Legal Advisers of the Commission on the League, Presented by Mr. Lodge" and "Covenant for the League of Nations Showing the Preliminary Reported Draft and the Covenant as Finally Adopted at the Plenary Session," in John Eugene Harley, *The League of Nations and the New International Law* (New York, 1921); John Eppstein (comp.), *Ten Years' Life of the League of Nations: A History of the Origins of the League and of Its Development from A.D. 1919 to 1929* (London, 1929); H. Wilson Harris, *What the League of Nations Is* (London, 1925).

CHAPTER V

REFLECTIONS

IT IS not surprising that mankind made its greatest of all attempts to establish a new international order at the close of the World War of 1914–18. It would seem that every great war in history was followed by renewed interest in peace and by the presentation of plans to secure it. In 1513 the plan of William of Ciervia and John Sylvagius and a little later the work of Erasmus aimed at stopping the wars that were raging in Europe in those times. With the civil wars in France in the sixteenth century came the Grand Design of Henry IV. When the ambitions of Louis XIV threatened the security of other European states and plunged the world into sanguinary struggles, the peace plans of William Penn, John Bellers, and the Abbé de Saint-Pierre called for a new order. With the War of the Austrian Succession came the work of Rousseau, and with the wars of the French Revolution the treatise of Kant. The Napoleonic wars were followed by Alexander's Holy Alliance. With World War I came the largest number of peace plans occasioned by any war in history.

In our study of the most noted peace plans of history we have seen the idea of a league of nations evolve from simple beginnings to the final complex organization created in 1919. The early peace plans were not only simple and highly unified but were conceived as panaceas to be adopted by the world as originally framed. These schemes were inelastic and were to be accepted intact by the world; they did not allow for change, which is the universal law of history. Some

182

of the projects, such as that of Henry IV, looked to the aggrandizement of a single state, to the satisfaction of national selfishness. Peace was to follow only after the state had ascended to supreme power. Other conceptions, like that of Erasmus, looked to abstract justice—good in itself but not easily translated into a workable scheme for world organization. The majority of the authors realized that their schemes for world peace must be built upon the political order of the time and must be in tune with the historical development of international co-operation up to that point. Hence, medieval plans reflected the prevailing idea of the unity of Christendom. Later, with the growth of the national states, peace advocates proposed federations of kings and princes in which the representatives to the central government were to be the kings' ambassadors and were to do their will. With the coming of the age of democracy, peace treatises provided that the delegates were to represent the national governments, which in many cases were elected by the people and were responsible to them. In addition, recent schemes took into consideration the force of public opinion in support of the peace proposals. To study the peace plans of history, therefore, is to study the historical development of the processes of government.

Whereas early plans were simple in their conception and organization, modern proposals were complex and offered a wealth of detail. Political philosophers of recent days held that any adequate design for international organization must include separate and distinct legislative, administrative, and judicial organs. The early writings did not make this division; but we notice that, as the times changed, this separation was deemed all-important. The more modern works, without exception, incorporated this feature as essential. The earlier speculative plans gave way to the more practicable and workable suggestions of recent times, and the projects of the World War period of 1914–18 approached the realm of practical politics. These plans, in contrast to the earlier inelastic proposals, aimed to keep step with the changing times by providing for amendment and revision. At last a peace plan, infinitely complex and elaborate when compared with the early proposals, was broached and accepted as the hope of mankind. Such was the League of Nations Covenant.

One cannot help but wonder: "Why, with all these plans as a background, was the world unable to realize an international organization for peace before the twentieth century? Why were none of these peace plans of history adopted?" These projects were disregarded, it may be answered, because they were considered impracticable at the time of their conception. They were great ideas born into the world before the world was ready to receive them. The political philosophy of statesmen was the antithesis of a philosophy which would have made the realization of an effective peace plan possible. It is desirable that we turn here to a study of the means by which the world endeavored to maintain peace, not only that we may better judge the wisdom or the impracticability of the proffered peace projects in their attempts to correct the weaknesses and abuses in international relationships, but that we may better understand the reluctance of governments to adopt a more complete and wholehearted plan to insure universal peace. A study of peace plans would be incomplete without an analysis of the actual international order in which those peace plans would have to be worked out.

The system of alliances and the doctrine of the balance of power ruled the minds of modern statesmen, who trusted to them for the preservation of peace. History shows that their faith was ill-placed. Alliances themselves are as old as history. They were made for various purposes and often developed into general defensive alliances and sometimes offensive as well. But they have inherent weaknesses. They were sometimes manipulated by one party in its selfish interests. They were made for some temporary advantage and tended to dissolve when that advantage was gained. Alliances bred secret diplomacy and removed foreign relations from the control of the people, so that a nation might be plighted to go to war, all unknown to the people and without their consent. Secret diplomacy fostered suspicion and hatred and worked to disrupt mutual dependence and faith so necessary to peace.

The failure to maintain peace arose largely from the use of alliances to preserve the balance of power. It had long been a recognized policy that no state or union of states was to prevail over the others; and, if any state or union of states was likely to upset the political equilibrium of Europe, the threatened states were to combine to counterbalance the inequality. Such was the conception of the balance of power, a principle known even to the ancient Greeks and the Persians. The doctrine received its definite form in modern times in the alliances of the League of Venice in 1495 against Charles VIII, but not until the Peace of Westphalia was the basis laid for the application of the balance of power as a system. The principle was applied to thwart the ambitions of a Louis XIV and a Napoleon. The balance of power eventually divided Europe into armed camps, each increasingly suspicious of the other, each building up larger armaments to maintain the so-called "equality." For fear that the equilibrium of Europe might be upset to its disadvantage, a country was frequently compelled to uphold the interests of an ally, even to the point of going to war, no matter

186 PLANS FOR WORLD PEACE

how far removed those interests might appear. The balance of power was inextricably bound up with secret diplomacy, which fostered the growth of suspicion, distrust, and fear. The doctrine relied upon preserving an equilibrium of power to maintain peace—upon might rather than upon principles of justice.

Closely linked with the doctrine of the balance of power was the conception of the Concert of Europe, an attempt to secure some kind of unity for Europe under the dictatorship of the great powers. The Concert, it will be remembered, had its origin, at the close of the Napoleonic wars, in the Quadruple Alliance between Austria, Russia, Prussia, and England, to which France later adhered. The alliance aimed to suppress revolution, to maintain the status quo established by the treaties of Paris and Vienna, and in general to regulate the affairs of Europe. The principle of intervention was employed in the internal concerns of a country whose condition, it was held, threatened the peace of Europe. The attempt to win back for Spain her colonies in the New World led to the promulgation of the Monroe Doctrine, and the revolutions of 1830 and 1848 in Europe emphasized the principles of nationality and democracy, so that the principle of intervention by the Concert was invoked in the name of the rights of nationalities rather than the preservation of legitimacy and absolutism. The Concert of Europe through conferences or congresses repeatedly exercised its influence in European affairs. Examples are to be found not only in the congresses of Aix-la-Chapelle, Troppau, Laibach, and Verona but also in the Congress of Paris, 1856, and in the Congress of Berlin, 1878. On the one hand, the Concert of Europe was able to supervise the liberation of Greece from Turkey and to free Belgium from union with Holland. On the other hand, the Concert was unable to

prevent Prussia and Austria from taking Schleswig-Hol-
stein, and Prussia from expelling Austria from Germany.
From the last quarter of the nineteenth century the balance
of power produced a rivalry within the Concert of Europe
which greatly weakened its general action.

At the outbreak of World War I there did exist, then,
some sort of a concert of Europe. While the Concert did
make a real contribution to the development of international co-operation, it was unable to prevent numerous wars,
and its inadequacy is best proved by the number of major
wars in recent times. A tendency to disregard the claims of
smaller nations in order to preserve peacè among the great
powers was a serious weakness of the Concert. Its attempt
to preserve harmony was overshadowed by the workings of
the opposing factors of nationalism, imperialism, and militarism, which produced the inevitable fruits of distrust and
friction. Furthermore, the deficiencies of the conference
method were so great that beneficial effects could not always be realized. In addition to the factor of uncertain and
spasmodic appearances, the Concert and other conferences
that were called at intervals lacked organization and governing rules. The separation of the conferences into judicial,
legislative, and administrative organs was not followed.
This left the conferences with inadequate machinery to
grapple with the many and diverse problems that came before them. The work of the Concert was frequently limited
to "safe" subjects which did not get at the roots of war. The
diplomats of Europe relied upon their own efforts to settle
questions of "national honor and vital interests." The greatest weakness undoubtedly was the lack of a permanent authority to deal with emergencies. In 1914, when the dispute
arose between Austria and Serbia, there was no adequate
machinery in existence for the calling of the Concert of Eu-

rope. It was not upon the conference method that hopes for permanent peace could be based, for, in the last analysis, statesmen placed too little reliance upon it.

The modern world thus trusted for the preservation of peace to the system of alliances and the balance of power and, to a lesser degree, to the system of conferences and the Concert of Europe—all of which failed to prevent war. But it should be noticed that each method contained within it the idea of co-operation, the conception of union to maintain peace. Although not fully workable through the medium in which it was expressed, the idea was there—and that is important. The conception was a worthy contribution to the realization of a league for peace. The idea was sound, but it was nullified in large part by a philosophy which gave full vent to exaggerated nationalism, to selfish imperialism, and to almost unbridled militarism. Peace advocates saw the weaknesses in the execution of the idea of union for peace, and they strove to complete the idea in the establishment of the proper political machinery. They sought a fuller and closer union. Running through the peace plans of history there will be found insistence on this principle—the principle of federation. Plans differed, of course, on the strength of the union. Some preferred a weaker form, a confederation, while others planned a strong federation.

All the projects called for a central organ, whether termed a "congress," a "council," a "diet," or a "parliament." Some desired a permanent central government, like national governments, while others preferred it to be periodic, like conferences. The plans before the time of Ladd and Bentham united the functions of the court with the functions of the congress. These two writers separated the judicial and legislative functions by the establishment of a separate tribunal to which all justiciable disputes would be referred, and later writers adhered to this division. Recent plans made a distinction between justiciable and nonjusticiable disputes and, in general, provided that the former be referred to the court and the latter to the congress or council. The plans differed as to which nations were to be members. Some included all states, while others restricted the membership. There was also a divergence of opinion as to the number of votes to be given to each nation. In general, the plans provided for unequal representation in favor of the great powers. Many of the projects gave a wealth of details concerning their proposed international governments through which peace was to be maintained. Thus the authors of peace plans sought federation as the remedy to the international anarchy of the day; but the world clung to the system of alliances, to the balance of power, and to anemic conferences and refused to heed to pleas of peace advocates for a closer union.

In addition to the system of alliances and the balance of power and to the Concert of Europe the nations relied somewhat for the maintenance of peace upon the pacific settlement of disputes by mediation and arbitration. Arbitration was rare in the sixteenth, seventeenth, and eighteenth centuries. The eighteenth century was the century of mediation, and the nineteenth that of arbitration. States disinclined to diminish their sovereignty in the slightest degree were unwilling to submit their disputes to the decision of some paramount body, whether a court or council. Mediation presented to them a form of neutral intervention to aid in the conciliation of their controversy. A sensitive national honor, however, prevented a nation from seeking mediation when most needed, such as at a time when defeat in arms was certain; and diplomatists, with a supersensitive regard

for the dignity of the engaged states, hesitated and frequently inhibited their desire to offer their services as mediator.
An advance was made when states agreed to submit their
differences to arbitration. Arbitration clauses appeared in
treaties of peace referring compensation claims of subjects of
the belligerent states to a commission for adjudication.
Then came provisions for arbitration in the future in the
event of new disputes. The next step was a series of treaties
formulated in time of peace which looked forward to the
avoidance of war through the settlement of disputes by
arbitration.

The nineteenth century, as has been mentioned, was the
century of arbitration; for each successive decade the number of arbitration cases doubled. Between the Jay Treaty of
1794 and the year 1904 the United States was a party to
seventy-six arbitration cases. It is not surprising that the
Hague conferences called originally to discuss disarmament
dropped that issue and made their chief contribution in the
field of arbitration. At the time of the First Hague Conference the standing arbitration treaty had just begun to appear. The conferences gave a great impetus to the movement, and by 1910 ninety treaties for arbitration were communicated to The Hague, and one hundred were in force at
the outbreak of World War I. These treaties were of the
1903 type (between England and France), in which "differences between the two contracting parties of a judicial
order or relative to the interpretation of existing treaties,
which it may not have been possible to settle by diplomacy,
shall be submitted to the Permanent Court at The Hague."
All these treaties excluded questions involving "vital interests and independence or honor" of either state, the very
problems which would most easily lead to war. This explains the small role played by The Hague in preventing

war. The value of arbitration as a pacific means for the settlement of disputes was largely nullified by a sensitive nationalism. The fundamental principle of arbitration was sound—a regulation of relations between states by general rules applied in particular cases by an independent judicial body. Yet arbitration failed to prevent war. It was not the principle of arbitration that was at fault but the application of that principle. Once a dispute arose and passions were aroused, there was the practical difficulty of getting nations to agree to arbitrate their differences. A high sense of nationalism prevented the submission of the very questions that result in war.

The authors of peace treatises turned their attention to the weaknesses indicated, and in perusing the peace plans of history it will be found that all of them contemplated the pacific settlement of disputes, whether by a council or a court or both. The plans before Bentham and Ladd would refer the disputes to the congress, council, or diet for settlement by the representatives of the states not members to the controversy. Most of these schemes provided for the use of force, if necessary, to carry out the decisions or to compel a state to abide by its treaty promises. Ladd and Bentham discarded force and relied upon public opinion. The schemes of the period of 1914–18, almost without exception, recommended the use of force, at least to secure a moratorium while the case in dispute was being considered; and they showed a particular preference for economic sanctions, a quite new feature. The failure of arbitration to preserve the peace of the world explains why the peace plans of the war period of 1914–18 demanded the compulsory submission of disputes to pacific settlement, to take the place of the independent action of states. Realizing the lack of adequate machinery for the arbitration of disputes, these plans emphasized the methods and means by which such settlement could be made.

It has been seen that the political philosophy of modern times was wanting, for it trusted particularly to, first, the system of alliances and the balance of power, a doctrine of might rather than right; second, arbitration, sound in principle but nullified in large part by an exaggerated sense of nationalism; and, third, the Concert of Europe, which presented no effectual organization. This was the working "peace plan" of the world before World War I; and, while it was being relied upon, no other plan—no matter how much more effectual it may have been—could be put into practice. The war of 1914–18 proved to the statesmen of the world how ineffectual was their reliance upon these three means. The system of alliances to maintain the balance of power served only to draw all the great nations into the conflict. Arbitration was not employed once "national honor" was at stake. Since no authority existed to call the Concert of Europe, nations relied upon independent action—and war followed.

The peace proposals of the World War period of 1914–18 attacked these problems with vigor. Instead of the loose organization of congresses and conferences, there was to be reared a league of nations which was expected to be an adequate organization to deal with all peace problems. A league of all nations to preserve peace was to end, as President Wilson said later, "the great game, now forever discredited, of the balance of power." To make the old state of international anarchy impossible, the authors of peace plans turned to federation, that is, the union of nations in a definite league. Since the nation cannot be self-sufficient, either politically or economically, international co-operation, they held, must be relied upon to maintain peace. The necessity of compulsory arbitration followed logically from this conception, and the peace projects devoted much attention to the pacific settlement of disputes, for former attempts had led to meager results. Fundamental in the faulty political philosophy of modern times, which made almost any true peace plan impossible of attainment, was the conception of the state. In *The Path to Peace* Nicholas Murray Butler says:

The analogy between the state in a society of states and the individual in a society of individuals is complete. . . . . In short, the individual human being enriches his nature, strengthens his moral life and adds to his own worth by that form of social and political association and service which is found in close and intimate contact with his fellow men. Truly, man is, as Aristotle so long ago said, a political animal. He is not truly man unless and until he finds himself to be a member of a social and political group.

Precisely the same considerations apply to the life and activity of nations. When two or more sovereign states agree together to promote some common and noble end, they do not limit their sovereignties; they rather enrich them. By this co-operation and association each sovereign state reveals the fact that it has a moral consciousness and a moral purpose. It makes it plain that it cannot, and will not, live for itself alone, but will do all that lies in its power to promote the common interest of mankind. This does not limit sovereignty; it increases the value of sovereignty by ennobling it.[1]

The state, like the individual, must be subject to law. International law, like domestic law, contains two elements: positive and natural. The positive law consists of treaties, customs, usages, and so forth, which states have accepted. The natural law comprises those principles drawn immediately from the moral law of nature, which is divine in its origin.[2] Modern legal writers have frequently ridiculed the idea of the natural law as being medieval and antiquated.

[1] Nicholas Murray Butler, *The Path to Peace: Essays and Addresses on Peace and Its Making* (New York, 1930), pp. 49–50.

[2] *International Ethics* (New York, 1928), p. 4.

This has arisen from a failure to understand and appreciate the meaning and significance of the conception. The natural law, based on the ordinance of God and made known to us through natural reason, has obvious effects when applied to interstatal relations. It means that international relations cannot be anarchical according to the nature of things but rather that they must be controlled by a higher law—not the mere will of a sovereign, but the order of nature, to which sovereigns as well are subject.[3] Thus the relations of nations must be ruled not by sheer will but by a law enjoining justice. Unfortunately, this medieval tradition was sacrificed at the beginnings of modern times and was distorted at the hands of political writers of the seventeenth and eighteenth centuries, to the detriment of the proper development of international law.

The moral foundation for any international structure was not sufficiently stressed by many of the recent peace plans; and the needed moral basis for the 1919 League of Nations was not, perhaps, fully appreciated.[4] Not until we regard the state as a moral person and not until we place international relations on a moral basis shall we have permanent peace. That states, like individuals, are subject to moral precepts must be fully accepted,[5] not only in theory, but in the actual relations of nations with each other. International conduct must be ruled by ethical standards. If permanent peace is to be attained, men must turn to God for guidance and strength.

[3] J. L. Brierly, *The Law of Nations: An Introduction to the International Law of Peace* (Oxford, 1928), pp. 11–12.

[4] Lord Robert Cecil, in *The Moral Basis of the League of Nations* (London, 1923), holds that the League does have the proper moral basis.

[5] James Brown Scott, "A Single Standard of Morality for the Individual and the State," *Proceedings of the American Society of International Law at Its Twenty-sixth Annual Meeting Held at Washington, D.C., April 28–30, 1932*, pp. 10–36.

BIBLIOGRAPHY

BOOKS AND PAMPHLETS

ADAMS, HERBERT BAXTER. *Bluntschli's Life-Work.* Baltimore: privately printed, 1884.

ALEXANDER, WILLIAM MENZIES. *League of Nations in History.* ("Publications of the League of Nations Union," Ser. 2, No. 14.) London, 1918.

Appeals for Peace of Pope Benedict XV (August 1, 1917) and Pope Pius XI (December 24, 1930). Baltimore: Belvedere Press, 1931.

Appel-Programme, Statuts: Composition du conseil et du bureau. Paris: G. Cadet (Association française pour la Société des nations), 1918.

ASHBEE, C. R. *The American League To Enforce Peace: An English Interpretation.* With an Introduction by G. LOWES DICKINSON. London: Allen & Unwin, 1917.

ASQUITH, HERBERT H.; GREY, SIR EDWARD; *et al. The National Policy.* ("Publications of the Union of Democratic Control," No. 6.) London, n.d.

Attack upon Freedom of Speech, The: The Broken-up Meeting at the Memorial Hall, 29th November, 1915, an Elaborate Conspiracy and Its Origin; Full Text of the Speeches Which Were To Be Delivered. ("Publications of the Union of Democratic Control," No. 20b.) London, n.d.

Attack upon Freedom of Speech, The: Astounding Official Defense; House of Commons Sequel to the Broken-up Meeting at the Memorial Hall, November 29th, 1915. ("Publications of the Union of Democratic Control," No. 21b.) London, n.d.

AULARD, A. *La Paix future d'après la Révolution Française et Kant.* Paris: Librairie Armand Colin, 1915.

BALCH, THOMAS WILLING. *Éméric Crucé.* Philadelphia: Allen, Lane & Scott, 1900.

Basis of Permanent Peace, The: Outline Study of a League of Nations; the Background, Purpose and Problems of the Movement. New York: League To Enforce Peace, n.d.

BASSETT, JOHN SPENCER. *The Lost Fruits of Waterloo.* New York: Macmillan, 1918.

BEALES, A. C. F. *The History of Peace: A Short Account of the Organised Movements for International Peace.* New York: Dial Press, 1931.

195

BECKWITH, GEORGE C. *Eulogy on William Ladd, Late President of the American Peace Society.* Boston: Whipple & Damrell, 1841.

✕ BENTHAM, JEREMY. *Plan for an Universal and Perpetual Peace.* With an Introduction by C. JOHN COLOMBOS. ("Grotius Society Publications: Text for Students of International Relations," No. 6.) London: Sweet & Maxwell, 1927.

————. *The Works of Jeremy Bentham.* Published under the superintendence of his executor, JOHN BOWRING. 11 vols. Edinburgh: W. Tait, 1843.

BÉRARD, VICTOR. *De arbitrio inter liberas Graecorum civitates.* Lutetiae Parisiorum: Edebat E. Thorin, bibliopola, 1894.

Betrayal of the Peoples, The, Issued by the Executive Committee of the Union of Democratic Control (with Map Illustrating the Territorial Changes Involved in the Peace Treaty). ("Publications of the Union of Democratic Control," No. 37a.) London: St. Clements Press, n.d.

BLUNTSCHLI, J. C. *Gesammelte kleine Schriften: Aufsätze über Recht und Staat.* Nördlingen: C. H. Beck, 1879.

BOECKEL, FLORENCE BREWER. *Between War and Peace: A Handbook for Peace Workers.* New York: Macmillan, 1928.

BONNARD, LOUIS CARLE. *Essai sur la conception d'une société des nations avant le XXᵉ siècle.* Paris: Rousseau, 1921.

BOOTH, ARTHUR JOHN. *Saint-Simon and Saint-Simonism: A Chapter in the History of Socialism in France.* London: Longmans, Green; Reader & Dyer, 1871.

BOURNE, R. S. (ed.). *Towards an Enduring Peace: A Symposium of Peace Proposals and Programs, 1914–1916.* With an Introduction by FRANKLIN H. GIDDINGS. New York: American Association for International Conciliation, 1916.

BOYCE, MYRNA. *The Diplomatic Relations of England with the Quadruple Alliance, 1815–1830.* Iowa City: State University of Iowa, 1918.

BOYLE, HOMER L. *History of Peace, Compiled from Governmental Records, Official Reports, Treaties, Conventions, Peace Conferences and Arbitrations.* Grand Rapids, Mich.: History of Peace Pub. Co., 1902.

BRAILSFORD, HENRY N. *A League of Nations.* New York: Macmillan, 1917.

BRIERLY, J. L. *The Law of Nations: An Introduction to the International Law of Peace.* Oxford: Clarendon Press, 1928.

BRIOUT, EDGARD. *L'Idée de paix perpétuelle de Jérémie Bentham.* Paris: Edgard Briout, 1905.

BRYCE, VISCOUNT JAMES. *Essays and Addresses in War Time.* New York: Macmillan, 1918.

———. *The Holy Roman Empire.* New York: Macmillan, 1904.

———. *Proposals for the Avoidance of War (Private and Confidential, Not for Publication).* With a prefatory note by VISCOUNT BRYCE (as revised up to February 24, 1915). N.p., n.d.

BRYCE, JAMES, *et al. Proposals for the Prevention of Future Wars.* London: Allen & Unwin, 1918.

BUCHANAN, WILLIAM I. (report of). *The Central American Peace Conference, Held at Washington, D.C., 1907.* Washington, D.C.: U.S. Government Printing Office, 1908.

BUSTAMANTE, ANTONIO SANCHEZ, DE. *The World Court.* Translated by ELIZABETH F. READ. New York: Macmillan, 1926.

BUTLER, SIR GEOFFREY GILBERT. *Studies in Statecraft, Being Chapters, Biographical and Bibliographical, Mainly on the Sixteenth Century.* Cambridge, England: University Press, 1920.

BUTLER, NICHOLAS MURRAY. *The Path To Peace: Essays and Addresses on Peace and Its Making.* New York: Scribner's, 1930.

BUXTON, CHARLES RODEN. *Memorandum on Territorial Claims and Self-determination.* ("Publications of the Union of Democratic Control," No. 29a.) London, 1919.

CALDWELL, WALLACE E. *Hellenic Conceptions of Peace.* New York: Columbia University Press, 1919.

CALVO, CHARLES. *Le Droit international théorique et pratique: précédé d'un exposé historique des progrès de la science du droit des gens.* 4 vols. Paris: Guillaumin, 1880–81.

CECIL, LORD ROBERT. *The Moral Basis of the League of Nations.* London: Lindsey Press, 1923.

Central Organisation for a Durable Peace: Manifesto. The Hague: The Organisation, 1915.

CHAMBERLAIN, SIR AUSTEN. *The League of Nations.* Glasgow: Jackson Wylie, 1926.

CHEEVER, GEORGE BARRELL. *The True Christian Patriot: A Discourse on the Virtues and Public Services of the Late Judge Jay.* Delivered before the American Peace Society. Boston: American Peace Society, 1860.

CHOATE, JOSEPH HODGES. *The Two Hague Conferences.* With an Introduction by J. B. SCOTT. Princeton: Princeton University Press, 1913.

CHURCH, RICHARD WILLIAM. *Dante: An Essay. To Which Is Added a Translation of "De monarchia" by F. J. Church.* London: Macmillan, 1879.

CLARK, J. REUBEN. *Memorandum on the Monroe Doctrine.* ("Publications of the U.S. Department of State," No. 37.) Washington, D.C.: U.S. Government Printing Office, 1930.

CLIFFORD, JOHN. *The League of Free Nations: Facing the Facts.* ("Publications of the League of Nations Union," Ser. 2, No. 18.) London, 1918.

COBBAN, ALFRED BERT CARTER. *Rousseau and the Modern State.* London: Allen & Unwin, 1934.

Conférence internationale de la paix, La Haye 18 Mai–29 Juillet 1899. La Haye: Imprimerie nationale, 1899.

Constitution of the League, The. ("Publications of the League of Nations Union," No. 77.) London, 1918.

Contributions by Various Writers on the Project of a League of Nations. London: League of Nations Society, n.d.

COULTON, G. G. *The Main Illusions of Pacificism: A Criticism of Mr. Norman Angell and of the Union of Democratic Control.* Cambridge, England: Bowes & Bowes, 1916.

CREIGHTON, MANDELL. *A History of the Papacy during the Period of the Reformation.* 5 vols. London: Longmans, Green, 1882.

CRESSON, WILLIAM PENN. *The Holy Alliance, the European Background of the Monroe Doctrine.* ("Publications of the Carnegie Endowment for International Peace, Division of International Law.") New York: Oxford University Press, 1922.

CROSBY, OSCAR. *International War: Its Causes and Its Cure.* London: Macmillan & Co., Ltd., 1919.

CROZIER, ALFRED OWEN. *Nation of Nations: The Way to Permanent Peace.* Cincinnati: Stewart & Kidd, 1915.

CRUCÉ, ÉMÉRIC. *The New Cyneas of Éméric Crucé.* Edited with an Introduction and translated into English from the original French text of 1623 by THOMAS WILLING BALCH. Philadelphia: Allen, Lane & Scott, 1909.

———. *"Le Nouveau Cynée" ou discours d'estat représentant les occasions et moyens d'establir une paix générale et la liberté du commerce par tout le monde. Aux monarques et princes souverains de ce temps.* Paris: Chez Jacques Villery, 1623.

CURTI, MERLE EUGENE. *The American Peace Crusade, 1815–1860.* Durham, N.C.: Duke University Press, 1929.

DANTE ALIGHIERI. *The "De monarchia" of Dante Alighieri.* Edited with translation and notes by AURELIA HENRY. Boston and New York: Houghton Mifflin, 1904.

DARBY, WILLIAM EVANS. *International Tribunals.* London: Peace Society, 1899, 1900.

DAVIES, BARON DAVID. *The Problem of the Twentieth Century: A Study in International Relationships.* London: Ernest Benn, 1930.

———. *Some Problems of International Reconstruction and a League of Nations.* ("Publications of the League of Nations Union," Ser. 2, No. 23.) London, 1918.

DAVIS, H. W. C. (ed.). *Essays in History Presented to Reginald Lane Poole.* Oxford: Clarendon Press, 1927.

DEROCQUE, GILBERTE. *Le Projet de paix perpétuelle de l'Abbé de Saint-Pierre comparé au pacte de la Société des nations.* Paris: Rousseau, 1929.

DICKINSON, G. LOWES. *The Choice before Us.* New York: Dodd, Mead, 1917.

———. *The International Anarchy, 1904–1914.* New York: Century, 1926.

DICKINSON, W. H. *A League of Nations and Its Critics.* ("Publications of the League of Nations Society," No. 14.) London, 1917.

Documents Relating to the Program of the First Hague Peace Conference Laid before the Conference by the Netherland Government. Translation. ("Pamphlet Series of the Carnegie Endowment for International Peace, Division of International Law," No. 36.) Oxford: Clarendon Press, 1921.

Documents respecting the Limitation of Armaments, Laid before the First Hague Peace Conference of 1899 by the Government of the Netherlands. ("Division of International Law," Pamphlet No. 22.) Washington, D.C.: Carnegie Endowment for International Peace, 1916.

DREYFUS, FERDINAND: *L'Arbitrage international. Avec une préface de Frédéric Passy.* Paris: Ancienne maison Michel Lévy frères, 1892.

DUBOIS, PIERRE. *De recuperatione Terre Sancte: traité de politique générale, pub. d'après le manuscrit du Vatican par Charles V. Langlois.* Paris: A. Picard, 1891.

DUGGAN, STEPHEN PIERCE (ed.). *The League of Nations: The Principle and the Practice.* Boston: Atlantic Monthly Press, 1919.

DUVAL, FRÉDÉRIC. *De la paix de Dieu à la paix de fer.* Paris: Librairie Paillard, 1923.

EMERTON, EPHRAIM. *The "Defensor pacis" of Marsiglio of Padua: A Critical Study.* Cambridge, Mass.: Harvard University Press, 1920.

Enforced Peace: Proceedings of the First Annual National Assemblage of the League To Enforce Peace, Washington, May 26–27, 1916. New York: League To Enforce Peace, 1916.

EPPSTEIN, JOHN. *The Catholic Tradition of the Law of Nations*. Washington, D.C.: Catholic Association for International Peace (published for the Carnegie Endowment for International Peace), 1935.

——— (comp.). *Ten Years' Life of the League of Nations: A History of the Origins of the League and of Its Development from A.D. 1919 to 1929*. With an Introduction by VISCOUNT CECIL OF CHELWOOD and an Epilogue by GILBERT MURRAY. London: May Fair Press, 1929.

ERASMUS, DESIDERIUS. *The Complaint of Peace, to Which Is Added "Antipolemus" or "The Plea of Reason, Religion, and Humanity, against War."* Boston: Charles Williams, 1813.

———. *The Complaint of Peace: With a Digression on the Folly of Kings in Unlimited Monarchies*. Translated by VICESIMUS KNOX. London, 1795.

———. *Institutio principis Christiani*, chaps. iii–xi. Translated with an Introduction by PERCY ELLWOOD CORBETT. ("Grotius Society Publications: Texts for Students of International Relations," No. 1.) London: Sweet & Maxwell, 1921.

ERZBERGER, M. *The League of Nations: The Way to the World's Peace*. Translated by BERNARD MIALL. New York: Henry Holt, 1919.

FAY, SIDNEY BRADSHAW. *The Origins of the World War*. 2 vols. New York: Macmillan, 1930.

FAYLE, ERNEST C. *The Fourteenth Point: A Study of the League of Nations*. New York: Henry Holt, 1919.

FINCH, GEORGE A. *The Sources of Modern International Law*. ("Division of International Law, Monograph Series," No. 1.) Washington, D.C.: Carnegie Endowment for International Peace, 1937.

First Perpetual League, The, between the Swiss Cantons of Uri, Schwyz, and Unterwalden. ("Publications of the League of Nations Society," No. 3.) London, 1917.

Français, Les, à la recherche d'une société des nations depuis le roi Henri IV jusqu'aux combattants de 1914. Paris: Bureau de la "Civilisation française," 1920.

FREEMAN, EDWARD AUGUSTUS. *History of Federal Government in Greece and Italy*. London: Macmillan & Co., Ltd., 1893.

FRESCHOT, CASIMIR. *Compleat History of the Treaty of Utrecht . . . . , The*. 2 vols. London: Roper & Butler, 1715.

FREY, SIEGFRIED. *Das öffentlich-rechtliche Schiedsgericht in Oberitalien im XII. und XIII. Jahrhundert*. Luzern: Verlag Eugen Haag, 1928.

FRY, A. RUTH. *John Bellers, 1654–1725, Quaker, Economist and Social Reformer*. His writings reprinted with a memoir by A. RUTH FRY. London: Cassell, 1935.

GARGAZ, PIERRE-ANDRÉ. *A Project of Universal and Perpetual Peace.* Printed by BENJAMIN FRANKLIN at Passy in the year 1782; reprinted with an English version, Introduction, and typographical note by GEORGE SIMPSON EDDY. New York: George Simpson Eddy, 1922.

General Smuts and a League of Nations: Includes Also Speeches by Lord Bryce, the Archbishop of Canterbury, Lord Buckmaster, Lord Hugh Cecil, and Others, Report of Meeting Held at the Central Hall, Westminster, May 14, 1917. ("Publications of the League of Nations Society," No. 11.) London, 1917.

GENTILI, ALBERICO. *'De iure belli" libri tres.* 2 vols. ("The Classics of International Law," No. 16.) (The Carnegie Endowment for International Peace, Division of International Law.) Oxford: Clarendon Press; London: H. Milford, 1933.

GOLDSMITH, ROBERT. *A League To Enforce Peace.* With an Introduction by A. LAWRENCE LOWELL. New York: Macmillan, 1917.

GRADY, ELEANOR HUNSDON. *Epigraphic Sources of the Delphic Amphictyony.* Walton, N.Y.: Reporter Co., 1931.

GRANT, ARTHUR JAMES. *The Holy Alliance and the League of Nations.* With a Foreword by LORD ROBERT CECIL. ("Publications of the League of Nations Union," No. 112. London, 1923.

GREY, VISCOUNT, et al. *The League of Nations.* London: Oxford University Press, 1918, 1919.

GROTIUS, HUGO. *Hugonis Grotii " De iure belli ac pacis" libri tres.* Amsterdami: apud G. Blaevw, 1631.

———. *Hugonis Grotii " De iure belli ac pacis" libri tres.* Amsterdami: apud G. Blaev, 1632.

———. *Hugonis Grotii " De jure belli ac pacis."* The translation of Book I by FRANCIS W. KELSEY with the collaboration of A. E. R. BOAK et al., with an Introduction by JAMES BROWN SCOTT. Oxford, England: Clarendon Press, 1925.

———. *Hugonis Grotii " De jure belli ac pacis," libri tres.* Translated with an Introduction by W. S. M. KNIGHT. ("Grotius Society Publications: Texts for Students of International Relations," No. 3.) London: Sweet & Maxwell, 1922, 1925.

———. *Hugonis Grotii " De jure belli et pacis."* 3 vols. Translated by WILLIAM WHEWELL. Cambridge, England: University Press, 1853.

———. *The Rights of War and Peace, Including the Law of Nature and of Nations.* Translated by A. C. CAMPBELL. New York: M. W. Dunne, 1903.

Handbook for Speakers on a League of Nations, Compiled by the League of Nations Society for the Use of Students and Speakers. London: Allen & Unwin, 1918.

HARLEY, JOHN EUGENE. *The League of Nations and the New International Law.* New York: Oxford University Press, 1921.

HARRIS, H. WILSON. *What the League of Nations Is.* London: Allen & Unwin, 1925.

HEARNSHAW, F. J. C. (ed.). *The Social and Political Ideas of Some Great French Thinkers of the Age of Reason.* London: George G. Harrap, 1930.

——— (ed.). *The Social and Political Ideas of Some Great Medieval Thinkers.* London: George G. Harrap, 1923.

——— (ed.). *The Social and Political Ideas of Some Great Thinkers of the Renaissance and Reformation.* London: George G. Harrap, 1925.

——— (ed.). *The Social and Political Ideas of Some Great Thinkers of the Sixteenth and Seventeenth Centuries.* London: George G. Harrap, 1926.

HEMMENWAY, JOHN. *The Apostle of Peace: Memoir of William Ladd.* With an Introduction by ELIHU BURRITT. Boston: American Peace Society, 1872.

HERSHEY, AMOS S. *The Essentials of International Public Law and Organization.* New York: Macmillan, 1929.

HICKS, FREDERICK CHARLES. *The New World Order.* New York: Doubleday Page, 1920.

HIGGINS, A. PEARCE. *The Hague Peace Conferences and Other International Conferences concerning the Laws and Usages of War: Texts of Conventions with Commentaries.* Cambridge, England: University Press, 1909.

HILL, DAVID JAYNE. *The Second Hague Peace Conference.* (60th Cong., 1st sess., Senate Doc. No. 433.) Washington, D.C.: U.S. Government Printing Office, 1908.

HOBSON, J. A. *The New Holy Alliance: U.D.C. Memoranda on a Democratic Peace.* ("Publications of the Union of Democratic Control," No. 34a.) London: St. Clements Press, 1919.

———. *Towards International Government.* New York: Macmillan, 1915.

HODÉ, JACQUES. *L'Idée de fédération internationale dans l'histoire: les précurseurs de la société des nations.* Paris: Editions de la vie universitaire, 1921.

HUDSON, MANLEY O. *The World Court, 1921-1938.* Boston: World Peace Foundation, 1938.

HUGHAN, JESSIE WALLACE. *A Study of International Government.* New York: Thomas Y. Crowell, 1923.

HYDE, H. E. *The International Solution.* London: Allen & Unwin, 1918.

Independence Hall Conference Held in the City of Philadelphia, Bunker Hill Day (June 17th), 1915, Together with the Speeches Made at a Public Banquet in the Bellevue-Stratford Hotel on the Preceding Evening. New York: League To Enforce Peace, 1915.

International Ethics. New York: Paulist Press, 1928.

JAY, WILLIAM. *An Address Delivered before the American Peace Society at Its Annual Meeting, May 26, 1845.* Boston: American Peace Society, 1845.

———. *War and Peace: The Evils of the First and a Plan for Preserving the Last.* New York: Wiley & Putnam, 1842.

———. *War and Peace: The Evils of the First and a Plan for Preserving the Last.* Introductory note by JAMES BROWN SCOTT. New York: Oxford University Press, 1919. (Publications of the Carnegie Endowment for International Peace. Division of International Law.)

JESSUP, PHILIP C. *The United States and Treaties for the Avoidance of War.* ("International Conciliation," No. 239.) New York: Carnegie Endowment for International Peace, Division of Intercourse and Education, 1928.

JONES, SIR HENRY. *Form the League of Peace Now: An Appeal to My Fellow-Citizens.* ("Publications of the League of Nations Union," Ser. 2, No. 5.) London, 1918.

JONES, ROBERT, and SHERMAN, S. S. *The League of Nations from Idea to Reality.* London: Sir Isaac Pitman & Sons, 1927.

KALLEN, HORACE MEYER. *The League of Nations—Today and Tomorrow: A Discussion of International Organization Present and To Come.* Boston: Marshall Jones, 1919.

KÄMPF, HELLMUT. *Pierre Dubois und die geistigen Grundlagen des französischen Nationalbewusstseins um 1300.* Leipzig und Berlin: B. G. Teubner, 1935.

KAMAROWSKY, COMTE L. *Le Tribunal international.* Traduit par SERGE DE WESTMAN; introduction par JULES LACOINTA. Paris: G. Pedone-Lauriel, 1887.

KANT, IMMANUEL. *Eternal Peace and Other International Essays.* Translated by W. HASTIE. Edinburgh: T. and T. Clark, 1891; Boston: World Peace Foundation, 1914.

———. *Perpetual Peace.* Translated by BENJAMIN F. TRUEBLOOD. Boston: American Peace Society, 1897.

———. *Perpetual Peace.* Translated with an Introduction by M. CAMPBELL SMITH. New York: Macmillan; London: Allen & Unwin, 1903, 1915.

204   PLANS FOR WORLD PEACE

KANT, IMMANUEL. *Perpetual Peace.* With an Introduction by NICHOLAS MURRAY BUTLER. New York: Columbia University Press, 1939.

———. *Perpetual Peace: A Philosophical Proposal.* Translated by HELEN O'BRIEN with an Introduction by JESSIE H. BUCKLAND. ("Grotius Society Publications: Texts for Students of International Relations," No. 7.) London: Sweet & Maxwell, 1927.

———. *Project for a Perpetual Peace: A Philosophical Essay, by Emanuel Kant.* . . . . Translated from the German. London: Vernor & Hood, 1796.

———. *Projet de paix perpétuelle: essai philosophique par Emanuel Kant.* Traduit de l'allemand avec un nouveau supplément de l'auteur. Königsberg: Chez F. Nicolovius, 1796.

X   ———. *Zum ewigen Frieden: Ein philosophischer Entwurf von Immanuel Kant.* Königsberg: F. Nicolovius, 1795.

———. *Zum ewigen Frieden.* Mit Ergänzungen aus Kants übrigen Schriften und einer ausführlichen Einleitung über die Entwicklung des Friedensgedankens herausgegeben von KARL VORLÄNDER. Leipzig: Verlag von Felix Meiner, 1914.

———. *Zum ewigen Frieden: Ein philosophischer Entwurf von Immanuel Kant. Text der Ausgabe A (1795) unter Berücksichtigung des Manuscriptes, der Ausgaben A a (1795) und B (1796).* Hrsg. von KARL KEHRBACH. Leipzig: P. Reclam jun., 1905.

KAPRAS, JOHN. *The Peace League of George Poděbrad, King of Bohemia.* Vol. II, Part V. Prague: Czecho-Slovak Foreigners' Office, 1919.

KEEN, FRANK NOEL. *Hammering Out the Details.* London: A. C. Fifield, 1917.

———. *The World in Alliance: A Plan for Preventing Future Wars.* London: Walter Southwood, 1915.

KLUYVER, C. A. (comp.). *Documents on the League of Nations.* Leiden: A. W. Sijthoff, 1920.

KNIGHT, W. S. M. *The Life and Works of Hugo Grotius.* ("Grotius Society Publications," No. 4.) London: Sweet & Maxwell, 1925.

LADD, WILLIAM. *Address Delivered at the Tenth Anniversary of the Massachusetts Peace Society, December 25, 1825.* Boston: Isaac R. Butts, 1826.

——— (PHILANTHROPOS [pseud.]). *A Brief Illustration of the Principles of War and Peace.* Albany: Packard & Van Benthuysen, 1831.

——— (PHILANTHROPOS [pseud.]). *A Dissertation on a Congress of Nations.* N.p.: Press of James Loring, 1832.

————. *An Essay on a Congress of Nations, for the Adjustment of International Disputes without Resort to Arms.* London: T. Ward & Co., 1840.

————. *An Essay on a Congress of Nations for the Adjustment of International Disputes without Resort to Arms.* With an Introduction by JAMES BROWN SCOTT. New York: Oxford University Press, 1916. (Carnegie Endowment for International Peace. Division of International Law.)

————. *An Essay on a Congress of Nations, for the Adjustment of International Disputes without Resort to Arms, Together with a Sixth Essay Comprising the Substance of the Rejected Essays.* Boston: Whipple & Damrell, 1840.

———— (PHILANTHROPOS [pseud.]). *A Solemn Appeal to Christians of All Denominations in Favor of the Cause of Permanent and Universal Peace.* New York: American Peace Society, 1834.

LA FONTAINE, HENRI. *The Great Solution: Magnissima charta.* Boston: World Peace Foundation, 1916.

LANGDON-DAVIES, B. N. *The A.B.C. of U.D.C.* London: Union of Democratic Control, n.d.

LANGE, C. L. *Exposé des travaux de l'organisation.* The Hague: Central Organization for a Durable Peace, 1917.

————. *Histoire de l'internationalisme.* ("Publications de l'Institut Nobel norvégien," Tome IV.) Kristiania: H. Aschehoug; New York: G. P. Putnam's Sons, 1919.

LAS CASES, COMTE EMMANUEL. *Journal de la vie privée et des conversations de l'Empéreur Napoléon à Sainte Hélène.* 8 vols. London, 1823.

LAURENT, F. *Histoire du droit des gens.* 2 vols. Brussels: Meline Cans et Cie, 1861.

LAWRENCE, F. W. PETHICK. *Making Germany Pay: U.D.C. Memoranda on a Democratic Peace.* ("Publications of the Union of Democratic Control," No. 30a.) London, 1919.

LAWRENCE, T. J. *The Society of Nations: Its Past, Present, and Possible Future.* New York: Oxford University Press, 1919.

League Bulletin, The. New York: Issued weekly by the League To Enforce Peace, No. 48 (August 17, 1917), No. 52 (September 14, 1917), No. 116 (December 7, 1918), No. 115 (November 30, 1918).

League of Free Nations Association: Statement of Principles. New York: League of Free Nations Association, 1918.

League of Nations, A. ("International Conciliation," No. 134.) New York: American Association for International Conciliation, 1919.

League of Nations: Comparison of the Plan for the League of Nations Showing the Original Draft as Presented to the Commission Constituted by the Preliminary

206PLANS FOR WORLD PEACE

Peace Conference in Session at Versailles, France, Together with the Covenant as Finally Reported and Adopted at the Plenary Session of the Peace Conference, Also the Presentation Speeches of the President of the United States Relating Thereto. Washington, D.C.: U.S. Government Printing Office, 1919.

League of Nations, The: "The Final Triumph of Justice and Fair Dealing," Speech by President Wilson, New York, Sept. 27, 1918. ("Publications of the League of Nations Society," No. 43.) London, 1918.

League of Nations: Scheme of Organisation Prepared by a Sub Committee of the League of Nations Society. With a Foreword by the RT. HON. SIR W. H DICKINSON. ("Publications of the League of Nations Society," No. 42.) London, 1918.

League of Nations Society, The. ("Publications of the League of Nations Society," No. 2.) London, 1917.

League of Nations Union, The. ("Publications of the League of Nations Union," Ser. 2, No. 10.) London, 1918.

League To Enforce Peace. Foreword by W. R. BOYD, JR. New York: League To Enforce Peace, n.d.

LEVERMORE, CHARLES H. (prepared by). *Plans for International Organization: Sixteen of the Best Known Proposals since 1603: An Outline.* Washington, D.C.: American Peace Society, 1917.

LODER, B. C. J. (presented by). *Institutions judiciaires et de conciliation: rapport.* The Hague: Central Organization for a Durable Peace, 1917.

LORIMER, JAMES. *The Institutes of the Law of Nations: A Treatise of the Jural Relations of Separate Political Communities.* 2 vols. Edinburgh and London: William Blackwood & Sons, 1884.

LOUIS-LUCAS, PIERRE. *Un Plan de paix générale et de liberté du commerce au XVIIe siècle: "Le nouveau Cynée" d'Éméric Crucé (1623).* Paris: L. Tenin, 1919.

LYSEN, A. *Hugo Grotius, Essays on His Life and Works, Selected for the Occasion of the Tercentenary of His "De iure belli ac pacis," 1625–1925.* With a Preface by JACOB TER MEULEN. Leyden: A. W. Sythoff's Pub. Co., 1925.

McCURDY, G. A. *The League of Free Nations.* ("Publications of the League of Nations Union," Ser. 2, No. 3.) London, 1918.

MACDONNELL, SIR JOHN, and MANSON, EDWARD (eds.). *Great Jurists of the World.* With an Introduction by VAN VECHTEN VEEDER. Boston: Little, Brown & Co., 1914.

McKENNA, C. H. *Francis de Vitoria, Founder of International Law.* ("Publications of the Catholic Association for International Peace," No. 5.) New York: Paulist Press, 1930.

MARBURG, THEODORE. *Development of the League of Nations Idea: Documents and Correspondence of Theodore Marburg*, edited by JOHN H. LATANÉ. 2 vols. New York: Macmillan, 1932.

——. *League of Nations: A Chapter in the History of the Movement.* New York: Macmillan, 1917.

——. *League of Nations: Its Principles Examined.* New York: Macmillan, 1918.

—— (description and comment by). *Draft Convention for League of Nations by Group of American Jurists and Publicists.* New York: Macmillan, 1918.

MARBURG, THEODORE, and FLACK, HORACE E. (eds.). *Taft Papers on League of Nations.* New York: Macmillan, 1920.

MARRIOTT, J. A. R. *Commonwealth or Anarchy? A Survey of Projects of Peace from the Sixteenth to the Twentieth Century.* London: P. Allan, 1937.

——. *The European Commonwealth.* Oxford: Clarendon Press, 1918.

MARSILIUS OF PADUA. *Defensor pacis, herausgegeben von Richard Scholz.* Hannover: Hahnsche Buchhandlung, 1932-33.

——. *The "Defensor pacis" of Marsilius of Padua.* Edited by C. W. PREVITÉ-ORTON. Cambridge, England: University Press, 1928.

——. *Marsilius von Padua" Defensor pacis": Erstes Buch nach dem Erstdruck für Seminarübungen, hrsg. von Alexander Cartellieri.* Leipzig: Dyk, 1913.

MARVIN, F. S. (ed.). *The Evolution of World-Peace.* London: Oxford University Press, 1921.

MATHIEU, MARIE. *L'Evolution de l'idée de la société des nations.* Nancy: Imprimerie Lorraine, Rigot, 1923.

MATTHEWS, MARY ALICE (comp.). *Peace Projects: Select List of References on Plans for the Preservation of Peace from Medieval Times to the Present Day.* (Carnegie Endowment for International Peace, Reading List No. 36.) Washington, D.C., 1936.

MEAD, EDWIN D. *Organize the World.* Boston: International School of Peace, n.d.

MÉRIGNHAC, A. *Traité théorique et pratique de l'arbitrage international.* Paris: Larose, 1895.

MEULEN, JACOB TER. *Der Gedanke der internationalen Organisation in seiner Entwicklung*, Vol. I: *1300-1800;* Vol. II: *1789-1889.* The Hague: Martinus Nijhoff, 1917 (Vol. I); 1929 (Vol. II).

MILLER, DAVID HUNTER. *The Drafting of the Covenant.* With an Introduction by NICHOLAS MURRAY BUTLER. 2 vols. New York: G. P. Putnam's Sons, 1928.

208   PLANS FOR WORLD PEACE

MINOR, RALEIGH C. *A Republic of Nations: A Study of the Organization of a Federal League of Nations.* New York: Oxford University Press, 1918.

MOLINARI, GUSTAVE DE. *L'Abbé de Saint-Pierre, membre exclu de l'Académie française: sa vie et ses œuvres, précédés d'une appréciation et d'un précis historique de l'idée de la paix perpétuelle suivies du jugement de Rousseau sur le projet de paix perpétuelle et la polysynodie ainsi que du projet attribué à Henri IV, et du plan d'Emmanuel Kant pour rendre la paix universelle etc. etc., avec des notes et des éclaircissements par M. G. de Molinari.* Paris: Guillaumin et Cⁱᵉ, 1857.

———. *The Society of Tomorrow: A Forecast of Its Political and Economic Organisation.* Translated by P. H. LEE WARNER with an Introduction by HODGSON PRATT and a letter to the publishers from FRÉDÉRIC PASSY, with an Appendix containing tables on the cost of war and of preparation for war, from 1898 to 1904, compiled by EDWARD ATKINSON. New York: G. P. Putnam's Sons; London: T. Fisher Unwin, 1904.

MONTGELAS, MAXIMILIAN. *Beiträge zur Völkerbundfrage.* Leipzig: Der neue Geist Verlag, 1919.

MOORE, JOHN BASSETT. *History and Digest of the International Arbitration to Which the United States Has Been a Party.* 6 vols. (53d Cong., 2d sess., H.R. Mis. Doc. No. 212.) Washington, D.C.: U.S. Government Printing Office, 1898.

———. *The Peace Problem: Address on the Peace Problem, Delivered at the Twentieth Celebration of Founders' Day, Held at Carnegie Institute, in Pittsburgh, Pa., on April 27, 1916.* (64th Cong., 2d sess., Sen. Doc. No. 700.) Washington, D.C.: U.S. Government Printing Office, 1917.

MOREL, E. D. *The Fruits of Victory: Have Our Statesmen Won the Peace Our Soldiers Fought For?* ("Publications of the Union of Democratic Control," No. 39a.) London, 1919.

———. *The Union of Democratic Control.* ("Publications of the Union of Democratic Control," No. 13.) London: Contemporary Review Co., n.d.

MORLEY, JOHN. *Rousseau.* New York: Scribner & Welford, 1878.

MORROW, DWIGHT WHITNEY. *The Society of Free States.* New York: Harper & Bros., 1919.

Morrow of the War, The. ("Publications of the Union of Democratic Control," No. 1.) London, n.d.

MÜLLER, JOSEPH. *Das Friedenswerk der Kirche in den letzten drei jahrhunderten (1598–1917).* Berlin: Deutsche Verlagsgesellschaft für Politik und Geschichte m.b.H., 1927.

MUIR, RAMSAY. *Nationalism and Internationalism*. London: Constable, 1916.

MUNCH, P. (director). *Les Origines et l'œuvre de la société des nations*. 2 vols. Copenhagen: Gyldendalske Boghandel-Nordisk Forlag, 1923.

MURRAY, GILBERT. *The League of Nations and the Democratic Idea*. New York: Oxford University Press, 1918.

Nations Unite! Speeches on a League of Nations. ("Publications of the League of Nations Society," No. 23.) London, 1918.

NOVACOVITCH, MILETA. *Les Compromis et les arbitrages internationaux du XIIe au XVe siècle*. Paris: Pedone, 1905.

NYS, ERNEST. *Le Droit des gens et les anciens jurisconsultes espagnols*. La Haye: Martinus Nijhoff, 1914.

———. *Etudes de droit international et de droit politique*. 2 vols. Brussels: A. Castaigne, 1896–1901.

OPPENHEIM, LASSA. *The League of Nations and Its Problems: Three Lectures*. London: Longmans Green, 1919.

PAISH, GEORGE. *A Permanent League of Nations*. London: T. Fisher Unwin, 1918.

Paix durable, Une: commentaire officiel du Programme-Minimum. La Haye: Organisation centrale pour une paix durable, n.d.

PAJOT, HUBERT. *Un Rêveur de paix sous Louis XIII: Éméric Crucé, Parisien*. Paris: Les Presses universitaires de France, 1924.

PAULSEN, FRIEDRICH. *Immanuel Kant: His Life and Doctrine*. Translated from the revised German edition by J. E. CREIGHTON and ALBERT LEFEVRE. New York: Charles Scribner's Sons, 1902.

PEASE, EDWARD R. *The History of the Fabian Society*. New York: International Publishers, 1926.

PENN, WILLIAM. *An Essay towards the Present and Future Peace of Europe*. Washington, D.C.: American Peace Society, 1912.

———. *An Essay towards the Present and Future Peace of Europe*. Gloucester: J. Bellows, 1914.

———. *The Peace of Europe: the Fruits of Solitude and Other Writings by William Penn*. With an Introduction by JOSEPH BESSE. ("Everyman's Library," No. 724.) New York: E. P. Dutton & Co., n.d.

———. *William Penn's Plan for the Peace of Europe*. ("Old South Leaflets," No. 75.) Boston: Directors of the Old South Work, 1896.

PHELPS, EDITH M. (comp.). *A League of Nations*. New York: H. W. Wilson, 1919.

210   PLANS FOR WORLD PEACE

PHILLIMORE, BARON WALTER G. F., *Schemes for Maintaining General Peace.* ("[Great Britain] Foreign Office Handbooks . . . ," No. 160) ("Peace Handbooks," Vol. XXV, [No. 3].) London: H. M. Stationery Office, 1920.

PHILLIPS, WALTER ALISON. *The Confederation of Europe: A Study of the European Alliance, 1813–1823, as an Experiment in the International Organization of Peace.* London and New York: Longmans Green, 1914, 1920.

PHILLIPSON, COLEMAN. *The International Law and Custom of Ancient Greece and Rome.* 2 vols. London: Macmillan & Co., 1911.

POLLARD, A. F. *The League of Nations in History.* London: Oxford University Press, 1918.

POLLOCK, SIR FREDERICK. *The League of Nations and the Coming Rule of Law.* London: Oxford University Press, 1918.

PONSONBY, ARTHUR. *The Control of Foreign Policy.* ("Publications of the Union of Democratic Control," No. 5a.) London, 1918.

———. *The Covenant of the League of Nations: An Analysis with Full Text.* ("Publications of the Union of Democratic Control," No. 41a.) Letchworth, England: Garden City Press, 1920.

———. *Parliament and Foreign Policy.* ("Publications of the Union of Democratic Control," No. 5.) London, n.d.

POWICKE, FREDERICK MAURICE. "Pierre Dubois: A Medieval Radical," *Owens College Historical Essays* (London, 1902).

Prize Essays on a Congress of Nations, for the Adjustment of International Disputes, and for the Promotion of Universal Peace without Resort to Arms, Together with a Sixth Essay Comprising the Substance of the Rejected Essays. Boston: Whipple & Damrell, 1840.

Problems of a League of Nations, The. ("Publications of the League of Nations Union," Ser. 1, No. 1.) London, 1918.

Problems of the International Settlement. London: Allen & Unwin, 1918.

Proceedings of the First Annual Meeting Held at the Caxton Hall, July 20th, 1917. ("Publications of the League of Nations Society," No. 16.) London, 1917.

Project Relative to a Court of Arbitral Justice, The: Draft Convention and Report Adopted by the Second Hague Peace Conference of 1907. With an introductory note by JAMES BROWN SCOTT, technical delegate of the United States. ("Pamphlet Series of the Carnegie Endowment for International Peace, Division of International Law," No. 34.) Washington, D.C.: The Endowment, 1920.

Pronouncements of Leading Statesmen. ("Publications of the League of Nations Society," No. 12.) London, 1917.

Pronouncements on a League of Nations. ("Publications of the League of Nations Society," No. 24.) London, 1918.

RAEDER, ANTON H. *L'Arbitrage international chez les Hellènes.* New York: G. P. Putnam's Sons, 1912.

RALSTON, JACKSON HARVEY. *International Arbitration from Athens to Locarno.* Stanford, Calif.: University Press, 1929.

Recueil de rapports sur les différents points du Programme-Minimum, Vols. I–IV. La Haye: Martinus Nijhoff, 1916 (Vols. I, II); 1917 (Vol. III); 1918 (Vol. IV).

REICHEL, HARRY R. *Why a League of Free Nations?* ("Publications of the League of Nations Union," Ser. 2, No. 21.) London, 1918.

Report of the Executive Committee, League To Enforce Peace, to the National Committee and League Members at the Biennial Meeting in Connection with the "Win the War for Permanent Peace" Convention, Philadelphia, May 15–17, 1918. N.p., n.d.

REVON, MICHEL. *L'Arbitrage international.* Paris: Rousseau, 1892.

Rex v. E. D. Morel, Being a Verbatim [sic] Report of the Court Proceedings at Bow Street, on Sept. 1 and 4, 1917 before Mr. E. W. Garrett. ("Publications of the Union of Democratic Control," No. 24a.) London, n.d.

ROEMER, WILLIAM F., and ELLIS, JOHN TRACY. *The Catholic Church and Peace Efforts.* ("Studies Presented to the Catholic Association for International Peace by the History Committee," No. 14.) New York: Paulist Press, 1934.

ROUARD DE CARD, M. E. *L'Arbitrage international dans le passé, le présent et l'avenir.* Paris: A. Durand et Pedone-Lauriel, 1877.

ROUSSEAU, JEAN JACQUES. *"L'Etat de guerre" and "Projet de paix perpétuelle."* With Introduction and notes by SHIRLEY G. PATTERSON and Foreword by GEORGE HAVEN PUTNAM. New York: G. P. Putnam's Sons, 1920.

———. *Extrait du projet de paix perpétuelle de Monsieur l'abbé de Saint-Pierre.* [N.p.], par J. J. Rousseau, 1761.

———. *A Lasting Peace through the Federation of Europe and the State of War.* Translated by C. E. VAUGHAN. London: Constable, 1917.

———. *A Project for Perpetual Peace.* Translated from the French with a Preface by the translator. London: Printed for M. Cooper, 1761.

———. *"A Project of Perpetual Peace," Rousseau's Essay.* Translated by EDITH M. NUTTALL and printed in French and English, with an Introduction by G. LOWES DICKINSON. London: R. Cobden-Sanderson 1927.

Rousseau, Jean Jacques. *A Treatise on the Social Compact, or the Principles of Political Law: A Project for a Perpetual Peace.* London: D. I. Eaton, 1795.

Saint-Pierre, Charles Irénée Castel, Abbé de. *Mémoires pour rendre la paix perpétuelle en Europe.* Cologne: Chez Jaques le Pacifique, 1712.

————. *Projet pour rendre la paix perpétuelle en Europe.* 2 vols. Utrecht: Chez Antoine Schouten, marchand libraire, 1713.

————. *A Project for Settling an Everlasting Peace in Europe, First Proposed by Henry IV of France, and Approved of by Queen Elizabeth, and Most of the Then Princes of Europe, and Now Discussed at Large, and Made Practicable.* London, 1714.

————. *Projet de traité pour rendre la paix perpétuelle entre les souverains chrétiens.* Utrecht: Antoine Schouten, 1717. (Vol. III of his *Projet pour rendre la paix perpétuelle en Europe.*)

————. *Selections from the Second Edition of the " Abrégé du projet de paix perpétuelle." By C. I. Castel de Saint-Pierre. ... 1738.* Translated by H. Hale Bellot, with an Introduction by Paul Collinet. ("Grotius Society Publications: Texts for Students of International Relations," No. 5.) London: Sweet & Maxwell, 1927.

————. *Der Traktat vom ewigen Frieden, 1713, herausgegeben und mit einer einleitung versehen von Wolfgang Michael.* Berlin, Hobbing, 1922.

Saint-Simon, Comte Claude Henri. *L'Œuvre d'Henri de Saint-Simon.* Textes choisis avec une introduction par C. Bouglé; notice bibliographique de Alfred Péreire. Paris: Librairie Félix Alcan, 1925.

————. *De la réorganisation de la société européenne ou de la nécessité et des moyens de rassembler les peuples de l'Europe en un seul corps politique en conservant à chacun son indépendance nationale, par A. Thierry, son élève (Octobre 1814),* publié avec une introduction et des notes par Alfred Péreire. Paris: Les Presses françaises, 1925.

Scheme for the World League, A: Speech Delivered by the Late Lord Parker in the House of Lords on March 19, 1918. ("Publications of the League of Nations Union," Ser. 2, No. 16.) London, 1918.

Schwarzenberger, Georg. *William Ladd: An Examination of an American Proposal for an International Equity Tribunal.* With a Preface by James Brown Scott. ("New Commonwealth Institute Monographs," Ser. B, No. 3.) London: Constable & Co., 1935.

Schwitsky, Ernst. *Der europäische Fürstenbund Georgs von Poděbrad: Ein Beitrag zur Geschichte der Weltfriedensidee.* Borna-Leipzig: Buchdruckerei Robert Noske, 1907.

Scott, James Brown (ed.). *American Addresses at the Second Hague Peace Conference Delivered by Joseph H. Choate, General Horace Porter, James Brown Scott.* Boston: Ginn, 1910.

———. *The Catholic Conception of International Law: Francisco de Vitoria, Founder of the Modern Law of Nations; Francisco Suárez, Founder of the Modern Philosophy of Law in General and in Particular of the Law of Nations.* Washington, D.C.: Georgetown University Press, 1934.

——— (ed.). *The Hague Conventions and Declarations, of 1899 and 1907, Accompanied by Tables of Signatures, Ratifications and Adhesions of the Various Powers and Texts of Reservations.* New York: Oxford University Press, 1915. (Carnegie Endowment for International Peace. Division of International Law.)

———. *The Hague Peace Conferences of 1899 and 1907: A Series of Lectures Delivered before the Johns Hopkins University in the Year 1908.* 2 vols. Baltimore: Johns Hopkins Press, 1909.

———. (ed.). *Instructions to the American Delegates to the Hague Peace Conferences and Their Official Reports.* With an Introduction by James Brown Scott. New York: Oxford University Press, 1916. (Carnegie Endowment for International Peace, Division of International Law.)

———. *Law, the State, and the International Community.* 2 vols. New York: Columbia University Press, 1939.

———. *Peace through Justice.* New York: Oxford University Press, 1917.

——— (under the supervision of). *The Proceedings of the Hague Peace Conferences, Translation of the Official Texts.* Prepared in the Division of International Law of the Carnegie Endowment for International Peace. 4 vols. New York: Oxford University Press, 1920–21.

———. *The Spanish Conception of International Law and of Sanctions.* ("Pamphlet Series of the Carnegie Endowment for International Peace, Division of International Law," No. 54.) Washington, D.C.: Carnegie Endowment for International Peace, 1934.

———. *The Spanish Origin of International Law.* Washington, D.C.: School of Foreign Service, Georgetown University, 1928.

Secret Diplomacy as a Menace to the Security of the State: The National and Imperial Problem (from a speech by Mr. E. D. Morel at the Christian Institute, Glasgow, November 23, 1915). ("Publications of the Union of Democratic Control," No. 19b.) London, n.d.

Seroux d'Agincourt, Camille. *Exposé des projets de paix perpétuelle de l'Abbé Saint-Pierre (et de Henri IV) de Bentham et de Kant.* Paris: Henri Jouve, 1905.

214   PLANS FOR WORLD PEACE

SHAW, LORD (of Dunfermline). *An Address at a General Meeting of the Society, 15th December, 1916.* ("Publications of the League of Nations Society," No. 7.) London, 1916.

———— (of Dunfermline). Speech: *The League of Nations in the House of Lords, June 26th, 1918.* ("Publications of the League of Nations Society," No. 39.) London, 1918.

SHORT, WILLIAM H. *Program and Policies of the League To Enforce Peace: A Handbook for Officers, Speakers, and Editors.* New York: League To Enforce Peace, 1916.

SHOTWELL, JAMES T. *Plans and Protocols To End War: Historical Outline and Guide.* ("International Conciliation," No. 208.) New York: Carnegie Endowment for International Peace, Division of Intercourse and Education, March, 1925.

SMUTS, J. C. *The League of Nations: A Practical Suggestion.* London: Hodder & Stoughton, 1918.

SOULEYMAN, ELIZABETH V. *The Vision of World Peace in Seventeenth and Eighteenth-Century France.* New York: G. P. Putnam's Sons, 1941.

SPALDING, H. N. *What a League of Nations Means.* ("Publications of the League of Nations Society," No. 22.) London, 1918.

STAWELL, F. MELIAN. *The Growth of International Thought.* ("Home University Library of Modern Knowledge," No. 143.) London: Thornton Butterworth, 1929.

STEPHEN, KARIN. *Arbitration in History.* ("Publications of the League of Nations Society," No. 40.) London, 1918.

STRATMANN, FRANZISKUS. *The Church and War: A Catholic Study.* New York: P. J. Kennedy & Sons, 1929.

SUAREZ, FRANCISCO. *De divina gratia.* Moguntiae: sumptibus H. M. Birckmanni, 1620–51.

Suggestions for League Speakers, Taken from the Organization Speech Delivered by Justice S. Harrison White, Colorado Supreme Court, at the Win-the-War-for-Permanent-Peace Convention, Colorado Branch, League To Enforce Peace, Denver, September 20, 1918. New York: League To Enforce Peace, 1918.

SULLY, MAXIMILIEN DE BÉTHUNE, DUC DE. *Mémoires du duc de Sully.* Nouvelle édition. 6 vols. Paris: E. Ledoux, 1827.

———. *Mémoires des sages et royalles œconomies d'estat, domestiques, politiques et militaires de Henry le Grand.... Et des servitvdes utiles obéissances conuenables & administrations loyales de Maximilian de Bethvne....* 4 vols. in 2. A Amstelredam: Chez Alethinosgraphe de Clearetimelee, & Graphexechon de Pistariste, [1638]–62.

Sully's Grand Design of Henry IV, from the Memoirs of Maximilien de Béthune, duc de Sully. With an Introduction by DAVID OGG. ("Grotius Society Publications: Texts for Students of International Relations," No. 2.) London: Sweet & Maxwell, 1921.

SWANWICK, H. M. *Builders of Peace, Being Ten Years' History of the Union of Democratic Control*. London: Swarthmore Press, 1924.

SYMONDS, JOHN ADDINGTON. *An Introduction to the Study of Dante*. Edinburgh: A. and C. Black, 1890.

TAFT, WILLIAM HOWARD. *The Obligations of Victory: An Address Delivered at the Convention of the League To Enforce Peace, at Madison, Wisconsin, under the Auspices of the University of Wisconsin, November 9, 1918*. New York: League To Enforce Peace, n.d.

——. *Why a League of Nations Is Necessary*. New York: League To Enforce Peace, n.d.

TAFT, WILLIAM HOWARD, and BRYAN, WILLIAM JENNINGS. *World Peace: A Written Debate between William Howard Taft and William Jennings Bryan*. New York: George H. Doran, 1917.

Tentative Draft Convention by an American Committee. ("Publications of the League of Nations Society," No. 30.) London, 1918.

TERASAKI, TARO. *William Penn et la paix*. Paris: A. Pedone, 1926.

Three Notable Protests against the Peace Treaty: A Christian Protest by Canon Peter Green; an Historical Protest by Dr. Charles Sarolea; a University Protest by the Bishop of Oxford (and Others). ("Publications of the Union of Democratic Control," No. 38a.) London, 1919.

TOD, MARCUS NIEBUHR. *International Arbitration amongst the Greeks*. Oxford: Clarendon Press, 1913.

TOUT, THOMAS FREDERICK. *The Empire and the Papacy, 918–1273*. London: Rivingtons, 1914.

Treaties for the Advancement of Peace between the United States and Other Powers Negotiated by the Honourable William J. Bryan, Secretary of State of the United States. ("Publications of the Carnegie Endowment for International Peace, Division of International Law.") With an Introduction by JAMES BROWN SCOTT. New York: Oxford University Press, 1920.

TREVELYAN, CHARLES. *The Union of Democratic Control (an Organisation Created To Secure the Control over Their Foreign Policy by the British People, and for the Promotion of International Understanding), Founded in November, 1914: Its History and Its Policy*. London: Simpson & Co., 1919; Hertford, Simpson & Co., 1921.

Union of Democratic Control, The: Its Motives, Object, and Policy. ("Publications of the Union of Democratic Control," No. 23*b*.) London, 1916.

Union of Democratic Control, The: Rules and Constitution, 1917–1918. London: Union of Democratic Control, n.d.

Union of Democratic Control, The: What It Is and What It Is Not. ("Publications of the Union of Democratic Control," No. 14*b*.) London, 1915.

UNWIN, RAYMOND. *Functions of a League of Nations.* ("Publications of the League of Nations Society," No. 19.) London, 1917.

VICTORIA, FRANCISCI DE. *De Indis et de iure belli relectiones.* Edited by ERNEST NYS. ("The Classics of International Law," edited by J. B. Scott.) Washington, D.C.: Carnegie Institution of Washington, 1917.

Views of War and Peace, Designed Especially for the Consideration of Statesmen. Boston: American Peace Society, n.d.

Vindication of Mr. Morel in the House of Commons. ("Publications of the Union of Democratic Control," No. 42*b*.) London: St. Clements Press, n.d.

Viscount Grey on a League of Nations, at a Meeting Held at Central Hall Westminster, October 10, 1918. ("Publications of the League of Nations Society," No. 44.) London, 1918.

VOLLENHOVEN, C. VAN: 'Grotius and Geneva," in *Bibliotheca visseriana: dissertationum ius internationale illustrantium,* Vol. VI, Part XIII. Leiden: E. J. Brill, 1926.

———. *The Law of Peace.* Translated by W. HORSFALL CARTER; Preface by JONKHEER W. J. M. VAN EYSINGA. London: Macmillan & Co., Ltd., 1936.

VREELAND, HAMILTON, JR. *Hugo Grotius, the Father of the Modern Science of International Law.* New York: Oxford University Press, 1917.

WALKER, JAMES, and PETRE, M. D. *State Morality and a League of Nations.* London: T. Fisher Unwin, 1919.

WALLIS, JOHN EYRE W. *The Sword of Justice or the Christian Philosophy of War Completed in the Idea of a League of Nations.* Oxford: B. H. Blackwell, 1920.

WALSH, EDMUND A. (ed.). *The History and Nature of International Relations.* New York: Macmillan, 1922.

WALSTON, SIR CHARLES. *The Next War, Wilsonism and Anti-Wilsonism, with an Open Letter to Col. Theodore Roosevelt.* Cambridge, England: University Press, 1918.

War after War: The Inaugural Meeting of the League of Free Nations Associa-

tion Held in the Town Hall, at Northampton on September 13, 1918; Speech by Viscount Bryce. ("Publications of the League of Nations Union," No. 13.) London, 1918.

WEBSTER, CHARLES KINGSLEY. *The Foreign Policy of Castlereagh, 1815–1822: Britain and the European Alliance.* London: G. Bell & Sons, 1925.

WEHBERG, HANS. *The Limitation of Armaments.* Translated by EDWIN H. ZEYDEL. ("Division of International Law," Pamphlet No. 46.) Washington, D.C.: Carnegie Endowment for International Peace, 1921.

WELLS, H. G., and OTHERS. *The Idea of a League of Nations.* Boston: Atlantic Monthly Press, 1919.

WHEATON, HENRY. *History of the Law of Nations in Europe and America.* New York: Gould, Banks, 1845.

WILGUS, ALVA CURTIS (ed.). *Modern Hispanic America*, With a Foreword by CLOYD HECK MARVIN. ("Studies in Hispanic American Affairs," Vol. I [1932].) Washington, D.C.: George Washington University Press, 1933.

WILLIAMS, ANEURIN. *A League of Nations: How To Begin It.* ("Publications of the League of Nations Society," No. 8.) London, 1917.

———. *The Minimum of Machinery.* ("Publications of the League of Nations Society," No. 18.) London, 1917.

WILSON, FLORENCE. *The Origins of the League Covenant: Documentary History of Its Drafting.* London: Hogarth Press, 1928.

WILSON, GEORGE GRAFTON (ed.). *The Hague Arbitration Cases: Compromis and Awards with Maps in Cases Decided under the Provisions of the Hague Conventions of 1899 and 1907 for the Pacific Settlement of International Disputes and Texts of the Conventions.* Boston: Ginn, 1915.

WOOLF, LEONARD S. *A Durable Settlement after the War by Means of a League of Nations.* ("Publications of the League of Nations Society," No. 21.) London, 1917.

———. *The Framework of a Lasting Peace.* London: Allen & Unwin, 1917.

———. *International Government: Two Reports, Prepared for the Fabian Research Department, Together with a Project by a Fabian Committee for a Supernational Authority That Will Prevent War.* New York: Brentano's, 1916.

WORCESTER, NOAH (PHILO PACIFICUS [pseud.]). *A Solemn Review of the Custom of War Showing That War Is the Effect of Popular Delusion and Proposing a Remedy.* N.p., 1814.

World-Wide Support for a League of Nations. ("Publications of the League of Nations Society," No. 34.) London, 1918.

WRIGHT, HERBERT FRANCIS. *Francisci de Victoria "De iure belli relectio."* Washington, D.C.: Catholic University, 1916.

WRIGHT, R. F. *Medieval Internationalism, the Contribution of the Medieval Church to International Law and Peace.* London: Williams & Norgate, 1930.

YORK, ELIZABETH. *Leagues of Nations: Ancient, Mediaeval, and Modern.* London: Swarthmore Press, 1919.

YOUNGHUSBAND, SIR FRANCIS. *Sense of a Community of Nations, A: An Address by Sir Francis Younghusband.* ("Publications of the League of Nations Society," No. 13.) London, 1917.

ARTICLES

ANDERSON, LUIS. "The Peace Conference of Central America," *American Journal of International Law* (New York), II, No. 1 (January, 1908), 144–51.

ANDREWS, FANNIE FERN. "The Central Organization for a Durable Peace," *Journal of the National Institute of Social Sciences* (New York), III (January, 1917), 119–25.

BAFF, WILLIAM E. "The Evolution of Peace by Arbitration," *American Law Review* (New York), LIII (1919), 229–68.

BURNS, C. DELISLE. "A Medieval Internationalist: Pierre Dubois," *Monist* (Chicago), XXVII (1917), 105–13.

CALL, ARTHUR D. "The Will To End War," *Advocate of Peace* (Washington, D.C.), LXXXVI, No. 4 (April, 1924), 228–38; No. 5 (May, 1924), 297–309.

CARTWRIGHT, JOHN K. "Contributions of the Papacy to International Peace," *Catholic Historical Review* (Washington, D.C.), VIII (April, 1928), 157–68.

DARBY, W. EVANS. "Some European Leagues of Peace," in *Problems of the War* (Vol. IV [1919] of the *Transactions of the Grotius Society* [London]), pp. 169–98.

DECLAREUIL, J. "Kant, le droit public et la société des nations," *Revue générale de droit international public* (Paris), XXV (1918), 113–43.

DELBOS, VICTOR. "Les Idées de Kant sur la paix perpétuelle," *Nouvelle revue,* CXIX (August, 1899), 410–29.

DE WULF, MAURICE. "The Society of Nations in the Thirteenth Century," *International Journal of Ethics* (Concord, N.H.), XXIX (January, 1919), 210–29.

FOX, SAMUEL. "Sixtus V's League of Nations" (reprinted from the *London Universe*), *Catholic Mind* (New York), XVI (1918), 560–62.

BIBLIOGRAPHY 219

FRASER, HENRY S. "A Sketch of the History of International Arbitration," *Cornell Law Quarterly*, XI, No. 2 (February, 1926), 179–208.

GRUBER, JOHN. "The Peace Negotiations of the Avignon Popes," *Catholic Historical Review* (Washington, D.C.), XIX, No. 2 (July, 1933), 190–99.

HARLEY, JOHN EUGENE. "America Joins the Quest for Peace," *World Affairs Interpreter* (Los Angeles), V (1935), 341–54.

HARRISON, AUSTIN. "Kant on the League of Nations," *English Review* (London), XXIX (November, 1919), 454–62.

HEMLEBEN, SYLVESTER JOHN. "Henry Fourth's Plan for a League of Nations," *Alumnae News of the College of New Rochelle* (New Rochelle, N.Y.), IX, No. 2 (April, 1932), 7–10.

HICKS, FREDERICK C. "The Literature of Abortive Schemes of World Organization," *American Library Institute: Papers and Proceedings, 1919* (Chicago, 1920), pp. 160–78.

HIGGINS, A. PEARCE. "James Lorimer," *Juridical Review* (Edinburgh), XLV, No. 3 (September, 1933), 239–56.

HUDSON, MANLEY O. "The Central American Court of Justice," *American Journal of International Law* (New York), XXVI, No. 4 (October, 1932), 759–86.

———. "The Permanent Court of Arbitration," *ibid.*, XXVII, No. 3 (July, 1933), 440–60.

KREY, AUGUST C. "The International State of the Middle Ages: Some Reasons for Its Failure," *American Historical Review*, XXVIII, No. 1 (October, 1922), 1–12.

LANGE, CHRISTIAN L. "Histoire de la doctrine pacifique et de son influence sur le développement du droit international," in *Academy of International Law*, The Hague, *Recueil dès cours, 1926, III* (Paris), XIII de la Collection (1927), 171–426.

LEVERMORE, CHARLES H. "Synopsis of Plans for International Organization," *Advocate of Peace* (Washington, D.C.), LXXXI, Nos. 7, 8 (July–August, 1919), 216–25, 252–66.

LEWIS, V. J. "The Bohemian Project of 1464," *New Commonwealth* (London), II, No. 3 (December, 1933), 10.

———. "Dante," *ibid.*, II, No. 1 (October, 1933), 8.

———. "John Bellers," *ibid.*, III, No. 1 (October, 1934), 197.

———. "Leibnitz," *ibid.*, III, No. 5 (February, 1935), 276–77.

———. "The Peloponnesian League," *ibid.*, I, No. 6 (March, 1933), 10.

———. "Pierre du Bois," *ibid.*, I, No. 12 (September, 1933), 10.

———. "Rousseau," *ibid.*, IV, No. 2 (November, 1935), 438.

220 PLANS FOR WORLD PEACE

LEWIS, V. J. "Saint-Pierre," *ibid.*, III, No. 3 (December, 1934), 234–35.
———. "William Penn," *ibid.*, II, No. 12 (September, 1934), 177.
M., J. O. (J. O. M.). "Alexander I and the Holy Alliance," *New Commonwealth* (London), V, No. 4 (January, 1937), 58–59.
———. "Immanuel Kant," *ibid.*, V, No. 1 (October, 1936), 4; No. 2 (November, 1936), p. 25.
———. "Jeremy Bentham," *ibid.*, V, No. 3 (December, 1936), 41.
MCGRANE, R. C. "A Sixteenth Century League of Nations," *Nation* (New York), CVIII (March 8, 1919), 372.
MACKINNEY, LOREN C. "The People and Public Opinion in the Eleventh Century Peace Movement," *Speculum* (Cambridge, Mass.), V (April, 1930), 181–206.
MANDERE, H. CH. G. J. VAN DER. "Hugo Grotius, Founder of Modern International Law: 1625–1925," *Contemporary Review* (New York), CXXVII (1925), 755–59.
MATTHAEI, LOUISE E. "The Place of Arbitration and Mediation in Ancient Systems of International Ethics," *Classical Quarterly* (London), II (October, 1908), 241–64.
MEAD, EDWIN D. "An Early Scheme To Organize the World," *Independent* (New York), LXIII (August 29, 1907), 497–99.
———. "Immanuel Kant's Internationalism," *Contemporary Review* (London), CVII (February, 1915), 226–32.
MÜLLER, JOSEPH. "L'Œuvre de toutes les confessions Chrétiennes (Eglises) pour la paix internationale," in Academy of International Law, The Hague, *Recueil dès cours, 1930, I* (Paris), XXXI de la *Collection* (1931), 293–392.
MYERS, DENYS P. "The Origin of the Hague Arbitral Courts," *American Journal of International Law* (New York), VIII (1914), 769–801; X (1916), 270–311.
NYS, ERNEST. "The Necessity of a Permanent Tribunal," in *Judicial Settlement of International Disputes*, pp. 3–28. ("Publications of the American Society for Judicial Settlement of International Disputes," No. 2 [with Supplement].) Baltimore, November, 1910.
ORZÁBAL QUINTANA, ARTURO. "Kant y la paz perpetua," *Nosotros* (Buenos Aires), Año 18, XLVI, No. 179 (April, 1924), 441–57.
PFISTER, CHRISTIAN. "Les 'Economies royales' de Sully et le Grand Dessein de Henry IV," in *Revue historique*, LIV (January–April, 1894), 300–324; LV (May–August, 1894), 66–82, 291–302; LVI (September–December, 1894), 39–48, 304–39.

PHILLIPSON, COLEMAN. "Franciscus a Victoria (1480–1546), 'International Law and War,'" *Society of Comparative Legislation Journal* (London), XV (1915), 175–97.

POLITIS, N. "The Work of the Hague Court," in *Judicial Settlement of International Disputes*, pp. 3–17. ("Publications of the American Society for Judicial Settlement of International Disputes," No. 6.) Baltimore, November, 1911.

PUECH, J. L. "La Société des nations et ses précurseurs socialistes," *Revue politique et littéraire, Revue bleue* (Paris), LIX, No. 3 (February 5, 1921), pp. 82–85; No. 5 (March 5, 1921), pp. 147–51.

PYLE, JOSEPH GILPIN. "An Earlier League To Enforce Peace," *Unpopular Review* (New York), X, No. 20 (October–December, 1918), 244–54.

RAGG, LONSDALE. "Dante and a League of Nations," *Anglo-Italian Review* (London), II, No. 8 (December, 1918), 327–35.

ROBINSON, PASCHAL. "Peace Laws and Institutions of the Medieval Church," *Ecclesiastical Review* (Philadelphia), LII (1915), 523–36.

SCOTT, JAMES BROWN. "The Central American Peace Conference of 1907," *American Journal of International Law* (New York), II, No. 1 (January, 1908), 121–43.

———. "The Court of Arbitral Justice, Approved by the Second Hague Peace Conference (1907) and Recommended by the Institute of International Law (1912)," in *Judicial Settlement of International Disputes*, pp. 3–12. ("Publications of the American Society for Judicial Settlement of International Disputes," No. 10.) Baltimore, November, 1912.

———. "Grotius' *De jure belli ac pacis;* libri tres: The Work of a Lawyer, Statesman and Theologian," *American Journal of International Law* (New York), XIX (1925), 461–68.

———. "A Single Standard of Morality for the Individual and the State," *Proceedings of the American Society of International Law at Its Twenty-sixth Annual Meeting Held at Washington, D.C., April 28–30, 1932* (Washington, D.C., 1932), pp. 10–36.

——— (ed.). *Proceedings of Fourth National Conference, American Society for Judicial Settlement of International Disputes, December 4–6, 1913, Washington, D.C.* Baltimore: Williams & Wilkins, 1914.

SPENDER, HAROLD. "The League of Nations: A Voice from the Past," *Contemporary Review* (New York), CXIV (1918), 407–14.

SULLIVAN, JAMES. "The Manuscripts and Date of Marsiglio of Padua's *Defensor pacis*," *English Historical Review* (London), XX (1905), 293–307.

TANSILL, CHARLES C. "Early Plans for World Peace," *Historical Outlook* (Philadelphia), XX, No. 7 (November, 1929), 321–24.

TARN, W. W. "Alexander the Great and the Unity of Mankind" (Raleigh Lecture on History), *Proceedings of the British Academy* (London), XIX (1933), 123–66.

TELFER, VERA. "Catholic Projects for a League of Nations," *Catholic World* (New York), CXX (October, 1924), 73–80.

TRYON, JAMES L. "Proposals for an International Court," *Proceedings of the American Society for Judicial Settlement of International Disputes, 1913* (Baltimore, 1914), pp. 96–128.

VESNITCH, MIL. R. "Cardinal Alberoni: An Italian Precursor of Pacifism and International Arbitration" (with the plan translated from the French by THEODORE HENCKELS of Washington, D.C.), *American Journal of International Law* (New York), VII (1913), 51–107.

VEVERKA, FERDINAND. "United Europe Idea" (letter to the editor of the *New York Times*), *New York Times*, March 23, 1930, sec. 3, p. 5.

VOLLENHOVEN, C. VAN. "On the genesis of 'De iure belli ac pacis (Grotius, 1625)," *Koninklijke Akademie van Wetenschappen. Mededeelingen. Afdeeling Letterkunde*, LVIII, Ser. B, No. 6, pp. 129–55. Amsterdam, 1924.

WESTERMANN, W. L. "Interstate Arbitration in Antiquity," *Classical Journal* (Chicago), II (1907), 197–211.

WILKINSON, CHARLTON. "Dante's Vision of International Peace," *Nation and the Athenaeum* (London), XXX, No. 3 (October 15, 1921), 111.

WILLIAMS, MARIE V. "Internationalism in Ancient Greece," *London Quarterly Review* (London), CLVI (July, 1931), 12–18.

WING, GEORGE C. "William Ladd, the Apostle of Peace," *Sprague's Journal of Maine History* (Dover, Me.), XI, No. 2 (1923), 53–60.

WISHART, ANDREW. "A Scottish Jurist and the League Idea," *Juridical Review* (Edinburgh), XXXIV (December, 1922), 331–37.

WRIGHT, HERBERT F. "St. Augustine on International Peace," *Catholic World* (New York), CV (September, 1917), 744–53.

INDEX

68996